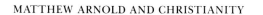

MATTHEW ARNOLD AND CHRISTIANITY

MATTHEW ARNOLD
and CHRISTIANITY:
His Religious Prose Writings

by JAMES C. LIVINGSTON

\\

UNIVERSITY OF SOUTH CAROLINA PRESS

#128080 48

Library of Congress Cataloging-in-Publication Data

Livingston, James C., 1930–
    Matthew Arnold and Christianity

    Includes index.
    1. Arnold, Matthew, 1822–1888—Prose. 2. Arnold,
Matthew, 1822–1888—Religion. 3. Christian literature,
English—History and criticism. 4. Theology, Doctrinal—
England—History—19th century. I. Title.
PR4024.L58 1985   828' .808   85-24121
ISBN 0-87249-462-4

To Sarah and Susannah

Contents

Preface

Howard Foster Lowry, the founder of Arnold studies in this century, predicted that once the definitive history of nineteenth-century thought was written, the unique and distinguished contribution of Arnold to religious thought would be recognized.[1] Biblical scholars have spoken of *Literature and Dogma* as a pioneer work in the field of religious hermeneutics, one which gives an early clue to the movement of religious thought in the generations following Arnold. This high regard for Arnold's contribution to modern religious thought has not, however, been widely shared. Arnold's position as a commanding literary and social critic is secure. He continues to be regarded, with Tennyson and Browning, as preeminent among the High Victorian poets. But his religious prose writings have, until recently, been largely dismissed as of little interest or importance. Moreover, those critics who have touched on Arnold's religious writings have, on the whole, either denounced or praised him for what they perceive to be a thoroughly humanistic exercise in theological reductionism, be it either aesthetic or psychological. The testing of this widely accepted view of Arnold's critical intention in his religious prose and the real nature of his own religious position has been the principal impetus for this study.

Arnold prided himself more for his work as a religious critic than for his poetry. Today we are more aware of the influence that *Literature and Dogma* had on the minds of Englishmen and Americans and on some Europeans struggling with the question of religious belief in the years before the Great War. Scores of distinguished biblical critics, theologians, bishops and other clergy—not to mention ordinary laymen—found in Arnold's religious books a way of preserving what they found to be fundamental to belief, of making it invulnerable to "scientific" criticism, and of establishing it on a new basis.

More recently there are signs that the historical importance and the inherent merits of Arnold's religious prose work are gaining recognition. Doubts as to whether Arnold has been rightly interpreted or given his due are now being heard. This sense that there is need for a reevaluation gained impetus in part through brief but highly sympathetic treatment of Arnold's religious prose by critics such as Basil Willey and Douglas Bush and, more recently, by the work of David DeLaura and Ruth ap-Roberts. The completion of the excellent critical edition, in 11 volumes, of *The Complete Prose Works of Matthew Arnold*, edited by R. H. Super, and the publication of Park Honan's biography, *Matthew Arnold: A Life*, have also contributed to this reconsideration. Honan remarks that "No other aspect of Arnold studies late in the twentieth century was livelier, more intelligent, or more in motion" than the study of his religious thought.[2] The historian John Kent suggests that, while dismissed by a long tradition of Anglican historical scholarship, Arnold offers the clearest evidence of what was going on in the minds of those who faced the religious ferment in Britain in the latter years of the nineteenth century.[3] Literary and theological critics, such as Nathan Scott, Jr., recently have pointed out the ongoing significance of Arnold's hermeneutical program.[4]

The nature of Arnold's religious hermeneutics and his reconception of the Bible and Christianity are the center of the present study. However, before these subjects can properly be explored and assessed, it is useful to examine briefly the reception that Arnold's religious prose writings have received. This will help to explain why a study of this side of Arnold is now appropriate. Chapter 1 looks at the religious aspect of Arnold's development from poet to mature critic, his growing sense of vocation, and some of the influences that shaped his thinking between the mid-1840s and the early 1870s. It is especially important in this regard to emphasize Arnold's persistent concern, from Oxford days onward, for religion and the importance of the spiritual quest. Without a sense of what was at work in Arnold's development during these crucial decades, it is difficult to get a true measure of the nature and intent of his religious thought and criticism. This first chapter is not, however, a study in sources. The tracing of sources, essentially a study in itself, carries us away from this book's concerns. Those readers familiar with the background of Arnold's development from poet to religious critic may wish to move directly to chapter 2.

Chapters 2 through 4 deal with several themes that are central to Arnold's hermeneutical program, including the role of the *Zeitgeist* and the idea of religious development, the relationship between religion and culture and, more specifically, between religion and the poetic imagination. This leads to a study of Arnold's conception of the nature and status of religious language and experience and his understanding of the truth of Christianity. Chapter 4 then outlines several functions of religious criticism that are fundamental to Arnold's interpretation of religious literature and the Bible in particular. In chapter 5 I attempt to look afresh at Arnold's substantive religious beliefs and to show that his views, while often dismissive of traditional conceptions and language, are nevertheless in accord with the mainstream of liberal and modernist Christian theology of the past century. Chapter 6 assays the difficult question of Arnold's place in the spectrum of religious thought in our modern period—a subject about which, I believe, little that is helpful has been written. In this concluding chapter I attempt to convey a sense of the qualities that constitute Arnold's unique spirituality and religious temper.

NOTES
1. H. F. Lowry, ed., *The Letters of Matthew Arnold to Arthur Hugh Clough* (London, 1932) 50.
2. Park Honan, *Matthew Arnold: A Life* (New York, 1981) 476.
3. J. Daniélou, A. H. Couratin, and John Kent, *The Pelican Guide to Modern Theology* II (Baltimore, 1969) 309.
4. Nathan Scott, Jr., "Arnold's Vision of Transcendence—the Vis Poetica," *The Journal of Religion* (July, 1979).

Acknowledgments

This study owes a large debt to many scholars and institutions. The critical editions of Arnold's prose and poetry as well as the editions of his letters and notebooks were, of course, essential. The extent of my dependence on the editorial work of R. H. Super, Kenneth Allott, C. B. Tinker, H. F. Lowry, K. Young, W. H. Dunn, and G. W. E. Russell is immeasurable. The studies of Arnold by Sidney Coulling, Dwight Culler, David DeLaura, William Madden, Park Honan, Fraser Neiman, William Robbins, Lionel Trilling, and Basil Willey were also crucial. From these works I derived not only a wealth of factual information but, more importantly, ideas and interpretations that launched my own reflection and helped to shape my own understanding of Arnold. This is also true of my encounter with the work of a number of literary critics, among them T. S. Eliot, Murray Krieger, and I. A. Richards, with whose interpretations of Arnold I found myself in disagreement, but whose work has been a great stimulus to my own thinking.

I am most grateful to David DeLaura, Park Honan, and Fraser Neiman for their advice at points in the book's progress. David DeLaura, Giles Gunn, Fraser Neiman, and R. H. Super read portions of earlier drafts. Their knowledge and their rigorous and candid criticism convinced me of the need to revise the text at a number of points, and I believe this has improved both the form and the substance of the essay. For the University of South Carolina Press, Kevin L. Lewis also gave the work a most critical scrutiny, and I am immensely grateful for this generous help. The interest and support which these scholars have accorded this work is especially appreciated, since I know that some of them do not subscribe to at least some of my central conclusions. I have not followed all the suggestions proffered by these scholars, and any faults or limitations in this essay remain my own responsibility. I would also like to note that Ruth apRoberts's important contribution to Arnold studies, *Arnold and God*, appeared when this book was in all essentials complete. Therefore, I have not taken detailed account of her essay. Those familiar with apRoberts's work will see, however, that we differ in our interpretation of Arnold's religious views.

My research and writing was notably eased and advanced by the considerate and efficient help of several libraries and librarians. I am indebted to the Swem Library of the College of William and Mary; the Bodleian Library, Balliol College Library, and the Pusey House Library, all in Oxford; the University Library, Cambridge; the Alderman Library of the University of Virginia; and the Princeton University Library, which granted permission to quote from an unpublished Arnold letter.

An extended period of time for research and writing was made possible through the award of a fellowship by the National Endowment for the Humanities and a research grant from the College of William and Mary. Without the assistance of these two institutions, the completion of this book would not have been possible. The Bross Foundation, Lake Forest College, Lake Forest, Illinois, honored me with the award of the decennial Bross Prize for the unpublished and earlier version of this study. The Bross Foundation has also generously assisted in the publication of this book.

I received valuable help from my student assistant, Marla Esten, and from Claudia Puglisi, who prepared major segments of the typescript. My wife, Jackie, also assisted in the typing and in a number of editorial tasks at every stage of the book's progress.

Abbreviations

The following abbreviations are used for works cited parenthetically in the text:

C —*The Poetry of Matthew Arnold: A Commentary*, C. B. Tinker and H. F. Lowry (London, 1940).

CL —*The Letters of Matthew Arnold to Arthur Hugh Clough*, ed. H. F. Lowry (London, 1932).

CPW—*Complete Prose Works of Matthew Arnold*, 11 vols., ed. R. H. Super (Ann Arbor, 1961-77).

L —*Letters of Matthew Arnold, 1848-88*, 2 vols., ed. G. W. E. Russell (London, 1895).

NB —*The Note-Books of Matthew Arnold*, ed. H. F. Lowry, K. Young, and W. H. Dunn (London, 1952).

P —*The Poems of Matthew Arnold*, ed. Kenneth Allott and Miriam Allott 2nd ed. (London, 1979).

UL —*Unpublished Letters of Matthew Arnold*, ed. A. Whitridge (New Haven, 1923).

MATTHEW ARNOLD AND CHRISTIANITY

Introduction

The decade of the 1860s was Matthew Arnold's most creative period as a critic. It was also a time when certain perceptions and judgments converged in his mind and set the course of his later life and direction as a writer. These sentiments and convictions were never entirely absent from Arnold, even as a young man. However, experiences and age now forced them upon him with a new intensity and fixed his resolve.

First, Arnold's profound sense of the unalterable flux and passage of life and of time took on a vivid personal meaning. Writing to his mother in December 1866, a few days after a birthday celebration, he confessed that "forty-four is indeed an age at which one may say 'The time past of our life may suffice us' to have trifled and idled, or worse, in. I more and more become conscious of having something to do, and of a resolution to do it" (L 1:400). Less than two years later, Arnold suffered the loss of his infant son, Basil, and his eldest son, 16-year-old Tommy. These tragic events he associated "with several awakenings and epoch-making things." "All these things," he wrote, "point to a new beginning, yet it may well be that I am near my end, as papa was at my age . . . and that there will be little time to carry far the new beginning. But that is all the more reason for carrying it as far as one can, while one lives" (L 1:466).

Arnold's feeling of "having something to do" was coupled with a deepening sense that the English spirit was undergoing a profound revolution or evolution in the last decades of the nineteenth century and that the hope of the future largely rested with the middle class—a middle class, however, delivered out of the commercial, mechanical, philistine spirit of Protestant Dissent. And so it was that Arnold entered a "new beginning" as social and religious critic, a task that was to continue virtually uninterrupted for almost a quarter of a century. Of the nine essays published in the first edition of *Essays in Criticism* (1865), six were wholly or in part devoted to religion, while the preface and major sections of Arnold's finest work of social criticism, *Culture and Anarchy* (1869), have to do with religious life and institutions. From the year 1862—at the age of 40—to the end of his life, Arnold was to write on religion. This output included four books and approximately 15 additional essays, not to mention the frequent discussion of religion in his many prefaces, his reports on schools, and those hundreds of jottings in the *Note-Books* which, as a collection of spiritual wisdom, rightfully can lay claim to a place "among the best of the books of devotion" (NB 13).

Arnold's religious writings received extensive review not only in the newspapers and the leading periodicals of the day—*The Fortnightly*, *The Contemporary Review*, *The Academy*, *Fraser's*, *The Spectator*, and the *Pall Mall Gazette*—but in dozens of church papers and magazines of all religious persuasions. Eminent critics—R. H. Hutton, Goldwin Smith, John Morley, Leslie Stephen, and J. C. Shairp, to name only some of the more prominent—wrote reviews and often extensive essays on Arnold's religious works, as did prominent Victorian philosophers, theologians, and ecclesiastics.[1]

On the whole, Arnold's paradoxically radical yet conservative effort at religious reconstruction was not well received. Religious liberals and freethinkers, such as W. R. Greg and Leslie Stephen, censured Arnold for his attempt to reconceive the old doctrines and his refusal to make a clean break with the ancient "materialized" language and belief. The doctrines should, in the words of Stephen, "be denounced openly, constantly, vigorously,"[2] rather than trusting that the old notions would decay of themselves or meld into genuinely experiential beliefs. The orthodox, on the other hand, whether of the Church or Dissent, charged Arnold with reductionism. This latter charge was, in fact, the common estimate, and not only that of his contemporaries; it became something of a received tradition of Arnold criticism until recently.

Despite this critical reception, a number of professional theologians and biblical scholars of the generation following Arnold's showed considerable appreciation of his theological knowledge and commended his hermeneutical effort. The response of F. C. Burkitt, Norris-Hulse Professor of Divinity in Cambridge and a leading New Testament scholar, represents the feeling of many of the new generation of Modernists. He wrote:

> It is now fashionable among literary people to deplore Arnold's incursions into biblical criticism. He is often supposed to have rushed in as a kind of dilettante theological amateur to regions where not but professors and clergymen should adventure. Most literary people do not know how well equipped he was for the work. He had the habit and experience of literary criticism and an excellent knowledge not only of the

works of modern theologians but—what is of much more importance—of the ancient sources also.[3]

Between roughly 1870 and 1920 Arnold's religious prose was widely read and his ideas were the subject of comment in the writings of many liberal theological scholars and ecclesiastics. However difficult it may be to weigh the extent of his influence on the broad direction of religious thought and, more especially, on particular thinkers between 1870 and 1920, it is clear that he had a real effect on the religious life and on the work of numerous prominent theologians and clergy, as well as unnumbered laity. This is well documented by a review of the best liberal theological literature to about 1920, throughout which are found references to Arnold's essays and his striking ideas. Scores of influential liberal clergy concurred with Llewelyn Davies's judgment that "there are characteristics of Mr. Arnold's creed which are likely to make it, to a large section of Englishmen, more attractive than any rival."[4] Those characteristics that most appealed to the two generations of churchmen following Arnold were his sense of the metaphorical nature and limits of religious language; his skepticism regarding dogmatic assertion and metaphysical speculation; his grounding of religious belief in experience, particularly in moral experience; his forthright spiritual interpretations of such doctrines as the resurrection and the last judgment; and his broad liberality with regard to Church Establishment and its national mission.

T. R. Glover, author of the popular *The Jesus of History* (1917), spoke with high favor of Arnold's method of experiential verification, reminding his readers that it was Matthew Arnold who pointed out that Jesus never touches on theory, "but bases Himself invariably upon experience."[5] The Modernist theologian C. W. Emmet appealed to the words of Arnold in insisting that "the Christian Church is founded, not on a correct speculative knowledge of the ideas of Paul, but on much surer ground: Let every one that nameth the name of Christ depart from iniquity."[6] Earlier W. H. Fremantle, in his Bampton Lectures for 1885, had commended to his audience the practical verification of Christianity since, as he confessed, one so often finds intellectual definition inadequate. "Who," Fremantle asked, "can define God or religion? These expressions are, to quote a writer of our own day, 'Words thrown out at a great subject.' "[7]

Arnold's correction of the one-sidedness of popular Evangelical theology was especially well received by Broad and High Church theologians alike. "The mystical resurrection," wrote W. J. Sparrow Simpson,

both of Christ and of the Christian, has been practically ef-
faced in much popular religion in favor of the more easily
grasped idea of bodily resurrection after physical death. . . .
Modern religion requires the restatement in its proper position of the sublime conception of mystical correspondence between the spiritual experience of our Lord and those of any
true disciple. So far as he insisted on this, Matthew Arnold has
done us real service.[8]

Modernist churchmen also were indebted to Arnold for his unre-
served, frank attack on the evidential value of miracles and prophecy
fulfillment. To those exploded traditional evidences H. D. A. Major offered the Modernist reply:

I know this is true because it *finds me*; in other words the
appeal which it makes to my moral and spiritual consciousness
. . . that is, to an unveiling of moral and spiritual truth. . . .
When Matthew Arnold wrote sarcastically, "to prove to you
that what I am writing is true, I propose to turn my pen into
a pen-wiper," he was not writing blasphemous nonsense but
justifiable criticism of a view of miracles which is now
discredited.[9]

Arnold's effort at religious reconstruction had influence beyond the
Church of England and even the Christian communion. His treatment
of Hebraism and Hellenism in *Culture and Anarchy* was of considerable
service to the eminent Talmudic scholar Emanuel Deutsch, who confided
to Arnold that without his help he could not have written his popular
essay on the Talmud for the *Quarterly*. Referring to Deutsch's expression
of gratitude, Arnold confessed to Lady deRothschild that he had "had no
such tribute to my powers of relaxing and dissolving yet paid. If we can
but dissolve what is bad without dissolving what is good!" (L 1:395). Mor-
decai Kaplan, the great Jewish philosopher and founder of the Recon-
structionist movement in Judaism in 1922, regarded *Literature and Dogma*
as a formative influence on his own reconception of the spiritual meaning
of the Hebrew scriptures. In a diary entry for 17 August 1905 he wrote:

An essay which I recently read with zest is Arnold's *Literature
and Dogma*. It did a great deal more to stimulate my Jewish
self-consciousness than anything I have ever read in English
or in Hebrew except the Bible. I am more convinced than ever
that Acad Haäm's conception of nationality, plus Arnold's
interpretation of Israel's [ancient] genius for righteousness

contain that which could form a positive expression of the Jewish spirit.[10]

The impress of Arnold's religious writings is detected not only in much of the liberal theological literature in the decades before the Great War but also on the personal lives of preeminent ecclesiastics and unsung laymen. His writings, the evidence makes clear, did reach and speak to people who had been "won by the modern spirit to habits of intellectual seriousness" and who had "stood near enough to the Christian religion to feel the attraction which a thing so very great . . . cannot but exercize" (CPW 7:392). H. H. Henson, Dean of Durham and Bishop of Hereford; William R. Inge, the formidable "gloomy Dean" of St. Paul's; and William Temple, perhaps the greatest Archbishop of Canterbury in this century— all liberal clergymen—were helped by their reading of Arnold during periods of religious crisis and honest doubt. Temple was deeply troubled about subscription to the Articles and Creeds before approaching his bishop on the possibility of ordination. His reading of Arnold helped him work through this difficulty. Freed of his disquiet, he wrote to a friend:

> It is the great wisdom of our Church that it was not founded to support any particular doctrines, as the Protestant bodies were. . . . Freedom of doctrine is the life-breath of the Church of England. Historically the thing is as clear as daylight. . . . The whole thing is admirably put by Matthew Arnold in "Puritanism and the Church," and "Modern Dissent" in the *St. Paul and Protestantism* volume.[11]

The personal spiritual help which his writings supplied to people in religious distress and uncertainty gave Arnold immense satisfaction. Late in life he wrote to his wife: "I get the strangest letters from people who have read and liked *Literature and Dogma*. One man writes to me to ask if I think he, having read and liked my book, can without hypocrisy serve the office of churchwarden. A mother from 'Norton Hall' in Gloucestershire has read the same book and wants my advice in educating her daughters" (L 2:380). A Catholic priest, formerly in the Roman Church but then ministering in the English Church, wrote that the fact that he retained "any sort of Christianity and continued to use and enjoy the Bible, I owe entirely to Matthew Arnold. . . . He undoubtedly saved me from leaving the Papal Church a dulled and blank materialist, thoroughly and violently anti-Christian; and his gentle influence tended me through the next ten years, until I mellowed for the process of reconstruction."[12]

Arnold was especially struck and delighted by the response to *Literature and Dogma* in America. From Boston he wrote to his sister: "*Literature and Dogma* has certainly done good here in New England; at a critical moment it has led many back again to the study of the Bible, and has given reality to the study of it" (L 2:270-71). "What strikes me in America," he writes from Cincinnati, "is the number of friends *Literature and Dogma* has made me, amongst ministers of religion especially—and how the effect of the book here is conservative" (L 2:301). This conservative, reconciling effect of *Literature and Dogma* Arnold attributed to the greater candor and absence of conventionality in American life. "The dread of seeing and saying that what is old has served its time and must be displaced is much less. . . . This being so, the mind is left free to consider the book on its real merits" (L 2:301).

As we know, Arnold preferred to be remembered for his work on behalf of religion rather than for his literary or political criticism. The reason for this is not difficult to grasp since he considered religion "the indispensable background," that which art, science, and political culture "rest against and imply." Both Arnold's interest in religion and his appeal to many of his contemporaries are to be understood in the light of what he perceived to be the reconciling function of his religious criticism in a time of conflict and division. His effort was one of reconstructing a synthesis of the scientific temper with religious and spiritual values in an age of the growing hegemony of science. And he was delighted that he saw so many signs that his work was having a salutary effect.

If Arnold's writings had influence on the religious life of many of the educated class in Britain and America for two generations after 1870, the same cannot be said about the period after 1920. Furthermore, his effort at religious reconstruction was received critically, and even with hostility, by many of the most prominent Victorian critics. The central charge against him was "aestheticism," the claim that he reduced the language of religion to poetry, to subjective psychological feelings and ideals—to emotion or pseudo-statement.

The charge of aestheticism was first advanced by Arnold's friend from Oxford days, Principal J. C. Shairp of St. Andrews, upon the publication of *Culture and Anarchy*. Shairp protested that Arnold appeared to regard religion as only one factor, and not necessarily the ruling element, in the quest for perfection. Perfection, Shairp wrote, was for Arnold the many-sided, harmonious development of human nature, "and to this end religion was only an important means."[13] On the basis of this judgment Shairp concluded that men like Arnold "who seek religion for culture's sake are aesthetic, not religious."[14]

Shairp's reproach of aestheticism carried with it the accusation of reductionism, that Arnold reduced religion to poetic emotion or to a moral subjectivism. Leslie Stephen read Arnold similarly. He was troubled by the fact that Arnold accepted a radical criticism of traditional orthodoxy as being in the right, and yet held that believers remain somehow justified in their belief. "Agree fully and frankly," he writes, "that the value of a creed is not to be tested by its historical and philosophical validity; that it really belongs to the sphere of poetry and provides symbols for the emotions, not truths for the understanding"[15] and one approximates Arnold's position. The weakness of such a poetic or imaginative treatment is, according to Stephen, "the tendency to confound a judgment of beauty with a judgment of fact. A creed is so charming . . . that it must be true."[16]

The Victorian figure whose judgment on Arnold's religious criticism remained most influential—largely through the cordial approbation of T. S. Eliot—is the philosopher F. H. Bradley, who also associated Arnold with moral subjectivism. Religion, Bradley rightly insists, is more than moral sentiment, for in the religious consciousness "we find the belief, however vague and indistinct, in an object, a not-myself; an object, further, which is real." Having concluded that Arnold's religion lacks such an objective reference, Bradley draws the inference that his "ideal of personal morality is not enough for religion."[17]

T. S. Eliot read deeply in Bradley, producing a dissertation on his metaphysics. He considered that Bradley's work had "an indubitable claim to permanence" and that *Ethical Studies* (1876) was the book which had "knocked the bottom out of *Literature and Dogma*." "Such criticism," asserted Eliot, "is final," the conclusive demonstration that "Arnold had made an excursion into a field for which he was not armed."[18]

Eliot's censure of Arnold's religious prose writings is not essentially different in kind from that proffered by Shairp and other Victorian critics a half century earlier: namely, that Arnold holds an inadequate view of the relation of religion and culture (the charge of aestheticism) and that Arnold transmutes the Christian religion into subjective feeling (the charge of reductionism). As to the first accusation, Eliot claims that in his books on Christianity, Arnold "seems only to say again and again—merely that the Christian faith is of course impossible to the man of culture," and that "the total effect of Arnold's philosophy is to set up Culture in the place of Religion." The result is that religion is left "to be laid waste by the anarchy of feeling."[19]

Eliot's charge of emotivism proved to be of momentous consequence in setting one important direction of Arnold criticism for over a half century. His indictment is notorious: the aim of Arnold's religious writings "is to affirm that the emotions of Christianity can and must be preserved without the belief," which is in effect "a counsel to get all the emotional kick out of Christianity one can, without the bother of believing it."[20]

Eliot's judgments on Arnold's religious criticism had a fateful influence. Yet Eliot's own understanding of the status and complex relationship of religious, poetic, and scientific language is unclear to many critics; he certainly did not work out these problems with the care required of one who wished to speak authoritatively on them. Furthermore, it is clear that Eliot's concern sharply to distinguish the nature and functions of poetry and religion contributed in no small measure, though unintentionally, to the positivist reduction of poetry and, in turn, of the language of religion to the status of emotion, as distinct from the language of fact and statement—with all the confusions and problems attendant on this positivist circumscription of all language into "emotive" and "scientific" terms.

It was I. A. Richards, in *Principles of Literary Criticism* (1924) and in his important essay *Science and Poetry* (1926), who formulated the positivist linguistic categories programmatically and who, like Eliot, explicitly associated Arnold with an emotivist interpretation of poetry, including religious literature. According to Richards, "We may either use words for the sake of the references they promote, or we may use them for the sake of the attitudes and emotions which ensue,"[21] poetry affording the clearest example of the subordination of reference to emotion. "It is," he asserts, "the supreme form of *emotive* language"[22] or "pseudo-statement." Poetry's "truth" simply depends on whether or not it "suits and serves some attitude or links together attitudes which on other grounds are desirable."[23]

Richards feared that our centuries-old identification of pseudo-statement—about God, the human soul, its nature and destiny—with belief and with knowledge was now irrevocably past. Since, for Richards, "it is fairly clear that genuine knowledge cannot serve us here and can only increase our practical control of Nature, [our task] is to cut our pseudo-statements free from belief, and yet retain them, in this released state, as the main instruments by which we order our attitudes to one another and to the world."[24]

By far the most influential criticism of this type is found in Lionel Trilling's masterful intellectual biography of Arnold, first published in 1939 and reissued twice since. Trilling faults Arnold for not verifying ("scientifically") his theological claims; but when he observes Arnold attempting a "scientific" mode of verification, he scolds him for departing from pragmatism and the emotive language of pseudo-statement.

Trilling's criticism focuses on the fundamental problem of truth and verification. "We hear the word 'verifiable' from Mr. Arnold pretty often," he quotes F. H. Bradley. "What is it to verify? Has Mr. Arnold put 'such a tyro's' question to himself?" Bradley's question, according to Trilling, "indicates the root of all Arnold's difficulties: he is basically confused about the nature of fact and verification."[25]

Trilling sets himself to clarify for Arnold "the nature of fact and verification" by calling not only upon Bradley but also upon I. A. Richards's discussion in *Science and Poetry*. A pseudo-statement, Trilling reminds us, "is a form of words which is justified entirely by its effect in releasing or organizing our impulses and attitudes. . . . A statement . . . is justified by its truth, i.e., it's correspondence, in a highly technical sense, with a fact to which it points." Now, Trilling adds, "This says, of course, only what Arnold said when he contrasted scientific with literary language."[26] Here lies the crux of Trilling's misconception of Arnold's position, for, as we shall see, Arnold's distinction between scientific and literary language is *not* convertible to Richards's distinction between statement and pseudo-statement. Consequently, Arnold's notion of verification is distinct from that set down in Richards's essay and from Trilling's interpretation of Richards's intention.

According to Trilling's use of *Science and Poetry*, pseudo-statement or poetry makes no claim to truth; it remains in the sphere of subjective feeling; it is not verifiable. And here, Trilling asserts, Arnold's religion remains—and as such it is a mere dilettantism. "Dilettantism," he writes, "is exactly the charge which Santayana levels at the whole movement from which Arnold's thought proceeds." The movement referred to is Modernism, and a Modernist is one who "has ceased to be a Christian to become . . . a connoisseur of Christianity." "Modernism is the love of all Christianity in those who perceive that it is all fable."[27] The Modernist, Santayana continues, is one for "whom the hard and narrow realism of official Christianity is offensive just because it presupposes that Christianity is true."[28]

That Trilling's judgment of Arnold's position is consistent with Santayana's distorted view of Modernism is plain from the context. For Trilling continues: "That Christianity is true: that is, after all, the one thing that Arnold cannot really say. That Christianity contains the highest moral law, that Christianity is natural, that Christianity is lovely, that Christianity provides a poetry serving the highest good, that Christianity *contains* the truth—anything but that *Christianity* is true."[29] Arnold cannot say Christianity is true because, in Trilling's view, Arnold has reduced Christian language to poetry, i.e., to pseudo-statement, and pseudo-statement is confined within the bounds of feeling and is not verifiable. "Feeling is all," says Faust. But Trilling counters: "Gretchen knows what neither Faust nor Arnold knew, that feeling is *not* all in poetry and religion. The language she knows, *is* the feeling, and language *is* the *idea*."[30]

In short, Trilling's argument runs essentially as follows: Arnold contends that Christian language is the language of poetry, not science. But poetic language is the language of pseudo-statement. Pseudo-statement is purely emotive and subjective. It does not speak of facts, nor can it be verified; hence, it cannot be true. Since Arnold cannot say that Christianity is true, his use of Christian language is a mere dilettantism.

The cumulative weight of the judgments on Arnold's religious epistemology advanced by Eliot, Richards, and Trilling understandably has had a great influence. Until recently it carried something of the status of a "received" critical tradition. This is evident in the way in which scholars have referred to Richards's, Eliot's, or Trilling's judgments as a shorthand way of dealing with Arnold's religious position.[31] The reductionist, noncognitivist interpretation of Arnold's religious epistemology has, in recent decades, taken forms other than purely "emotivist" readings. Arnold has been identified with R. B. Braithwaite's conative theory of religious belief;[32] with Jamesian pragmatism;[33] and with Hans Vaihinger's theory of fictions.[34] The demands of conceptual clarity require, however, that terms such as aestheticism, emotivism, and pragmatism receive careful scrutiny and discrimination before being used to characterize Arnold's position. The failure to take such care has contributed in large part to the frequent misrepresentation of Arnold's religious epistemology. While occasionally uncertainty on the matter is acknowledged, it is often the case that when terms such as aestheticism are directed at Arnold, a noncognitivist, nonreferential employment of language is implied. But to read Arnold in these terms, I will attempt to show, is not only to misread his religious epistemology but to fail properly to grasp his understanding of the substance of Christian belief at a number of crucial points.

Before I embark on the analysis of Arnold's religious epistemology, his hermeneutics, and his interpretation of Christianity, by which these representations can best be considered, it will be useful to examine Arnold's development from young poet to mature critic, and the influences that played upon him in the crucial decades between the 1840s and 70s.

NOTES

1. The finest study, which I have found extremely helpful, of Arnold's contemporary critics and how his engagement with them advanced his own ideas, is Sidney Coulling's *Matthew Arnold and His Critics* (Athens, OH, 1974).

2. Leslie Stephen, "Mr. Matthew Arnold and the Church of England," *Fraser's Magazine*, ns 2, (1870): 429-30.

3. F. C. Burkitt, *Two Lectures on the Gospels* (London, 1901) 54-56.

4. J. Llewelyn Davies, "Mr. Matthew Arnold's New Religion of the Bible," *The Contemporary Review* 21 (1872-73): 842.

5. T. R. Glover, *The Christian Tradition and Its Verification* (London, 1913) 16.

6. C. W. Emmet, *Conscience, Creeds, and Critics* (London, 1918) 103.

7. W. H. Fremantle, *The World as the Subject of Redemption* (London, 1885) 363.

8. W. J. Sparrow Simpson, *The Resurrection and Modern Thought* (London, 1911) 315.

9. H. D. A. Major, *English Modernism* (Cambridge, MA, 1927) 132-33.

10. Cited Leslie Brisman, "The Romantic Faith and the Primitive Logia," *The Arnoldian* 5 (1978): 2.

11. F. A. Iremonger, *William Temple* (London, 1948) 106.

12. G. W. E. Russell, *Matthew Arnold* (London, 1894) 354-55.

13. J. C. Shairp, *Culture and Religion in Some of Their Relations* (Edinburgh, 1870) 60-61.

14. Shairp 62.

15. Leslie Stephen, *Studies of a Biographer* (New York, 1907) 2: 109-10.

16. Stephen 106.

17. F. H. Bradley, *Ethical Studies* (Oxford, 1927) 315-16.

18. T. S. Eliot, *Selected Essays 1917-1932* (London, 1932) 399, 398.

19. Eliot 382.

20. Eliot 349.

21. I. A. Richards, *Principles of Literary Criticism* (London, 1924) 267.

22. Richards, *Principles* 273.

23. I. A. Richards, *Science and Poetry* (London, 1926) 59.

24. Richards, *Science* 60-61.

25. Lionel Trilling, *Matthew Arnold* (London, 1963) 358.

26. Trilling 360.

27. Trilling 363.

28. Trilling 364.

29. Trilling 364.

30. Trilling 365.

31. M. H. Abrams, in *Literature and Belief* (New York, 1958) 4ff., links Arnold with Richards, who, we are reminded, has taught us "to free the emotional efficacy of poetry from belief," for poetry now must take over the function of ordering our emotional life hitherto performed by the pseudo-statements of religion.

Murray Krieger, in *The New Apologists for Poetry* (Minneapolis, 1956) 183ff., similarly subsumes Arnold's position within Richards's view of the aesthetic status of religious language and speaks of "Richards's Arnoldian view of the historical role of poetry as a substitute for religion" (185).

Some critics are so assured of the Richards-Trilling reading of Arnold that they merely invoke Trilling's judgment, confident that they have discharged their critical task. See, e.g., Michael Thorpe, *Matthew Arnold* (London, 1969) 159ff., and Hoxie Neale Fairchild, *Religious Trends in English Poetry* (New York, 1957) 4:499ff. Fairchild comments: "Lionel Trilling already performed it [the critical task] so admirably . . . it is fortunate for me as well as the reader that the work has been done" (499).

Two more recent and excellent studies of Arnold also invoke Richards's 1926 edition of *Science and Poetry* and interpret Arnold's view of religious language as the "purest aestheticism possible" or as essentially "affectivist," i.e., emotivist and subjective. William Madden, in *Matthew Arnold: A Study of the Aesthetic Temperament in Victorian England* (London, 1967), remarks that "Richards's concluding statement in *Science and Poetry* is to this extent an accurate and revealing paraphrase of the position set out in Arnold's late criticism" (194-95).

Peter A. Dale's valuable study of Arnold, *The Victorian Critic and the Idea of History* (London, 1977) 160ff., identifies Arnold's use of religious language with that of Santayana in that it has nothing to do with cognitive truth "but resides solely in the reader's immediate or intuitive emotional and moral response to that object" (160), the position later adopted by "I. A. Richards, who has produced a systematic elaboration of Arnold's fundamental position" (161).

32. See R. B. Braithwaite's influential Eddington Lecture, *An Empiricist's View of the Nature of Religious Belief* (Cambridge, 1955). Braithwaite is deeply impressed by Arnold's insight into the role of the religious imagination and sees Arnold as a precursor of his own conative theory. As we shall observe in chapter 3, Arnold's position has certain affinities with that of Braithwaite, but Arnold differs critically in wanting to make real theological assertions.

33. Vincent Buckley, in *Poetry and Morality* (London, 1959), sees Arnold as "a sort of pragmatist" in that Arnold "would judge the truth of Christianity by its inward effects, its power to stabilize man and fit him for moral action in the world" (52-53). E. San Juan, in "Arnold and the Poetics of Belief: Some Implications of Literature and Dogma," *Harvard Theological Review* 58, (1960), associates Arnold with William James's pragmatism since "the pragmatic or, in Arnold's term, 'experimental' value of any utterance lies in its capacity to help one realize his actions." (101). Pragmatism is not an inappropriate label for Arnold's experiential position, so long as one understands the true epistemological implications of experience in Arnold's radical empiricism.

34. See Harry M. Campbell, "Arnold's Religion and the Theory of Fictions," *Religion in Life* 36 (1967), and more recently Ruth apRoberts's full-scale study of Arnold's religious criticism, *Arnold and God* (Berkeley, 1983). I find apRoberts's treatment of religious language as "fictive," in her chapter on metaphor, to be epistemologically ambiguous. She appears to see religious metaphor as serving a genuine *cognitive* function, but elsewhere she associates Arnold with Richards's separation of referential and emotive discourse and with Wallace Stevens's "Supreme Fiction."

1 "A Return upon Himself": Arnold's Development from Poet to Religious Critic

Cognitavi vias meas, et converti pedes meas in testimonia Tua; I called mine own ways to remembrance, and turned my feet unto Thy testimonies. PS. CXIX.59

God and the Bible

He who sees that the ways of renunciation and of action are one, he sees truly.

Bhagavad Gita 5,5

Many of Arnold's contemporaries voiced the wish that he would cease writing prose like *Literature and Dogma* and would again give his English public the likes of "Thyrsis" and "The Scholar-Gipsy." The lament over Arnold's "giving up" poetry for a life of prosaic controversy was and is often accompanied by the claim that his abandonment of poetry was a willed sacrifice that left him divided and contradictory—"a study in conflict," as E. K. Brown called Arnold. This interpretation is strikingly conveyed in W. H. Auden's lines that Arnold

> thrust his gift in prison till it died
> And left him nothing but a jailer's voice and face.

The source of the death of Arnold's poetic gift, a gift nourished by youthful, Romantic enthusiasm at Oxford, is traced to that paternal reverence which finally caused the son to cry out,

> I am my father's forum and he shall be heard
> Nothing shall contradict his holy, final word.[1]

That Arnold experienced conflicts as a young man in his twenties and thirties is indisputable; and the fact is that uncertainties, longings, regrets were never entirely dispelled. But what else would one expect of a man of great imagination and sensitivity? Today Arnold scholars generally are agreed that too much has been made of the conflict between Arnold the poet and Arnold the social and religious critic. There is, in fact, not only a discernible continuity between Arnold's poetic efforts and his prose work, but one can see in his development from youthful Oxonian to middle-aged man-of-affairs the shaping of a self and the working out of a vocation that brought wholeness, "fixity," even a joy which came from a sense of satisfaction in seeing that his life and work were having a wide and fruitful effect.[2] That such a self and vocation involved the moderating of desire and the overmastering of Romantic strife, languor, and melancholy has to be seen as one of Arnold's distinctions—the psychological integration of a deeply sensitive, complex, and worldly man from fragmentariness into wholeness. That the serenity, cheerfulness, or even the joy of Arnold's maturity was never far removed from what Max Müller saw as a kind of understood, though seldom expressed, sadness does not detract from but only increases our sense of admiration. Arnold was a man who, indeed, did come to see life steadily and whole, through and despite all of its "daemonic" agitations as well as sublime delights, as steadily and whole as any man could hope to see life without falsifying experience.

To stress the kinship between Arnold the poet and Arnold the critic and the psychological and intellectual integration of the man is not to deny that especially during the 1840s Arnold was a divided self—

> But hardly have we, for one little hour,
> Been on our own line, have we been ourselves—   (P 290)

but rather to rectify the overemphasis on the fragmented Arnold with its often attendant failure to see the continuities as well as the form of the developing mind of the man as he sought to shape his life. As to his religious belief during the spiritually tumultuous decade between Oxford and his marriage, there is no doubt that he rejected many traditional formulations of orthodox Christian doctrine. His theological ideas were, as Charlotte Brontë observed, "vague and unsettled."[3] It is clear from the evidence in the poetry and elsewhere that Arnold at the least experimented with, and in some instances embraced, heterodox religious beliefs during these years. But it is also evident that he came to find many of these beliefs and the sentiments which they engendered to be inadequate, and that in his own intellectual and spiritual development he increasingly expressed appreciation for the traditional religious faith of Europe.

It is, therefore, misleading because too unqualified to say that Arnold gave up Christianity or was not in any acceptable sense a Christian during his most creative years as a poet. The evidence does not give us a definite answer. There is clear testimony, however, that he continued to speak with approbation about aspects of his youthful faith and that he identified with the faith of his father during these years. By his early forties Arnold endorsed a form of liberal Christian belief and participated, without dissembling, in the worship of the church. In any case, this study is in part an effort to substantiate the view that Arnold's mature religious position is avowedly and legitimately Christian; that his considered philosophy of life—including his covert metaphysics—is vitalized and permeated by distinctly Christian ideas and sentiments.

During his undergraduate years at Oxford, Arnold was liberated, to use today's idiom, from the religious orthodoxy of his youth through his reading of Emerson, Carlyle, Goethe, and the novels of George Sand. As Tom Arnold's daughter, Mrs. Humphry Ward, recalled, the Arnold brothers and their friends "discovered George Sand, Emerson, and Carlyle, and orthodox Christianity no longer seemed to them the sure refuge it had always been to the strong teacher who trained them as boys." Their "common Oxford passion" for George Sand's *Consuelo*, in particular, "was a revelation to the two young men brought up under the 'earnest' influence of Rugby. It seemed to open to them a world of artistic beauty and joy of which they had never dreamed."[4]

"RIGOROUS TEACHERS"

There is, however, another side to the story. We now know that from 1845 to 1847 Matthew Arnold undertook a regimen of philosophical reading that was directed at saving and restoring what he could of his religious beliefs. Unlike his brother Tom, Matthew "was concerned intimately at this period of his life primarily with the religious problem."[5] His preoccupation with it was personal and urgent. The "rigorous teachers" of the decade between the mid-1840s and the mid-1850s were those, as he was later to write of Emerson, who lived in "the life of the spirit": Goethe, Spinoza, the *Bhagavad Gita*, Marcus Aurelius, Lucretius, Senancour.* It is in the context of these "Continental" influences that one must find the clues not only to the struggles of the young poet but also to the spiritual connections, the continuities between the important poetry of 1849-53 and the prose of *Culture and Anarchy* and *Literature and Dogma*. Arnold's development as a poet in these crucial years is closely related to his working out a philosophy that would be spiritually satisfying; and it was, fundamentally, a struggle with the very Romantic temperament which he had

---

* These are the teachers that had the greatest hold on Arnold at this time and are reflected in the poems. During this period Arnold also read Plato, Kant, Berkeley, Descartes, Bacon, and Mill, as well as Plotinus, Augustine, Cudworth, Schelling, and Coleridge.

so recently found liberating. Park Honan has observed how after 1842 Arnold was occupied with the memory of his father, who had died in that year, and how in venerating Dr. Arnold the reformer "he aggravated a conflict in himself between the creative poet and the practical activist, the lyricist and the puritan, the imaginative man and the ethical man."[6] If "The Strayed Reveller" is, as Lionel Trilling has written, "Arnold's celebration of the painful glories of man's bondage to the strength of the emotions,"[7] most of the poems written between 1849 and the suppression of "Empedocles on Etna" in 1853 are expressions of various attempts to find release from "the doubts, disputes, distractions, fears," the "sick hurry" that Arnold associates with that Romantic spirit which so infected his world and his own person.

In the Stoics and the *Bhagavad Gita*, in Spinoza and Senancour, Arnold found "an unblamed serenity . . . freed from passions." While they varied, each of these forms of spiritual "liberation" implied a distinctive notion of the self and its relation to the world. Arnold came under the spell of the medievalism and sentimentalism of Senancour, "thou sadder sage," but the French *solitaire's* "air of languor" and "feeling chill" could not finally satisfy him, although he never escaped it fully. In bidding farewell to Senancour, Arnold was declaring, though with reluctance, that he could not accept the view that spiritual deliverance demands absenting oneself in solitude from the world of men and public duty. "I in the world must live," Arnold asserts. (P 142).

In the Stoics and the *Bhagavad Gita*, Arnold found, for a time, a truer teaching. "The Indians," he writes to Clough in 1848, "distinguish between meditation or absorption—and knowledge: and between abandoning practice, and abandoning the fruits of action. . . . This last is a supreme step" (CL 71). What attracted Arnold was the idea "of toil unsevered from tranquility." The poems of the period show Arnold's acquiescence in the knowledge that our life and freedom of action are circumscribed—and yet that we *must act*.* Wisdom should teach us of the

> Uno'erleap'd Mountains of Necessity,
> Sparing us narrower margin than we deem.   (P 109)

We must not claim

> To too exact a steering of our way;
> Let us not fret and fear to miss our aim.   (P 146)

---

* Here I believe Trilling and others have misread Arnold. Arnold advocates, like Krishna's advice to Arjuna, a disinterested action, an action free of anxiety about externals or results.

The fretting and fearing are expressive of a self still under the illusions of a Romantic, unfettered egoism, a self which does not yet know its true nature and, hence, its limits—the self of Hegel's "unhappy consciousness." The wise man can "admire uncravingly," for

> Before him he sees life unroll,
> A placid and continuous whole—
> That general life, which does not cease,
> Whose secret is not joy, but peace.   (P 96)

The general life is being at one with nature, the Stoic *phusis*—universal, impersonal, detached—the life which alone is abiding and imperturbable. Such a life of renunciation, of spiritual freedom, is first of all an attitude of mind, not a denial of the active life. As Krishna remarks, "He who sees that the ways of renunciation and of action are one, he sees truly" (*Bhagavad Gita* 5,5). Secondly, it involves a "resolve to be thyself,"—that is, attaining a true judgment about what lies within and beyond one's nature. But since man is by nature a social being, he must carry out those duties which the natural order of society requires, though in a spirit of inner freedom.

Arnold came to see in Arthur Clough's Romantic storm and stress, in his failure to be disinterested, the essential weakness of his age and also the weakness in himself. It was a failure to conquer desire, to be free of morbid emotions, and to attain tranquillity of soul. "For God's sake," he writes to Clough, "don't mope, for from that no good can come." When Clough asked him where he thought he had gone wrong, Arnold gave him this candid and self-reflective answer:

> In this: that you would never take your assiette as something determined final and unchangeable for you and proceed to work away on the basis of that: but were always poking and patching and cobbling at the assiette itself—could never finally, as it seemed—"resolve to be thyself"—but were looking for this and that experience, and doubting whether you ought not to adopt this or that mode of being of persons *qui ne vous valaient pas* because it might possibly be nearer the truth than you own. . . . It is what I call your morbid conscientiousness. . . . It spoils your action (CL 130).

The dominant personal themes in the poems of 1849-52 are the distraction and weariness brought on by Romantic self-absorption and the growing perception, observed in the Stoic and Hindu life of detachment and *apatheia*, of a way of truly *being* himself and losing his misery. A close reading of the early poems reveals, however, that there is more in Arnold's spiritual intimations of the real self than Stoic detachment and repose. This oriental wisdom is infused with the sentiment preached so powerfully by Carlyle in *Sartor Resartus:* "The folly of that impossible Precept, *Know thyself*; til it will be translated into this partially possible one, *Know what thou canst work at*."[8] The poems disclose a more active, Carlylean, Goethean, biblical insistence on renouncement and selfless duty:

> He only lives with the world's life,
> Who hath renounced his own.   (P 140)

It was Carlyle who introduced Arnold to Goethe's supremely influential *Entsagen*: "Well did the wisest of our time write: 'It is only with renunciation [*Entsagen*] that Life, properly speaking, can be said to begin.'"[9] Yet from infancy, long before Arnold read Carlyle or Goethe, the biblical teaching of *necrosis*—of dying to the self—was bred in the bones of Matthew Arnold. *Necrosis* was to become the crux of his understanding of Christianity and that by which he himself found not only peace but joy. And so while Goethe's *Entsagen* is indisputably important, the roots of Arnold's mature intuition of the meaning of renunciation are to be found in his youthful Christian nurture.

Arnold's deep and extensive philosophical reading, while profoundly affecting him, left him unsatisfied; and the dissatisfaction had to do with an atrophy of feeling that philosophical reflection could not reverse. As early as September 1849, he acknowledged that his "one natural craving" was "not for profound thoughts, mighty spiritual workings, etc., etc. but a distinct seeing of my way as far as my own nature is concerned" (CL 110). The feeling is intensified when he writes to Clough in May 1854: "I feel immensely . . . what I have (I believe) lost and choked by my treatment of myself and the studies to which I have addicted myself" (CL 136). About the same time he notes: "I cannot conceal from myself the objection which really wounds and perplexes me from the religious side is that the service of reason is freezing to feeling, chilling to the religious mood. And feeling and the religious mood are eternally the deepest being of man, the ground of all joy and greatness for him" (Yale ms; cited P 277).

This new conviction that reason and learning may be freezing to feeling and that feeling—connected as it is to the religious sense, as "the deepest being of man"—must not be scorned, is voiced in the 1852 poem "Progress." Arnold is impatient with those advanced thinkers "Who cry aloud to lay the old world low," those rationalists who see in the ancient religions only "Religious fervours! ardour misapplied!" On the contrary, religion teaches the highest wisdom, energizes the will, and confers peace and refreshment:

> Which has not taught weak wills how much they can?
> Which has not fall'n on the dry heart like rain?
> Which has not cried to sunk, self-weary man:
> > *Thou must be born again!* (P 277-78)

A related sentiment is expressed in a letter to Clough of September 1853:

> If one loved what was beautiful and interesting in itself *passionately* enough, one would produce what was excellent without troubling oneself with religious dogmas at all. As it is, we are warm only when dealing with these last—and what is frigid is always bad. I would have others—most others stick to the old religious dogmas because I sincerely feel that this *warmth* is the great blessing and this frigidity the great curse—and on the old religious road they have still the best chance of getting the one and avoiding the other (CL 143).

Further evidence that his philosophical regimen left Arnold dissatisfied is present in the poem "The Second Best." Books read and schemes bred have, Arnold writes, strangled "nature's wish." He continues:

> So it *must* be! yet, while leading
> A strain'd life, while overfeeding,
> Like the rest, his wit with reading,
> > No small profit that man earns,
>
> Who through all he meets can steer him,
> Can reject what cannot clear him,
> Cling to what can truly cheer him;
> > Who each day more surely learns
>
> That an impulse, from the distance
> Of his deepest, best existence
> To the words, 'Hope, Light, Persistence,'
> > Strongly sets and truly burns. (P 296-97)

Arnold wants to cling only to that learning which can "cheer him," to reject all that cannot "clear him," but, better yet, he wants to learn to heed that impulse "from the distance / Of his deepest, best existence" which can stir "Hope, Light, Persistence." The way of the strayed reveller, the way of the quietist, even the way of the imperturbable sage does not appear to plumb that buried life which constitutes Arnold's true self. But, Arnold seems to be asking, can the buried, the true self be plumbed? Does it forever remain in that forest glade of Romantic innocence? Or is it an illusion? The fact is that, as A. Dwight Culler and others have pointed out,[10] the image of the subterranean buried self in the early poetry gives way in the prose and poetry of the 60s to the idea of the best self—a very different conception having to do with something objective, something outside the self, a will or life in obedience to which or in whose service one finds a perfect freedom or real self. Commenting on the best self, Culler writes: "We have moved from a romantic conception of things, where reality lies deep within the center and the outside is false, to a more religious conception, where the good is placed on high."[11]

Arnold's move from Romantic obsession with self-analysis and self-absorption through the idea of impersonality and detachment to the paradoxical shaping of a self through *necrosis*, the losing of the self, is not reflected in the early poetry. It does, however, emerge as a central theme of the later elegies, and it dominates the religious prose. And there are strong indications of such a spiritual turning in Arnold's letters of the early 1860s written to Clough and to his sister "K." Even in the poem "The Buried Life" there are intimations. Amid all the dialectical questionings about the true self, which convey "A melancholy into all our day," there is that rare occasion when "a belovéd hand is laid in ours" and "Our eyes can in another's eyes read clear"; and then "a lost pulse of feeling stirs again. . . . / And what we mean, we say, and what we would, we know" (P 290-91). Arnold is saying that not in inward searching but in the love of and life with another, feeling is restored and integrity achieved.

It is evident that in the early 1850s Arnold's search for a vision of life that, eschewing Romantic subjectivity would animate feeling, while channeling and fortifying a sense of vocation, was moving in the direction of the overtly religious poetry and prose of the 1860s. It is in Arnold's letters and essays of the early and mid-1850s—the time of his courtship and marriage to Frances Lucy Wightman, his appointment as inspector of schools, and his election as Professor of Poetry at Oxford—that his search for "fixity" and a sense of mission conjoined with "the highest Joy" is most fully revealed.

A letter of 1851 to his sister "K" gives an indication of Arnold's preoccupation at the time. He confesses that, while it is "a melancholy passage," the "aimless and unsettled, but also open and liberal state of our youth we *must* perhaps all leave" to take refuge in what he calls "our morality and character." The latter he identifies with those unworldly virtues and qualities which he observes in his family but also finds so naturally lacking in himself. He voices the wish to be with his family more often in order that he might be more readily apprised of his faults. "I intend not," he writes, "to give myself the rein in following my natural tendency, but to make war against it till he ceases to isolate me from you, and leaves me with the power to discern and adopt the good which you have and I have not' (L 1:14-15). In June 1852 he writes that despite "bad spirits" he must insist that "nothing can absolve us from the duty of doing all we can to keep alive our courage and activity" (CL 122-23).

Further evidence of Arnold's state of mind is revealed in his letter of August 1853 to Clough. He tells his friend that he finds an object lesson in the return of James Anthony Froude, the historian and author of the skeptical *Nemesis of Faith* (1849), to religious conformity, after a period of spiritual unrest, suffering, and notoriety. While he doubts that Froude "is altogether changed," as his friends suggest, he nevertheless sees the significance of Froude's action in his "having purified his moral being." By this Arnold means that "all that was mere fume and vanity and love of notoriety and opposition . . . [Froude] has abandoned and regrets." He sees Froude getting more solidly into his literary work; no longer is he "beating the air." "May we," Arnold exhorts, "follow his example!" (CL 140). And Arnold did follow Froude's example, for within two months he had completed the preface to *Poems* (1853) in which he repudiates "Empedocles on Etna."

The years 1852-57 were troubled years of transition for Arnold. They are associated with his publication and rejection of "Empedocles on Etna," the working out of a new poetics in "Sohrab and Rustum" and "Merope" and in the prefaces of 1852 and 1858, and the writing of poems such as "Stanzas from the Grande Chartreuse." It was a time of genuine "wandering between two worlds." However, the determination to suppress Romantic strife and languor is now firm; even a growing disenchantment with a profound Goethean and Stoic detachment and resignation is discernible; yet the urge to describe "the modern situation in its true *blankness* and *barrenness* and *unpoetrylessness*" (CL 126) is at war with his growing conviction that "only positive convictions and feelings are worth anything."

"Empedocles on Etna" stands as Arnold's fierce and heroic commitment to intellectual integrity, to [seeing] "things as they are . . . in their stern simplicity," and to rejecting the religious consolation of other men, "facile because adapted to their weaknesses" (P 154). Yet the poem's "dialogue of the mind with itself" dissatisfied Arnold profoundly, and it is this discontent that gives us the clue to his ultimate spiritual, as well as artistic, solution and the bridge to the emerging religious convictions of the mid-1860s.

Arnold's uncertainty about "Empedocles" is, revealingly, associated with Emerson. He writes to Clough: "You must tell me what Emerson says. Make him look at it. *You* in your heart are saying *mollis et exspes* [unstrung and hopeless] over again. But woe was upon me if I analyzed not my situation" (CL 126). Arnold knew, of course, what Emerson would think. The poem fails to speak of that joy and hope which are the great virtues of Emerson's own prose. In his recorded plans for the poem Arnold wrote that "the stern simplicity" is "capable of affording rapture and the purest peace."[12] But this, of course, is just what Empedocles is incapable of feeling:

> I alone
> Am dead to life and joy, therefore I read
> In all things my own deadness.   (P 199-200)

Empedocles, in spite of his insistence, cannot live in the world with joy, with an "immortal vigour." Arnold's rejection of Empedocles is crucial because it signals his own disillusion and his recognition that Lucretius, Marcus Aurelius, and Epictetus are not adequate guides. It also reflects Arnold's growing dissatisfaction with Carlyle's "gospel."[13] When in 1848 Clough, bidding Emerson farewell at Liverpool, said that "Carlyle has led us all out into the desert and left us there,"[14] he was, in effect, expressing Arnold's feelings as well. Arnold spoke of it years later in his "Emerson" address:

> Carlyle's perverse attitude toward happiness cuts him off from hope. He fiercely attacks the desire for happiness; his grand point in *Sartor*, his secret in which the soul may find rest, is that one shall cease to desire happiness, that one should learn to say to oneself: "What if thou wert born and predestined not to be happy, but to be unhappy!" He is wrong; St. Augustine is the better philosopher, who says: "Act we *must* in pursuance of what gives us most delight" (CPW 10:183).

It is this very gloom and lack of animation, joy, and hope—the absence of the Sophoclean "serious cheerfulness"—that is the mark of the "modern" but also the token of the failure of these "modern" poets to be *adequate*. In the inaugural lecture of 1857 Arnold speaks of Lucretius's noble attempts to penetrate to the nature of things. "But there is no peace, no cheerfulness for him either in the world from which he comes, or in the solitude to which he goes." He is "overstrained, gloom-weighted, morbid;

and he who is morbid is no adequate interpreter of his age" (CPW 1:33, 34). Arnold finds the same to be true of the great Stoics:

> It is impossible to rise from reading Epictetus or Marcus Aurelius without a sense of constraint and melancholy, without feeling that the burden laid upon man is well-nigh greater than he can bear. Honour to the sages who have felt this, and yet have borne it! Yet, even for the sage, this sense of labour and sorrow in his march toward the goal constitutes a relative inferiority; the noblest souls of whatever creed, the pagan Empedocles as well as the Christian Paul, have insisted on the necessity of an inspiration, a joyful emotion, to make moral action perfect (CPW 3: 134).

J. C. Shairp was certainly correct when in the summer of 1849 he wrote to Clough that "Empedocles on Etna" was "not so much about the man who leapt in the crater" as it was merely the name and outward circumstances "used for the drapery of [Arnold's] own thoughts" (C 287). But it is also true that while Empedocles threw himself into Etna, Arnold strove on. As Culler has put it, "Arnold threw his own personal Empedocles into the volcano and came back down, a whole man, to lead a useful life in the cities of the plain. Thus, although in one sense *Empedocles on Etna* dramatizes what Arnold did, in another it dramatizes what he did not do. It dramatizes what he was saved from doing by the fact that he did it vicariously in the realm of art."[15] Thus Arnold was entirely candid when in 1867 he wrote to Henry Dunn that "neither then nor now would my creed, if I wished or were able to draw it out in black and white, be by any means identical with that contained in the preachment of Empedocles"; for, he continues, "no critic appears to remark that if Empedocles throws himself into Etna his creed can hardly be meant to be one to live by" (C 288).

Kenneth Allott has appositely remarked on the paradox of "Empedocles on Etna" and the Matthew Arnold of the 1850s:

> "Empedocles on Etna" was rejected as a failure because it left Arnold with a hopeless antinomy: on the one hand, "the pale cold star of Truth" to be followed; on the other hand, the necessity of joy. But joy is impossible if "the service of reason" freezes "feeling and the religious mood"; and the price of joy is beyond the means of the sensitive and honest man if payment has to be made in the currency of illusion. However hard he tried, Arnold could not embrace "truth" and "joy" in a

single thought but was drawn back again and again to the nagging contradiction between them.[16]

Arnold was not one to waffle on matters of artistic or social import simply because he was savaged by a critic. But the criticisms of the early poems and especially of "Empedocles on Etna" by his sister "K" and by friends such as Clough, Froude, and Shairp were troubling because they focused on that "hopeless antinomy," the fact that Arnold could not reconcile truth and joy in a unified creative vision. "Anything," Shairp wrote of Arnold, "that so takes the life from out of things must be false. . . . If there's nothing else in the world but blank dejection, it's not worth while setting them to music."[17]

Charles Kingsley characteristically lectured Arnold but in such a personal manner as to sting his friend's already uneasy spirit. "Here is a man," Kingsley moralized,

> to whom God has given rare faculties and advantages. Let him be assured that he was meant to use them for God. . . . Let him rejoice in his youth, as the great Arnold told his Rugby scholars to do, and walk in the sight of his own eyes; but let him remember that for all these things God will bring him into judgment. For every work done in the strength of that youthful genius he must give account, whether it be good or evil.[18]

Kingsley's pious cautionary, crude as it was, nevertheless touched a sensitive chord in Arnold's own thought and feeling, which now were concentrated on his own new duties, his emergent reflections on the function of poetry, and, doubtless, on his growing sense of reconciliation with his father and attraction to his work and aims. While written years later, a letter of Arnold's to Henry Allon bespeaks the actual change that was taking place in Arnold in the years following the publication of the 1852 poems:

> As to praise of my poetry, I have indeed more than cause to be, as you say, satisfied: perhaps, as one advances in life, purely literary respects and literary praise seem not quite as much as they did when one was younger. . . . It so happens that I live chiefly with those to whom the remarks on the religious tendencies, or rather the want of them, in my poetry, will give more distress than the commendation of the poetry, much of it, as poetry, will give pleasure.[19]

Park Honan has emphasized the importance, not only of Dr. Arnold, but also of Matthew's mother and sister "K" in the development of his new poetics and his growing sense of social vocation. Mrs. Arnold's impatient feeling that her son, at 30, should take up his father's social causes clearly beset him.[20]

In the summer of 1853, a few months after completing "Sohrab and Rustum," Arnold went to Fox How and wrote the preface in which he explains the reasons for excluding "Empedocles on Etna" from the 1853 edition of the *Poems*. To him, the reason for the suppression is clear: in the poem "the suffering finds no vent in action"; "a continuous state of mental distress is prolonged, unrelieved by incident, hope, or resistance." When everything must be endured and nothing can be done, one contemplates a situation in which "there is inevitably something morbid." Such a representation is neither geniunely noble nor tragic. For, Arnold insists, in the presence of the most tragic circumstances, "the feeling of enjoyment may still subsist." Indeed, "the representation of the most utter calamity, of the liveliest anguish, is not sufficient to destroy it; the more tragic the situation, the deeper becomes the enjoyment." What then is demanded of a poem is not only that it should "add to the knowledge of men" but that it should "inspirit and rejoice the reader," that it should "infuse delight," give joy. "The right art is that alone, which creates the highest enjoyment" (CPW 1:2).

Taken in isolation, Arnold's new poetics could be read as banal or, worse, as a dishonest sop. But it is evident that he is in fact struggling to resolve the "hopeless antinomy," to work out the relation of knowledge, the truth of our situation, to such human necessities as love, hope, and joy. The happiness of which Arnold speaks is no crude eudaemonism or the result of the "power of positive thinking," for he links it with the truly tragic. It is here that the clue to the resolution of the antinomy and to Arnold's evolving religious vision is to be found: the convergence of tragedy and joy, "seeing things as they are" in their utter evil and terror and yet, paradoxically, recognizing that a life encompassed by such realities is "capable of affording rapture and the purest peace."

"Sohrab and Rustum" replaced "Empedocles on Etna" as the central poem of the 1853 volume and was, Arnold felt, partially successful in exemplifying the tenets of the 1853 preface. In November 1853 he writes to Clough: "Homer *animates*—Shakespeare *animates*—in its poor way I think Sohrab and Rustum *animates*—the Gipsy Scholar at best awakens a pleasing melancholy. But this is not what we want" (CL 146). As Trilling, Culler, and other critics have noted, while Arnold sought in "Sohrab and

Rustum" to illustrate his new poetic creed, its interest is found rather in the very personal meaning Arnold wished to forestall—a meaning associated with his father. Of the poem Trilling writes: "The strong son is slain by the mightier father, and in the end Sohrab draws his father's spear from his own side to let out his life and end the anguish. We watch Arnold in his later youth, and we must wonder if he is not, in a psychical sense, doing the same thing." Trilling interprets this as Arnold's desire no longer to seek the poise and equilibrium of his competing energies but to attain his father's fixity. "He stood ready," says Trilling, "to sacrifice poetic talent, formed in the solitude of the self, to the creation of character, formed in the crowding objectivity of the world."[21] How true Trilling's judgment is! And yet if the filial symbolism is to be employed personally, it may—as Culler has shown—reveal a more dialectical and reconciliatory meaning in the father-son relationship than Trilling perceives:

> For when Sohrab implores his father to come and sit beside him on the sand and call him son, we are told that Sohrab's voice "released the heart / Of Rustum," whose tears broke forth. "He cast / His arms around his son's neck, and wept aloud. . . ." Both he and Sohrab "poise" their lives by incorporating their opposites within themselves. Sohrab finds in Rustum a father and discovers that his father is not harsh, but soft and tender. And Rustum finds in Sohrab a son and acknowledges that this son is not effeminate but a true warrior. In this discovery they exchange symbols. . . . The true self of Sohrab contains the pillar as well as the garden, the true self of Rustum the garden as well as the pillar.
>
> The final reconciliation of the conflict is of course effected by the end-symbol of the river Oxus. Through the symbol our attention is turned away from the scene of death to one that signifies life, and we are told that life goes on despite this tragedy in which one life is extinguished.[22]

Culler's reading of the poem may be more in accord with the *Tüchtigkeit* which Trilling sees as Arnold's real hope and desire at this time, for this "excellence" involves the psychic health which, as Goethe says, is a sign that the Muse has taken her abode "with those who upon their entrance into active and effective, if sometimes unhappy life, cheerfully give up their dreams, accept what each hour brings in its season, learn to assuage their own sorrows, and look for opportunities to lighten the sorrows and foster the joys of others."[23] Here one is closer to that convergence of tragedy and joy, to that fixity or resolve, "the true sign of the Law" that Arnold now perceives both in the teaching of the Buddha and in the way of his own father.

Arnold opened his inaugural lecture in the Poetry Chair at Oxford in November 1857 by citing the advice of Gautama to a disciple: "Go then, O Pourna, having been delivered, deliver; having been consoled, console; being arrived thyself at the farther bank, enable others to arrive there also" (CPW 1:19). In this same month Arnold finished "Merope," which he told his sister he hoped would "have what Buddha called the character of Fixity" (L 1:57). Significantly, November was also the month Arnold assigned as the date of "Rugby Chapel," the elegy in memory of his father. Most of the elegies written in the decade prior to *New Poems* (1867), and which make up the best of Arnold's poetic output of this late period, tell us more about Arnold than they do about the subjects of the poems. "Rugby Chapel" is essentially the setting forth of a third path or way beyond Romanticism and Stoicism. In terms of the self it represents not only a repudiation of the ordinary self but the searchings for the buried self. It bears witness to the mystery that true healing and deliverance come only to those who, freed from obsession with the subjective self, find strength and joy in the best self. Culler has called attention to the fact that the elegy distinguishes among three ways of life: ". . . the majority of men, who 'eddy about / Here and there' (like the gipsies); the few, who make for some clear-purposed goal (like the questers); and then, not the poet sitting removed from it all on the mountain-top, but the Servant or Son of God, who saves others along with himself."[24]

The questers who strain on alone in the storm are asked when they reach the lonely inn: "Whom in our party we bring? / Whom we have left in the snow?" And they reply: "We bring / Only ourselves! we lost / Sight of the rest in the storm." Arnold clearly sees in the figure of his father a more excellent way, the way of the "Sons of God" who, though toil and dejection have tried their spirits, remain nevertheless "cheerful, and helpful, and firm." Arnold sees these three virtues as interdependent; the fixity and cheerfulness are the fruit of self-loss, but, paradoxically, the latter comes only when, forsaking languor, the soul is "tempered with fire." The sons of God, those children of the second birth, are for the world "beacons of hope," the "helpers and friends of mankind."

It is not until the poems of the early 1860s, however, that the figure of the best self is explicitly associated with Christian imagery. In "East London," Arnold comments on the ill and overworked clergyman in the East End:

O human soul! as long as thou canst so
Set up a mark of everlasting light,
Above the howling senses' ebb and flow,

To cheer thee, and to right thee if thou roam—
Not with lost toil thou labourest through the night!
Thou mak'st the heaven thou hop'st indeed thy home.

(P 525)

By the time "East London" was written, Arnold was already beginning, with the help of some new "masters of the mind," that reconstruction of Christian belief that was to occupy him for the next 15 years. He now emerges out of that limbo "between two worlds" in which he had been immobilized for much of the previous decade. He envisions hope in a new birth of Christianity that will unite the antique and the modern in a new synthesis. "Obermann Once More" is the expression of this transition and of Arnold's slowly ripened conviction of the dawning of a renewed, reconstructed Christianity and his resolve to serve its cause. "Obermann Once More," like the elegy to his father, marks a crucial stage in Arnold's own spiritual journey. It marks, as Tinker and Lowry have suggested, a twofold transition in Arnold's life: "First of all, there is the evidence— though rigorously repressed in the poem, as it should be—of that relatively new conviction about Christianity which was now to form the centre of Arnold's life. At least this much may be fairly said: the wandering between two worlds was over. In the second place, the poem is a monument to Arnold's transition from poetry to prose. The break was now clearly made, and this poem quietly attests the reasons" (C 272).

The light and warmth that Arnold had long sought he now discovers is "shining still." "Death's frozen hour is done," and with what time and strength is left, he will employ himself

That end to help attain:
One common wave of thought and joy
Lifting mankind again!   (P 576)

The joy Arnold envisions is not the joy of the forest glade, a joy born of "sweet illusions," but a "joy whose grounds are true." As Culler remarks, "The faculty through which we are able to find this, according to Arnold, is the imaginative reason,"[25]—that is, the union of intellect and feeling which uniquely marks the modern spirit. In Arnold's religious reconstruction it is the synthesis of Romanticism and rationalism, which issues in a new Christian humanism.

"NEW MASTERS OF THE MIND"

Arnold's resolve that he "in the world must live" was strengthened between the early 1850s and 60s, but so also was his feeling that the time left to employ himself may be brief. "His tensions were increased by a sense of time passing, by the breaking up of that solid establishment the Arnold family, and even by a grave warning. Consulting a doctor, Matthew was blandly told in 1847 or 1848 that he had inherited his father's heart defect."[26]
Arnold's sense of time passing, coupled with his new duties as head of his own growing family, his career responsibilities, and his stature as established writer and public figure made him increasingly aware of a new kind of distractedness and the need for self-discipline and a concentration of direction. "I have also lately had a stronger wish than usual not to vacillate and be helpless, but to do my duty," he wrote to his mother in December 1854 (L 1:41). The death of friends gave the new sense of public duty a troubling urgency. "How the days slip away, and how little one does in them! That is more and more my thought in hearing of every fresh death among those whom I have known," he confided to his sister "K" in June 1855 (L 1:45). What he desperately wished was to introduce some method into his life (L 1:54). From the mid-1850s the notebooks record entries that show the intensity of Arnold's resolve to accept the claim of duty and to give his life that sense of fixity which he was discovering in the teachings of the religious saints and sages. In each year between 1857 and 1859, and again from 1863 to 1869, the notebook entries near the beginning of each year repeat the words of Thomas à Kempis: *Semper aliquid certi pro ponendum est* (We should always form a fixed resolution). In 1858 he records: "The 3 things that improve genius: proper exertion, frequent exertion, and successful exertion" (NB 6). From the *Mānava-Dharmaśāstra* he reminds himself of "the misery attached to embodied spirits from a violation of their duties, and the imperishable bliss attached to them from their abundant performance of all duties" (NB 10). Duties can best be carried out if some method is imposed on life's multifariousness, so Arnold jots down his resolution:

up at 7
breakfast 8 ½ off by 10 to 10
bed at 11
write out plan for next day night before   (NB 38).

By the early 1860s Arnold's severe effort at discipline and self-direction was graced with a sense of renewal that lifted his spirits and gave him new strength. In 1863 he wrote to his mother: "Today I am forty-one, the middle of my life, in any case, and for me, perhaps much more than the middle. I have ripened, and am ripening so slowly that I should be glad of as much time as possible, yet I can feel, I rejoice to say, an inward spring which seems more and more to gain strength" (L 1:213). A few years later he was able to write: "I more and more have the satisfaction of seeing that what I do produces its effect, and this inspirits me to try to keep myself at my best" (L 1:420).

Arnold's feeling of growing accomplishment in the 1860s was accompanied, however, by a series of personal disappointments and tragedies that, rather than disheartening and distracting him, appear to have strengthened his determination to be freed of all self-will and to concentrate on what he now refers to as a higher will or higher nature. After 1865 and well into the 1870s the notebook entries have chiefly to do with the religious life and draw heavily on the Bible, Thomas à Kempis, and Arnold's favorite Stoic-Christian, Bishop Wilson. The dominate note is the eradication of what John Henry Newman called "personal preference." The two following notebook jottings for 1867 are highly representative:

From Plato—

> We must learn to sacrifice all individual will to reason, to that higher nature which is incapable of being the object of selfish impulse.

And from Bishop Wilson—

> They that deny themselves will be sure to find their strength increased, the affections raised, and their inward peace continually increased (NB 54).

The passage from Wilson is repeated six times in the next few years.

In the essays of the early 1860s one notes the growing dissatisfaction with the spiritual counsel of those "rigorous teachers" of his early years. The influence of new "masters of the mind," now prominent in the reading lists and notebooks, is increasingly apparent. Arnold's reading of the pagan classics, as well as Goethe, Spinoza, and Sainte-Beuve, now is reinforced by regular reading from the Bible, Dante, and the *Imitation of Christ*. After 1860 and for the next 15 years his habitual reading of these latter texts is augmented by the study of the works of a wide array of religious writers of the modern period, among them Renan, Joubert, the Guerins,

Revillé, Bishop Wilson, Frederick Robertson, Lacordaire, Montalembert, Alexandre Vinet, the Abbé Migne, Bossuet, Isaac Barrow, Herder, Ewald, Reuss, de Maistre, Scherer, Bunsen, D. F. Strauss, F. C. Baur, and Newman. These are the guides who instructed, fortified, and consoled Arnold intellectually and spiritually.

It would be a mistake, however, to think that Arnold executed a turnabout and wholly repudiated his earlier mentors. He judged the greatest of these—for example, Sophocles and Goethe—as not fully adequate and in need of the counterbalance of opposing ideas and tendencies. He was able to absorb what is real and enduring in those toward whom—for example, Carlyle—he was increasingly severe and dismissive. Hence, it is quite wrong to view Arnold as entirely rejecting the influence of those of whom he now disapproved. Nevertheless, new perceptions and convictions increasingly informed and shaped Arnold's vision and his critical agenda in the 1860s. His relation to the sources of his own intellectual and spiritual development remained rigorously critical and dialectical. He enlisted and used what he could for his own purposes. His approach to his teachers' doctrines can be likened to an Hegelian *aufhebung*, a critical negating, while at the same time a preserving of ideas in new terms. And nowhere is this more evident than in his treatment of the earlier teachers. Nowhere, perhaps, is Arnold's emerging Christian humanism, the joining of the classical and Christian visions, more perfectly exhibited.

Between 1863 and 1865 Arnold published 13 essays, eight of which have to do wholly or in part with religion. They reflect his growing conviction that, while an "intellectual deliverance" is required, intellect is barren when not touched, indeed infused, with the moral and religious sentiment. This conviction is explored in Arnold's subtle analysis of the insufficiency of the pagan wisdom of his previous spiritual guides.

I have spoken of Arnold's response to the lassitude, the incurable "depression and ennui" which he found to be such a distinctive quality of Lucretius's great poem and which infected the character of Marcus Aurelius—so beautiful and yet bound by "something melancholy, circumscribed, and ineffectual." Doubtless, thinking of his comments on his father in "Rugby Chapel" ("But thou would'st not *alone* / Be saved, my father!") Arnold writes of the great Roman: "[He] saved his own soul by his righteousness, and he could do no more. Happy they who can do this! but still happier, who can do more!" (CPW 3:146). Comparing the moral teaching of Epictetus with that of Jesus, Arnold concludes that, while the Christian morality propounds the maxim of loving one's neighbor with no "closer reasoning" or "truer sincerity" than does the Stoic, it nevertheless "propounds this maxim with an inspiration which wonderfully catches the hearer and makes him act upon it" (CPW 3:135-36). The gentle and tender sentiment of these great pagan teachers was, Arnold finds, "less than joy and more than resignation," sublime, dignified, yet reaching out for something more: "What an affinity for Christianity had this persecutor [Marcus Aurelius] of the Christians! The effusion of Christianity, its relieving tears, its happy self-sacrifice, were the very element, one feels, for which his soul longed. . . . We see him wise, just, self-governed, tender, thankful, blameless, yet with all this, agitated, stretching out his arms for something beyond" (CPW 3:156-57).

It was the "effusion" and the "happy self-sacrifice" in Christianity that affected Arnold deeply, but he could, of course, see even these virtues moving toward their excess in the Methodist chapel or in the mortifications of the later St. Francis. Christianity had lived by the heart and the imagination, but this alone would not suffice for the modern spirit. There is another side of man that must balance the religious sentiment.

Arnold had discovered the paradoxical concurrence of self-sacrifice, of suffering, with a joy that mysteriously transfigures the world of necessity. But he was acutely aware that the modern spirit demands not only the heart and the imagination but the senses and understanding as well. And so while the Hebrew genius is henceforth to hold the paramount place in Arnold's view of life, it would be a Hebraism always tempered and balanced by the genius of Hellenism. His search for a reconstructed Christianity is a search for the religious embodiment of the imaginative reason.

"PUTTING ON THE ARMOUR OF LIGHT"

The new intellectual and religious influences were connected with personal and public events that touched Arnold's life in the decade of the 1860s. All of these converged to give a new shape and a new direction to his life and to his vocation as writer. And yet there are clearly discernible continuities with the concerns of the previous decade. The themes of the new essays—the role of the poet and of criticism, of culture and the remnant, of the self and its vocation, and religion—have their beginnings in Arnold's poetry and earlier prose. His reflections on the self in poems such as "Empedocles on Etna" and "The Buried Life" are connected with those on the "best self" in *Culture and Anarchy*. The response to the early religious essay on "The Bishop and the Philosopher" forced Arnold to clarify his ideas of criticism in "The Function of Criticism." The concerns expressed about the aristocracy and the middle class in *England and the*

Italian Question (1859), in *The Popular Education of France* (1861), and in "Heinrich Heine" (1863) are worked out in *Culture and Anarchy* and *St. Paul and Protestantism* later in the decade. Arnold's reflections about culture have to do with religion, which has to do with criticism, which in turn has to do with education, which again relates to culture. England's middle classes lack culture because of their narrow religion; hence *Culture and Anarchy* is followed by *St. Paul and Protestantism*, which, by raising questions of the status of religious language and interpretation, finds its natural progression in *Literature and Dogma*. Arnold's criticism thus reveals a remarkable wholeness. The continuity and direction of his work is even more striking and intelligible when it is seen in the context of the personal and public events that played on his mind and agitated and affected him deeply in the years during which the religious books were composed.

During 1866 and 1867 Arnold experienced professional disappointments. On 4 January 1868 his infant son, Basil, died. After telling his sister of the circumstances of his son's death, he writes:

> And so this loss comes to me just after my forty-fifth birthday, with so much other "suffering in the flesh," the departure of youth, cares of many kinds, an almost painful anxiety about public matters—to remind me that the time past of our life may suffice us!—words which have haunted me for the last year or two, and that "we should no longer live the rest of our time in the flesh to the lusts of men, but to the will of God." However different the interpretation we put on much of the facts and history of Christianity, we may unite in the bond of this call, which is true for all of us, and for me above all, how full of meaning and warning (L 1:382).

Twelve months later, only a few weeks after the death of his son Tommy, a Harrow schoolboy, Arnold wrote to his mother, as was his habit, on his birthday. He is reminded that he is now within one year of his father's age when his life was ended—and, painfully, how much his father had accomplished in his relatively short life. The death of his two sons, "the gradual settlement of [his] own thoughts"—all these things now point to a new beginning.

Culture and Anarchy appeared within a few weeks of Arnold's birthday letter. He now was about to undertake the writing of *St. Paul and Protestantism*, the first of the larger religious works that would occupy his critical energies for the next decade. He had been reading the *Memoir* of Baron Bunsen and the *Life and Sermons* of Frederick Robertson. The lives of these men, given to the service of liberal religion, moved Arnold, and the notebook entries of 1868 from their works stand as keynotes of his new undertaking. From Robertson's sermon "The Irreparable Past" he records: "Rise, be going; count your resources; learn what you are not fit for and give up wishing for it; learn what you can do, and do it with the energy of a man" (NB 85). What he recently had learned he *could* accomplish ("I am astonished . . . at the favorable reception what I have said meets with [L 1:392])—more significantly, what he now desired to accomplish for the nation and in the field of religion—was to demonstrate the interdependence of religion and culture. He wished to show that a narrow and utilitarian culture will yield a fixed and mechanical interpretation of religion, which in turn will reinforce the ignorance, the lack of urbanity, and coarseness of the nation's life. The future of England lay in the hands of the vigorous and fast-growing middle class. The lifeblood of that class was religion—but a form of Christianity that, Arnold believed, was parochial and doomed. Arnold gave the next decade of his life to demonstrating that Christianity was not tethered to such a false and misleading view of the Bible and the church, which had such dire consequences for English life.

For Arnold to expose the limitations of middle-class religion meant that he must uncover those same deficiencies in Dissent, the religion of English Calvinism and Puritanism. And Arnold knew Protestant Dissent first-hand. "For fifteen years," he wrote to Gladstone in 1869, "I have seen the Protestant Dissenters close, from inspecting their schools; and have more and more observed how their real need is not more voluntarism and separation for their religious organizations, but a larger existence and more sense of public responsibility" (CPW 6:417).

In the background of *St. Paul and Protestantism* lay Arnold's criticism, in "The Bishop and the Philosopher," of Bishop J.W. Colenso's crudely literal and rationalistic interpretation of the Bible in his *The Pentateuch and the Book of Joshua Critically Examined* (1862), as well as Arnold's reflections in subsequent essays on what he considered more adequate principles of religious criticism.* *St. Paul and Protestantism* was not, however, solely concerned with the proper interpretation of the Bible. The book devoted equal attention to issues of Protestant Dissent and particularly to the justification of its separation from the Established Church. Arnold had been

---

* Succeeding chapters will have much to say about this, as well as about the relations of religion and culture and of Hebraism and Hellenism as developed in *Culture and Anarchy*. All of this served as critical background for themes carried forward in *St. Paul and Protestantism*.

roundly criticized for, among other things, misrepresenting Puritanism and its offspring, modern Dissent, in *Culture and Anarchy*, and he now sought to redress these criticisms and enlarge on the issues. However, it is likely that in the background of sections of *Culture and Anarchy* and of *St. Paul and Protestantism* was the Bicentenary Controversy of 1861-62.[27]

A more immediate and certain inducement for the writing of *St. Paul and Protestantism* was Arnold's reading of two French critics during 1869. In that year Ernest Renan published *Saint Paul* as the third volume of his *History of the Origins of Christianity*. Renan summed up his assessment of Paul, as Arnold reports it, by saying: "After having been for three hundred years, thanks to Protestantism, the Christian doctor *par excellence*, Paul is now coming to the end of his reign" (CPW 6:5). Renan viewed Paul as a restless, irrational, fanatical, and gloomy man—all that he perceived in the Augustinian Jansenists and the Calvinist Puritans, both of whom repelled him.

In the summer of 1869 Arnold also came upon the volumes of Eduard Reuss's *Histoire de la théologie chrétienne au siècle apostolique*, which offered a very different picture of Paul and his doctrine. According to Reuss, it was the schoolmen who turned Paul's spiritual insights into the hard and juridical language of the law court and the commercial transaction, a language fatefully adopted by Calvin and later by the Puritans. What if Reuss had shown that the language and doctrine of Puritanism are not characteristic of Paul? Why, then the whole doctrinal foundation of Dissent is undermined! Paul now coming to the end of his reign? "Precisely the contrary," writes Arnold, opening the argument of *St. Paul and Protestantism:*

> The Protestantism which had so used and abused St. Paul is coming to an end; its organizations, strong and active as they look, are touched with the finger of death; its fundamental ideas, sounding forth still every week from thousands of pulpits, have in them no significance and no power for the progressive thought of humanity. But the reign of the real St. Paul is only beginning; his fundamental ideas . . . will have an influence in the future greater than any which they have yet had—an influence proportioned to their correspondence with a number of the deepest and most permanent facts of human nature itself (CPW 6:5).

Having shown the genuinely living and existential nature of Paul's thought and thereby, in his opinion, having demonstrated the falseness of the Puritan theology in the first two papers that were to make up *St.*

Paul and Protestantism, Arnold wrote to his mother in November 1869 concerning his latest plan:

> I shall have a last paper at Christmas called "Puritanism and the Church of England," to show how the Church, though holding certain doctrines like justification in common with Puritanism, has gained not by pinning itself to those doctrines and nothing else, but by resting on Catholic antiquity, historic Christianity, development, and so on, which open to it an escape from all single doctrines as they are outgrown (L 2:21).

A few weeks later Arnold reported to his mother: "I think nearly all the new periodicals have something or other about me, which show how much more what I write is coming into vogue" (L 2:24). Mrs. Arnold now received newspaper clippings from her son, demonstrating how well he was reaching the Puritan class. Arnold proudly confides: "I should like to have shown you some of the Nonconformist speeches at the recent May meetings, full of comments on my preface to *St. Paul and Protestantism.* We shall see great changes in the Dissenters before very long" (L 2:30).

Arnold clearly was now doing what he enjoyed and what he could do well. He was energized by his sense of accomplishment. Friends' comments further encouraged him to proceed. T. H. Huxley wrote that he was "picking up many good things" in *St. Paul and Protestantism*: "One of the best is what you say . . . about science gradually conquering the materialism of popular religion."[28] Huxley's laudation doubtless gave Arnold pause, for while he saw the materializing of theology as a dangerous threat, he was becoming increasingly concerned over the growing clamor for science and scientific education at the expense of humane letters.

It was a worry that was to be further aggravated by an event which in turn helped to quicken Arnold's resolve to write the articles for the *Cornhill* that were to become the basis of *Literature and Dogma.* On 23 June 1870 Arnold attended the formal dedication of Keble College at Oxford. The new college was named for John Keble, one of the leaders of the Oxford Movement and Matthew Arnold's godfather. It was a time of great rejoicing among the Anglo-Catholic party. At the close of the formal dedication of the college Lord Salisbury, the Chancellor of the University of Oxford, spoke to a public meeting on behalf of the Keble Memorial Fund. Salisbury was a High Churchman and, apropos the occasion, addressed the following remarks to his audience:

> I think this college exists to pledge us to a religion which shall not be the formless, shapeless creature of fable such as

goes by the name of unsectarian religion—but shall be unsectarian in the higher sense because it is thoroughly Catholic; and that there shall be no more within these walls the idea of severing religion and dogma than there is the idea of severing the daylight from the sun.[29]

Arnold was appalled by the speech and a few days later wrote his mother a letter that revealed both his motivation in writing *Literature and Dogma* and some of its central themes. Speaking of Salisbury's address at Oxford, he comments:

> Religion he knows, and physical science he knows, but the immense work between the two, which is for literature to accomplish, he knows nothing of, and all his speeches at Oxford pointed this way. On the one hand, he was full of the great future for physical science, and begging the University to make up her mind to it, and to resign much of her literary studies; on the other hand, he was full, almost defiantly full, of counsels and resolves for retaining and upholding the old ecclesiastical and dogmatic form of religion. From a juxtaposition of this kind nothing but shocks and collisions can come; and I know no one, indeed, more likely to provoke shock and collisions than men like Lord Salisbury. All this pressed a good deal upon my mind at Oxford, and made me anxious, but I do hope that what influence I have may be of some use in the troubled times which I see are before us as a healing and reconciling influence, and it is this which makes me glad to find— what I find more and more—that I *have* influence (L 2:35).

Arnold had gone to Oxford to pay homage to a leader of the Oxford Movement and to witness the dedication of a college devoted to upholding Anglo-Catholic doctrine. He came away with the idea and the stimulus for writing a book antithetical to the Anglo-Catholic conception of Christianity, a book that he was later to consider his most important and that was to be more in demand than anything else he was to write.

There were, however, other stimulants—primarily religious controversies—that engaged the public's attention between 1870 and 1872, which gave Arnold both the incentive and the ammunition further to pursue his religious criticism. The first of these occasions was the debate over the Forster Education Bill of 1870. The question raised by the bill was whether religious instruction in tax-supported schools should be secular or sectarian—whether, in Arnold's terms, it should be literary or dogmatic. The

National Education League was dedicated to a universal public education that would be compulsory and secular. Other parties were calling for the inclusion of the catechism and religious formularies in the instruction of the tax-supported schools—a demand that was defeated.

The Forster Education Bill debate was finally to focus on the question of whether and how the Bible should be used as a regular part of the school curriculum. That the issue was no longer a mere "family quarrel" among Christians was remarked by T. H. Huxley in a speech before the London School Board in February 1871. Huxley warned the board that it was a cardinal error to consider the matter of religious instruction as simply an intra-Christian contest. In addition to the Christian antagonists, "there was a third party growing up and daily increasing in significance, which has nothing to do with either, but which has its own religion and morality that rests in no way whatever on the foundation of the other two." [30]

What especially struck Arnold about Huxley's reported speech was the suggestion that this third party had lost all allegiance to the Bible. Huxley had remarked that "if these islands had no religion at all, it would not enter into his mind to introduce the religious idea by the agency of the Bible." Arnold was as aware as Huxley of the growing numbers of people for whom the Bible was a mere anachronism, if not a downright evil. But Arnold interpreted this widespread contempt for the Bible as due not only to the new science but to the crude and "materialized" interpretations of clergymen—men of narrow training, lacking any appreciation of letters.

At the time of the Forster Education Bill debate another controversy was raging that also engaged Arnold's attention and influenced substantially the argument of *Literature and Dogma*—especially the book's polemic against "dogmatic" Christianity. Arnold's friend Arthur P. Stanley, the Dean of Westminster, had invited a Unitarian named Vance Smith to receive Holy Communion at Westminster Abbey on 22 June 1870. The occasion was a meeting of a group named by the Convocation of Bishops to consider the question of revising the English version of the Bible. The group included not only Anglicans but Scottish Presbyterians, Nonconformists, and the Unitarian Smith; these men were asked to cooperate in the project because of their eminent scholarship. At the first meeting of the revision committee Stanley invited all present to participate in the celebration of Holy Communion. High Churchmen were horrified at Stanley's action, which they considered contrary to the rubrics of the Prayer Book, which held the vows of confirmation as a prerequisite to receiving Communion. The scandal was brought before Convocation at its next meeting, and letters and memorials poured in denouncing Stanley and demanding his excommunication for such "a gross profanation of the Sacrament."[31]

The controversy reached its zenith at the meeting of Convocation in February 1871. Samuel Wilberforce, Bishop of Winchester, moved "that no person who denies the Godhead of our Lord Jesus Christ ought to be invited to join either Company to which is committed the revision of the Authorized Version of Holy Scripture." Wilberforce pointed out that his reason for wishing to exclude Vance Smith was not that he was a separatist from the Church of England, but that he was "a denier of our Lord's Godhead." Wilberforce explained to his peers that in approving his motion, "you enhance in the sight of all your own estimate of the difference between being unhappily separated from your outward community, *but being separated from you in that infinite separation for time and for eternity which is involved in declaring the Eternal Son to be a mere creature; and you have the evidence before you that he rejects the Godhead of the Eternal Son.*"[32]

Wilberforce's efforts were zealously supported by the Bishop of Gloucester, who lectured Convocation on the necessity of holding proper conceptions of the personality of the Holy Trinity, and who shortly thereafter was to write an essay for a book entitled *Modern Scepticism* in which he offered his belief in "the blessed truth that the God of the universe is a PERSON." It was the action of the Bishops of Winchester and Gloucester, "in doing something for the honour of Our Lord's Godhead," as Arnold was to put it (CPW 6:240), and their pretentious claims to know the exact nature of the Deity that incensed Arnold and brought his mocking wrath down upon their heads time and time again in *Literature and Dogma*.

The High Church party's opposition to Stanley did not end with the meeting of Convocation early in 1871. Throughout the 1850s and 60s, High Churchmen held the majority of votes in Congregation at Oxford. As a result they had long controlled many academic appointments at the university. During this period such distinguished scholars as Mark Pattison, Max Müller, and Benjamin Jowett were denied positions because of their liberal theological views. The abolition of the Universities Test Act in 1871 reduced the Anglo-Catholics' control of Oxford, but their opposition to latitudinarian theology in the university continued unabated. In December 1872 Dean Stanley was nominated one of the Select Preachers of the University. The High Churchmen once again joined forces and were set on defeating Stanley's appointment. However, they were defeated in turn by 349 to 287 votes. In protest of Stanley's election the Dean of Norwich resigned his own position as Select Preacher, and in his letter of resignation to the vice-chancellor he remarked that "if the pulpit of the University is to be turned into a vehicle for conveying to our youth a nerveless religion, without the bone and sinew of doctrine, a religion which can hardly be called faith so much as a mere Christianized morality, I for one must decline to stand there."[33] Professor Blackburn has shown that Arnold took several phrases directly from the Dean of Norwich's letter and used them in *Literature and Dogma* as exemplifying the narrow dogmatic mentality against which his book was directed.

A third controversy of the period that influenced Arnold in the writing of *Literature and Dogma* also involved Dean Stanley. The issue had to do with the retention of the Athanasian Creed in the *Book of Common Prayer*. A Ritual Commission had been charged with examining the Prayer Book with regard to its directions and use. The commission's study brought them face to face with Article 8 and the Athanasian Creed. The liberal party, led by Stanley, thought that because of the "damnatory clauses" attached to it the use of the Athanasian Creed in services should be made optional.

Again Bishop Wilberforce led the opposition, supported by the leading Anglo-Catholic theologians, E. B. Pusey and H. P. Liddon. This time the High Church party prevailed, and the commission recommended that the Athanasian Creed be retained and that an explanatory note be appended to it making clear that "the condemnations in this Confession of Faith are to be no otherwise understood than a solemn warning of the peril of those who willfully rejected the Catholic Faith."[34] A number of the commissioners dissented from the commission's report, and the controversy continued for almost three years. On 7 May 1873 the bishops, meeting in Convocation, issued a declaration holding that the anathemas of the creed were in accordance with those of Holy Scripture.

Literature and Dogma appeared several months before the bishops' Synodical Declaration, but Arnold was clearly aware of what direction the bishops' action would take. In the book he remarked that the Athanasian Creed "has fought and got ruffled by fighting, and is fiercely dictatorial now that it has won." Arnold had a very real dislike for the Athanasian Creed and the dogmatic conception of religion which it epitomized. Whereas *Literature and Dogma* speaks disparagingly of the Nicene Creed as "learned science," it characterizes the Athanasian Creed as "learned science *with a strong dash of violent and vindictive temper*" (CPW 6:343).

In the summer and autumn of 1871 Arnold began publishing articles that would serve as the basis of *Literature and Dogma*. However, only two articles were to appear in the *Cornhill* under its new editor, Leslie Stephen.

The finished book was not published until February 1873. Arnold wished to make it clear that his purpose was not to establish a bulwark against the impact of the scientific *Zeitgeist*. The scientific spirit was already having its effect in weakening traditional Christian belief and, in Arnold's view, the time-spirit could not and should not be stayed. Neither did Arnold address himself to those who were content with the older theology or to those freethinkers who had abandoned Christianity completely. *Literature and Dogma* was written for those who

> won by the modern spirit to habits of intellectual seriousness, cannot receive what sets these habits at nought, and will not try to force themselves to do so; but who have stood near enough to the Christian religion to feel the attraction which a thing so very great, when one stands really near to it, cannot but exercize, and who have some familiarity with the Bible and some practice in using it (CPW 7:392).

Arnold believed that those who felt both the irresistible character of the *Zeitgeist* and the incomparable greatness of biblical religion must now seek to place the truth of that religion on "a new experimental basis." For Arnold that meant establishing the truths of Christianity on the unassailable ground of human experience. The preliminary step to such a reconception of Christianity involved recognition of the fact that the language of the Bible is not to be confused with the language of science. Biblical language is not "rigid and fixed" but "fluid, passing, literary"; it is language "thrown out," as Arnold was so often to remark. It is a language of image and metaphor, symbol and myth. To appreciate the true character of the biblical literature one needs the help not of science and metaphysics, but of culture—of literary taste, which alone can save the reader from an indiscriminate literalizing of everything he reads. Only a broad acquaintance with culture will, in Arnold's opinion, spare men from the philistine pretension of equating truth exclusively with scientific statement.

If this preliminary step is observed, Arnold believed that one would go to the Bible and discover that the ancient Hebrews had no intention of being read as scientists or metaphysicians. For Israel, God was not the conclusion of a logical process. What the Isrealites did discover, and passed on to us as a matchless heritage, was the experience that "righteousness tendeth to life." "No people ever felt so strongly that succeeding, going right, hitting the mark in this great concern, was *the way of peace*, the highest possible satisfaction" (CPW 6:180). This eternal law of righteousness the Israelites experienced as a power not of their own making, which they personified as God. However, the God of the ancient Hebrews, whom Arnold called "the Eternal not ourselves that makes for righteousness," was not the God of the Bishops of Gloucester and Winchester; not a metaphysical construct. The "Eternal not ourselves" was attested to and verified by the inescapable experience of the moral life; that the eternal law of righteousness tendeth to life, to happiness, and to peace.

In time Israel lost sight of its original intuition. It began to look not to the law of righteousness but to supernatural, miraculous intervention as its only hope of salvation. Hence, to its sublime insight Israel proceeded to add *Aberglaube*, or "extra-beliefs,"* particularly those speculative eschatological prophecies of a future Messiah. Belief was no longer grounded in certain experience. Israel's faith became otherworldly and miraculous. And so what was needed was a restoration of the personal and experiential—religion newly imbued with deep feeling, inwardness, and authenticity. This was what Jesus provided.

According to Arnold, Jesus accomplished this renewal by a "method" of inwardness (*metanoia*, repentance, change of heart) and a "secret" of self-renouncement (*necrosis*, dying to the old self), which he combined with his unique mildness and "sweet-reasonableness." By this method and secret Jesus "made his followers feel that in these qualities lay the secret of their best self; that to attain them was in the highest degree requisite and natural, and that a man's whole happiness depended upon it" (CPW 6:220).

However, once again spiritual truth was overladen with a "materializing mythology," with popular *Aberglaube*. Jesus' own disciples did not understand him. He was too far above them. Jesus, it is true, used the popular mythology of his day, but in a *spiritual sense*. However, his meaning was lost on his followers, and they portrayed him as a thaumaturgist and apocalyptical visionary. And with the passing of time Christianity fixed more and more on these purely miraculous and otherworldly elements in the Gospels. Christianity rested no longer on its natural truth—that righteousness makes for life and for peace—but on the proofs of prophecy and miracle.

Even greater place was given to the miraculous and the metaphysical as Christianity spread through the Hellenistic world. Finally these "extra-beliefs" were formalized and reduced to scientific exactitude in the Apostles' and Nicene Creeds—the "popular" and "learned" sciences of Chris-

---

* Arnold regularly rendered the German word *Aberglaube* as "extra-belief." *Aberglaube* is usually translated as "superstition."

tianity. The distance traveled from the Bible to these creeds was very great, and this dogmatizing process has left us with beliefs that are neither sure nor verifiable. It has foisted upon us "extra-beliefs" that were falsely constructed "by taking certain great names and great promises too literally and materially."

Thus has Christianity remained to Arnold's day—its truth defended on the tenuous ground of *Aberglaube*. But, says Arnold, "there is always a drawback to a man's advantage in thus treating, when he deals with religion and conduct, what is extra-belief, and not certain, as if it were a matter of certainty, and in making it his ground of action. *He pays for it.* The time comes when he discovers that it is *not* certain; and then the whole certainty of religion seems discredited, and the basis of conduct gone" (CPW 6:232).

Arnold believed that Christianity was now paying for its false proofs from miracle and prophecy and its materialized dogmas by seeing the Bible and its incomparable truths increasingly discredited in the minds of the people. What had happened was that religion was "made to stand on its apex, instead of on its base. Righteousness is supported on ecclesiastical dogma, instead of ecclesiastical dogma being supported on righteousness" (CPW 6:350).

Arnold considered the loss of the Bible's influence on the nation as tragic, for he viewed the secular alternatives of Spencer, Comte, Bradlaugh, and Leslie Stephen as either fatuous nonsense or unctuous truism when compared with the sublimity and the morally transforming power of the biblical literature. What Arnold called for was a reading of the Bible anew in its original, natural light. So read, the Bible, he believed, would no longer be viewed as "prescientific error" but as that which must remain as the indispensable complement to our scientific work—without which our lives would become selfish and narrow, lacking all spiritual grace and vision.

NOTES

1. W. H. Auden, "Matthew Arnold," *The Collected Poetry of W. H. Auden* (New York, 1945) 54.

2. The continuity of Arnold's vocation and religious concerns has been stressed most recently by apRoberts, *Arnold and God*.

3. Kathleen Tillotson, *Brontë Society Transaction*; quoted Honan, *Matthew Arnold* 220.

4. Mrs. Humphry Ward, *A Writers Recollections* (London, 1918) 12.

5. Kenneth Allott, "Matthew Arnold's Reading-Lists in Three Early Diaries," *Victorian Studies* 2 (1959): 265.

6. Honan 127.

7. Trilling, *Matthew Arnold* 99-100

8. Thomas Carlyle, *Works*, ed. H. D. Traill 1:132.

9. Carlyle 153.

10. A. Dwight Culler, *Imaginative Reason: The Poetry of Matthew Arnold* (New Haven, 1966) esp. chap. 8.

11. Culler 269.

12. The Yale ms, cited Kenneth Allott, "A Background for Empedocles on Etna," *Essays and Studies 1968* (London, 1968) 94.

13. See David DeLaura, "Arnold and Carlyle" *PMLA* 69 (1964): 104-29. DeLaura also sees Carlyle as an important continuing influence on Arnold. See his "Carlyle and Arnold: The Religious Issue," *Carlyle Past and Present: A Collection of New Essays*, ed K. J. Fielding and Rodger L. Tarr, (New York, 1976).

14. Cited Katherine Chorley, *Arthur Hugh Clough: The Uncommitted Mind* (Oxford, 1962) 132.

15. Culler 154.

16. Allott, "Background for Empedocles," 96.

17. F. L. Mulhauser, ed., *The Correspondence of Arthur Hugh Clough* (Oxford, 1957) 2:401.

18. Charles Kingsley, "Recent Poetry, and Recent Verse," *Fraser's Magazine* 39 (1849): 579; cited Coulling, *Matthew Arnold and His Critics*, 38.

19. Coulling 215.

20. Honan 285 and passim.

21. Trilling 135-36.

22. Culler 211-12.

23. Trilling 135-36. (Goethe's *Wohlgemeinte Erwiderung*, Weimar edition, 41.2: 375-78.)

24. Culler 277.

25. Culler 282.

26. Honan 122.

27. The controversy had to do with the decision of the Congregational Union, supported by other Evangelical Nonconformists, to celebrate the bicentenary of the expulsion of the nonjuring clergy from their livings under the Act of Uniformity of 1662. The Anglican Evangelicals spoke out in opposition to the celebration. It is likely that Arnold's defense of the integrity of the Evangelical churchmen and the Establishment and his criticism of separatism on the grounds of doctrinal differences were provoked by the controversy. For this, see Jean A. Smallbone's researches in her London dissertation, "*St. Paul and Protestantism:* Its Place in the Development of Matthew Arnold's Thought" and "Matthew Arnold and the Bicentenary of 1862," *Baptist Quarterly*, ns 14 (1952): 222-26.

28. *Life and Letters of Thomas Henry Huxley*, ed. Leonard Huxley, (London, 1900) 1:329.

29. *Guardian*, 25 (1870): 762; cited William Blackburn "The Background of Arnold's *Literature and Dogma*," *Modern Philology* Nov. 1945: 131. I am indebted to Blackburn for much that follows concerning the immediate background of *Literature and Dogma*.

30. Blackburn 133.

31. Blackburn 133.

32. Blackburn 135-36; italics added.

33. R. E. Prothero, *The Life and Correspondence of Arthur Penrhyn Stanley* (London, 1893) 2:228.

34. Blackburn 138.

2 "To Make Reason and the Will of God Prevail": Arnold on Religion and Culture

> The revelations of God to man were gradual and adapted to his state at the several periods when they were successively made.
>
> Thomas Arnold

> No man who knows nothing else, knows even his Bible.
>
> *Culture and Anarchy*

The preceding chapter shows how, in the 1860s and 70s, the concern for religion became, in Basil Willey's term, the "centre of gravity" of Arnold's work in defending the imaginative reason against the claims of the old religious orthodoxy, the new science, and aestheticism. Formulating a series of hermeneutical principles and proposing a reconceived vision of Christianity in response to the rising crisis of belief became Arnold's major preoccupation in the decade 1865-75. This and subsequent chapters will be concerned with his program of reconstruction itself. This includes consideration of Arnold's understanding of the *Zeitgeist* and the development of religious doctrine, as well as the implications of this understanding for his grasp of the interdependence of religion and culture. These matters will lead into the critical and often misunderstood subject of Arnold's conception of the relationship between religion and poetry, which, in turn, leads to a consideration of Arnold's understanding of religious language, experience, and truth.

THE *ZEITGEIST* AND DEVELOPMENT

The two movements of mind that best characterize English thought in the second half of the nineteenth century are evolution and agnosticism concerning man's knowledge of the ultimate objects of metaphysical and theological belief. Arnold's intellectual development reveals the deep impress of these ideas on his mind and on his understanding of the directions that any religious reconstruction must take. The two movements are, of course, but the reverse sides of the same intellectual phenomenon. The profound sense of change, movement, and development as constitutive of reality implied that the forms and words men use to apprehend and speak of what is "real" or "ultimate" or "true" are themselves fluid, partial, symbolic.

The intellectual question that troubled the age was: Does the fact that the means which we use to shape and communicate our experience of the world are ever changing imply that *what* we experience is relative? For some, such as Pater, the answer was affirmative; for others, and Arnold was one of them, the answer remained negative. And yet, for those who wished to maintain both the fact of historical change and relativity as well as the enduring truth of certain religious or metaphysical beliefs, the challenge was very great indeed. The problem obviously is much with us still.

Arnold possessed a deep-rooted historical consciousness, a sense of the relativistic spirit of the age and the workings of the *Zeitgeist*. Yet by the time he reached his middle years his historicism was accommodated to a distinctly progressive view of historical development. Three particularly important influences were determinative in Arnold's developing theory of history: Goethe and Carlyle, Thomas Arnold and the liberal Anglican philosophy of history, and Newman.

Carlyle was one of the four "voices" that most impressed Arnold while at Oxford. Doubtless it was Carlyle's use of the term *Zeitgeist*, both in "Characteristics" (1831) and in *Sartor Resartus* (1833-34) that, with Goethe, influenced Arnold's use of the term[1]. In a letter to Arthur Clough in July 1848, Arnold refers to Goethe's saying "that the *Zeitgeist* when he was young caused everyone to adopt the Wolfian theories about Homer, himself included: and that when he was in middle age the same *Zeitgeist* caused them to leave these theories for the hypothesis of one poem and one author: inferring that in these matters there is no certainty, but alternating dispositions" (CL 86). Arnold tells Clough that he finds this relativity of intellectual judgment "congenial" and applies it to the reception of Clough's poem "Adam and Eve," which had not suited Arnold but which, he is confident, is "calculated to suit others." Arnold thus sees the time-spirit as productive of an inescapable temper of mind which informs an age. It is a force that cannot be ignored and that can, therefore, pose a severe challenge to beliefs and values which have their source in other times and cultural settings.

The *Zeitgeist* of his own present age, Arnold believed, signaled a movement of mind and a new sensibility which demanded that the ancient beliefs and values be apprehended in a new key if they were to endure. Here Matthew was very much his father's son, for Thomas Arnold also believed that to attempt to preserve the old state of things in their ancient forms was to court disaster. He maintained that the natural law of history is what he called the principle of accommodation, providence's adjustment of society and religion to the state of knowledge and moral conduct reached in the course of historical development. For example, Thomas Arnold was convinced that as men grow in moral and intellectual stature, the need for miracles as religious sanction and explanation recedes. It is the ability of religion to adapt itself, to follow the principle of accommodation, that is a sign of its strength and truth. In the words of Thomas Arnold's disciple, Arthur Stanley, "The everlasting mountains are everlasting not because they are unchanged but because they go on changing their form, their substance with the wear and tear of years. 'The Everlasting Gospel' is everlasting not because it remains stationary, but because, being the same, it can adapt itself to the constant change of society, of civilization, of humanity itself."[2] Thomas Arnold wrote that "It is worse than kicking against the pricks to oppose our vain efforts to an eternal and universal law of God's Providence."[3]

Matthew Arnold shared this Liberal Anglican philosophy of history. He believed that the *forms* in which doctrines come to us are under the dominion of the time-spirit; men cannot help taking them as self-evident, yet they are also liable to significant historical development and change. In the essay "Dr. Stanley's Lectures on the Jewish Church" (1863), Arnold writes: "Intellectual ideas are not the essence of the religious life; still the religious life connects itself . . . with certain intellectual ideas, and all intellectual ideas follow a development independent of the religious life" (CPW 3:76-77). Thus it is that the Articles of the Church of England are intellectual ideas with which the church, at the time of the Reformation, connected itself. But as ideas of the English Reformers they are ideas *of their time*, requiring development and adaptation. The time-spirit makes their inadequacy plain, but "as this consciousness becomes more and more distinct, it becomes more and more irksome." The moment arrives when the religious man finds himself in a false position, and "it is natural that he should try to defend his position, that he should long prefer defending his position to confessing it untenable, and demanding to have it changed" (CPW 3:77). But reconstruction becomes inevitable, difficult as is the challenge, and the times when these changes are wrought are the epochal movements of religious history, and the agents of these intellectual revolutions are the great religious reformers. For Arnold, the importance of these men is not to be found "in their having these new ideas, in their originating them. The ideas are in the world. . . . They are put into circulation by the spirit of the time. The greatness of a religious reformer consists in his reconciling them with the religious life, in starting this life upon a fresh period in company with them" (CPW 3:69).

Arnold's profound sense of the work of the *Zeitgeist* has been viewed as a weakness, an excessive present-mindedness. It was, and perhaps still is, fashionable to associate Arnold's recognition of the *Zeitgeist* with Dean Inge's damning quip: "He who marries the spirit of the age will soon find himself a widower." Yet for Arnold the *Zeitgeist* does not involve being carried away by every wind of doctrine. Rather, the time-spirit brings with it those emergent models or paradigms which, as T. E. Hulme pointed out, an entire culture assumes as foundational:

> There are certain doctrines which for a particular period seem not doctrines, but inevitable categories of the human mind. Men do not look at them merely as correct opinion, for they have become so much a part of the mind, and lie so far back, that they are never really conscious of them at all. They do not see them, but other things through them. . . . There are in each period certain doctrines, a denial of which is looked on by the men of that period just as we might look on the assertion that two and two make five.[4]

For Arnold the *Zeitgeist* presents us with those beliefs that Hulme refers to as "*doctrines* felt as facts." What is at work here can perhaps best be illustrated by reference to a historian's recent exploration of the question of intellectual change in a culture. In his impressive study of *Religion and the Decline of Magic*, in sixteenth- and seventeenth-century England, Keith Thomas makes the following observation:

> Religion ultimately outlived its magical competitors. The wizards and astrologers lost their prestige during the seventeenth century, whereas the Church has continued. . . . But this process was not simply a matter of religion driving out its rivals, for the religion which survived the decline of magic was not the religion of Tudor England. When the Devil was banished to Hell, God himself was confined to working through natural causes. . . . So although our period ended with the triumph of religion over magic, it was religion with a difference.[5]

The shift in theological belief in the seventeenth century was the imperceptible accompaniment of a momentous cultural change—i.e., the decline of magic brought about by numerous, complex, interrelated factors. The new theological beliefs were grounded in these new cultural assumptions which became, quite unconsciously, authoritative. Thomas comments on this phenomenon by first quoting from the psychoanalyst Ernest Jones:

"The average man today . . . does not hesitate to reject the same evidence of witchcraft that was so convincing to the man of three centuries ago, though he usually knows no more about the true explanation than the latter did." Most of those millions of persons who today would laugh at the idea of magic or miracles would have difficulty in explaining why. They are victims of society's constant pressure towards intellectual conformity.[6]

This intellectual conformity is a product of the spirit of the age, but it is also rooted in that set of foundational concepts indispensable to all other forms of description and action in the intellectual and social life of the time. Here Thomas Kuhn's important discussion of scientific paradigms and paradigm shifts is germane. Scientific paradigms are those "universally recognized scientific achievements that for a time provided model problems and solutions to a community of practitioners."[7] As Kuhn points out, "normal science" consists of those times when the paradigm is working, when it sets the rules of the game. When these rules begin to be challenged, science moves into a period of crisis. The outcome of the crisis is the emergence of a new paradigm to replace the old one—what Kuhn calls a paradigm shift. This is similar to what Michel Foucault refers to as *mutation epistemologique*[8] and what Bernard Lonergan speaks of as transcultural shift, to indicate what happens when ideas originated in one cultural milieu are transported into another very different one.[9]

According to Arnold, the *Zeitgeist* frames not only the questions but the paradigms or forms in which the answers are given. And Arnold perceived that the form in which Christianity had been taught and defended was unintelligible in terms of those categories of understanding current in his time. He recognized that most clergymen were in a false position when they attempted to speak forthrightly because Anglican theology was tied to an outmoded world view and psychology. In a letter written to his mother in 1862 he points out how troubled his father would be had he been living then as a young man. "His attention," writes Arnold,

would have been painfully awake to the truth that to profess
to see Christianity through the spectacles of a number of second or third-rate men who lived in Queen Elizabeth's time—
men whose works one never dreams of reading for the purpose of enlightening and edifying oneself—is an intolerable
absurdity, and that it is time to put the formularies of the Church
of England on a solider basis (L 1:178).

Arnold was fond of referring to Goethe's epigram: "Religion itself, like
time, like life and knowledge, is engaged in a constant process of advance
and evolution" (CPW 6:138).* It was the failure of the Dissenting churches
to grasp this fact that served as motivation for the writing of *St. Paul and
Protestantism*. Arnold believed that the Dissenters, as well as many orthodox churchmen, were simply riveted to their opinions, "opposed to that
development and gradual exhibiting of the full sense of the Bible and
Christianity, which is essential to religious progress" (CPW 6:85). They
exhibit their religious doctrines "as a sort of cast-iron product, rigid, definite, and complete, which they have got once and for all, and which can
no longer have anything added to it or anything withdrawn from it"
(CPW 6:111).

On the contrary, Arnold contends that time and experience, the movement of mind, has shown that the theological formularies of the sixteenth
century have "given way and cannot be restored," any more than the
Ptolemaic or the feudal systems or belief in magic can be restored. Arnold's understanding of the working of the time-spirit on the older theology—namely, on the proofs from prophecy, miracles, and on the inerrancy
of Scripture, as well as the claims of natural theology—takes up much of
Literature and Dogma and *God and the Bible* and need not be discussed here
in detail. One striking illustration with regard to miracle will characterize
his approach. He rejects the insistent demand of his critics that he engage
in a "proof" that miracles do not happen: "To engage in an *a priori* argument to prove that miracles are impossible, against an adversary who
argues *a priori* that they are possible, is the vainest labour in the world.
. . . The time for it is now past, because the human mind, whatever may
be said for or against miracles *a priori*, is now in fact losing its reliance
upon them" (CPW 7:164). Arnold is arguing that the belief in miracle has
given way not because of devastating logical arguments but because miracle is no longer part of that set of concepts regarded as necessary to those
modes of description used in our actual everyday thought and life. To

*This sentence is recorded in the *Note-Books* on three occasions.

refer back to Keith Thomas's example: miracles have gone the way of seventeenth-century magic. Arnold describes the process:

> Epiphanius tells us, that at each anniversary of the miracle of Cana, the water of the springs of Cibyra in Caria and Gerasa in Arabia was changed into wine; that he himself had drunk of the transformed water of Cibyra, and his brothers of that of Gerasa. Fifty years ago, a plain Englishman would have had no difficulty in thinking that the Cana miracle was true, and the other two miracles were fables. He is now irresistibly led to class all these occurrences in one category as unsubstantial tales of marvel. Scales seem to have fallen from his eyes in regard to miracles. . . . Mankind did not originally accept miracles because it had formal proof of them, but because its imperfect experience inclined it to them. Nor will mankind now drop miracles because it has formal proof against them, but because its more complete experience detaches it from them. The final result was inevitable, as soon as ever miracles began to embarrass people, began to be relegated . . . to a certain limited period long ago past and over (CPW 7:368).

When miracles no longer continued to play their explanatory role, they were simply relegated to the past since they were no longer needed. Once they had lost their "ordinary" explanatory function, they served no useful apologetic purpose. A similar example adduced by Arnold is the relation between the secularization of Aristotelian physics and the dispensing with the traditional proofs for the existence of God proffered by natural theology.

Arnold's awareness of the inevitable effect of the *Zeitgeist* on the forms of Christian apologetic was prescient. However, there remains the repeated charge that he looked upon the workings of the *Zeitgeist* as necessarily progressive, that for him there appears to be no intellectual backsliding, no retrogression in the ever-progressive movements of history. Like Hegel, Arnold did envision the ongoing funding of historical experience as essentially a progressive deepening of reality and truth, and this is because the historical process is the outworking of divine reason. He writes, for example, that

> thought and science follow their own law of development, they are slowly elaborated in the growth and forward pressure of humanity . . . and their ripeness and unripeness, as Dr. Newman most truly says, are not an effect of our wishing or resolving. Rather do they seem brought about by a power such

> as Goethe figures by the *Zeitgeist* or Time-Spirit, and St. Paul
> describes as a divine power *revealing* additions to what we pos-
> sess already" (CPW 6:92).

The charge against Arnold of an uncritical progressivism is, in my opinion, substantially just; and in this respect, as in others, Arnold was very
much a man of the mid-nineteenth century and the Liberal Anglican
philosophy of history. It is a serious charge, nevertheless, because it would
seem to reveal his failure to recognize the profound ironies and ambigu-
ities of history, as well as the relativistic character of *any and all* cultural
revolutions or new intellectual paradigm changes. The first charge will
hold, I believe, but the second will not. For while Arnold assumes that the
movement of history is progressive, he explicitly acknowledges—unlike
Hegel in this regard—that while his conceptions are "new and true and a
genuine product of the *Zeitgeist*," as historical forms of reconceiving the
tradition they are also partial and limited and will inevitably be superseded.
This is evident in his defense of his reading of St. Paul's doctrine against
his critics. While he argues that his interpretation of Paul is but the giving
of a plain, popular exposition of what "belongs to the *Zeitgeist*," that is,
what is in the air, anticipated and prepared for by others, nevertheless he
wishes to make clear that

> we by no means put forth our version of St. Paul's line of
> thought as true, in the same fashion as Puritanism puts forth
> its *Scriptural Protestantism*, or *gospel* as true. . . . Our rendering
> of St. Paul's thought we conceive rather as a product of nature,
> which has grown to be what it is and which will grow more;
> which will not stand just as we now exhibit it, but which will
> gain some aspects which we now fail to show in it, and will
> drop some which we now give to it. . . . Thus we present our
> conceptions neither as something quite new nor as something
> quite true (CPW 6:111-12).

To appreciate his sense of the *Zeitgeist* and its hermeneutical significance for religion, one needs to grasp not only Arnold's understanding
of the limits of language but also his theory of the development of doctrine. The question of language will be examined further in chapter 3.
The present chapter will focus on the concept of development, and here
the figure of Newman is important.

Arnold had read Newman's *Essay on the Development of Christian Doctrine*
prior to writing the essays that comprise *St. Paul and Protestantism*, and the
impress of Newman's essay is evident in Arnold's argument. In Novem-

ber 1869 Arnold had written to his mother about the church "resting on Catholic antiquity, historic Christianity, development, and so on, which open to it an escape from all single doctrines as they are outgrown" (L 2:21). He acknowledged that it was Newman who "has set forth, both persuasively and truly," a theory of development which no reading of church history could but convey. Arnold's choice of citations from Newman's *Essay* is instructive. They clearly reflect his own views and give important clues to the ideas that represent the ground principles of his hermeneutical program. Newman writes:

> We have to account for that apparent variation and growth of doctrine which embarrasses us when we would consult history for the true idea of Christianity. The increase and expansion of the Christian creed and ritual, and all the variations which have attended the process in the case of individual writers and churches, are the necessary attendants on any philosophy or polity which takes possession of the intellect and heart, and has any wide or extended dominion. From the nature of the human mind, time is necessary for the full comprehension and perfection of great ideas. The highest and most wonderful truths, though communicated to the world once for all by inspired teachers, could not be comprehended all at once by the recipients; but, as admitted and transmitted by minds not inspired, and through media which were human, have required only the longer time and deeper thought for their full elucidation. . . .
>
> Ideas may remain when the expression of them is indefinitely varied. Nay, one cause of corruption in religion is the refusal to follow the course of doctrine as it moves on, and an obstinacy in the notions of the past. So our Lord found his people precisians in their obedience to the letter, he condemned them for not being led on to its spirit—that is, its development. . . .
>
> It may be objected that inspired documents, such as the Holy Scriptures, at once determine doctrine without further trouble. But they were intended to create *an idea*, and that idea is not in the sacred text, but in the mind of the reader; and the question is, whether that idea is communicated to him in its completeness and minute accuracy on its first apprehension, or expands in his heart and intellect, and comes to perfection

in the course of time (CPW 6:86; Newman, *An Essay on the Development of Christian Doctrine* [London, 1845], 26-27, 60-62).

In these citations one can see *in nuce* several of the ideas that are formative in Arnold's working out of his own very different religious apologetic: that time is necessary for the full comprehension and perfection of ideas; that doctrines may be expressed with infinite variation, and therefore it is false to "rivet" doctrines to past formulations; and that in Newman's notion of the "idea" of Christianity one discerns the abiding truth within the flux of history. According to Newman, the development of Christian doctrine moves, in the first instance, from implicit, nonreflexive beliefs to the explicit articulation in doctrine. However, there remains the further historical stage of doctrinal expansion and elaboration, and, for Newman, in this process there is never a complete delineation of the idea of Christianity. Doctrinal development never reaches some exact linguistic completion; and yet, through the shifting historical process, the essential identity and continuity of the Christian idea remains.

Arnold had a far more radical sense than did Newman of the historical contingency of all dogma and was more sensitive to what he considered false developments. Nevertheless, he believed in the continuity of the Christian idea through the relativities of historical process and change. Like Newman, Arnold believed that no doctrine in its specific historical formulation nor any scriptural texts taken simply in their literal rendering could serve as the sum or essence, or idea, of Christianity as a historical religion. Though he is speaking of the method and secret of Jesus rather than of formal doctrine, Arnold nevertheless makes clear that Christianity is essentially a *source*:

> We can see why it is a mistake and may lead to much error, to exhibit any series of maxims, like those of the Sermon on the Mount, as the ultimate sum and formula into which Christianity may be run up. Maxims of this kind are but *applications* of the method and secret of Jesus; and the method and secret are capable of yet an infinite number more of such applications. Christianity is a *source*; no one supply of water and refreshment that comes from it can be called the sum of Christianity (CPW 6:299).

Newman did not, of course, equate development with Arnold's more sanguine view of intellectual and moral progress, and he required an authoritative ecclesiastical magisterium to serve as a necessary ballast to protect the irreducible core of dogma on its voyage down the unpredictable, often-tumultuous river of history. In this regard Arnold's view of the *Zeitgeist* and development, while fundamentally dependent on Newman, reveals a striking kinship with the more radical views formulated by the Catholic Modernists—often explicitly directed against Newman—twenty-five years after *Literature and Dogma*.

The Catholic Modernists saw Christianity essentially as a developmental and progressive phenomenon. It is, wrote George Tyrrell, "a sort of life that unfolds itself, like an organism, from age to age, that exhibits an immense variety of species and genera in different times and places, in all of which, collectively, its potentiality is progressively disclosed."[10] As one becomes more conscious of this process of development and approximation (though never attainment) of the idea of Christianity—that is, the more one apprehends "the idea and law of human progress"—the more, writes Tyrrell, "we shall necessarily appear more radical in our criticism, *being* all the while more conservative, more strongly assertive of the oldest laws and constitutions of our general life."[11]

It is this profound and, to critics, often perplexing union of radical historicism and religious conservativism that marks Arnold's kinship with the Modernists of the next generation. Both Arnold and the Modernists were willing to break with a purely Newmanian, homogeneous theory of development and to speak forthrightly of the possibility of basic *conceptual* change. "It is not indispensable to the authority of belief," writes Alfred Loisy,

> that it should be rigorously unchangeable in its intellectual form and its verbal expression. Such immutability is not compatible with the nature of human intelligence. Our most certain knowledge in the domain of nature and of science is always in movement, always relative, always perfectible. . . . Faith addresses itself to the unchangeable truth, through a formula, necessarily inadequate, capable of improvement, consequently of change.

And so it is that "neither the Christological dogma nor the dogma of grace nor that of the Church is to be taken as the summit of doctrine [or] intelligible for all generations, and equally applicable without any new translations or explanations, to all states, and to every advance of science, life, and human society."[12]

Both Arnold and the Catholic Modernists believed that significant intellectual shifts in paradigms, involving fundamentally different ways of looking at the world, may require a change that strains or breaks the notion of homogeneous development. Today this has become a common-place in Catholic writing on development.* The theory of an invariant evolution of Christian doctrine, writes Nicholas Lash, "has been finally destroyed not by 'denying' or 'disproving' it but rather by the collapse of that assumption of cultural homogeneity which was its tacit presupposition."[13] It is because this is now so widely recognized that contemporary Roman Catholic theologians, such as Maurice Bevenot, can speak of development by "pruning." Of doctrinal definition, Bevenot writes:

> Its instinct is sure enough, but it grasps its object only *grosso modo*, and can only express it in the categories and terms current at the time. . . . In the course of time, much that seemed to be necessarily included in the definition, comes to be recognized as not belonging to that core of truth which was the real intention of the definition. In such a situation, through the *deeper understanding* of the mystery in question, the development takes the form of a pruning and purgation of the previous definition, so that what it has previously been obligatory to hold, as being included in that definition, can now be called in question or even denied.[14]

Arnold would have found such a position congenial, since his approach to certain Christian beliefs often—but not always—involves the same kind of radical pruning or deeper understanding that involves a conceptual reinterpretation similar to what we find attempted by the Modernists. They sought to reinterpret Christian beliefs within a thoroughgoing modern explanatory scheme while maintaining continuity with the spiritual meaning of the doctrine.

Arnold attempts such a reinterpretation of several Christian doctrines. His comparison of the Cambridge Platonist John Smith's interpretation of witchcraft with St. Paul's understanding of the resurrection illustrates his approach. It is noteworthy that Arnold is conscious of the fact, demonstrated indisputably more recently by the New Testament scholar Rudolf Bultmann in his studies of St. Paul and St. John, that the process of reinterpretation or demythologization began in the New Testament itself—in Arnold's example, in the theology of St. Paul.

---

* This is not to imply that contemporary Catholic theologians, such as Lonergan, Schillebeeckx, Lash, and Bevenot share the Modernists' philosophical assumptions or doctrinal interpretations, but only that there are striking agreements and affinities in their theories of doctrinal development.

What Arnold intends to demonstrate in his comparison of St. Paul and John Smith is that men of veracity and judgment may believe in that which we deem incredible or about which we may remain agnostic and still teach us the truth of what in this other formulation we find unbelievable. Smith, a man of keen judgment and impeccable honesty, believed in witchcraft, since it was part of the very air he breathed in seventeenth-century England. "But it was [Smith's] nature to seek a firm ground for the ideas admitted by him. And for witchcraft and diabolical operation in the common conception of them as external things, he could find no solid ground, for there was none; and therefore he could not use them." And so, as Arnold shows, Smith was required to transform them. "After his exordium he makes an entirely fresh departure: 'When we say the devil is continually busy with us, I mean not only some apostate spirit as one particular being, but that spirit of apostasy, which is lodged in all men's natures'" (CPW 8:125-26). Arnold comments that "here in this *spirit of apostasy, which is lodged in all men's natures,* Smith had what was at bottom experimental and real" (CPW 8:126).

St. Paul, like the Cambridge Platonist,

> sought in an idea used for religion a side by which the idea could enter into his religious experience and become real to him. No such side could be afforded by the mere external fact and miracle of Christ's bodily resurrection. Paul, therefore . . . seized another aspect for the resurrection than the aspect of physical miracle. He presented resurrection as a spiritual rising which could be appropriated and enacted in our own living experience (CPW 8:128).

Arnold was confirmed in the belief that time and historical experience are the friends, not the enemies, of the spiritual life, and that this implies that the full elucidation and truth of religious doctrines cannot be contained within any particular formulation of the past. Religious doctrines must remain open to further adaptation required by time's ever-variable course, open to what Loisy called "the constantly changing condition of human life and intelligence." The fact that Arnold acted on his belief in doctrinal adaptation has caused critics to assert that he abandoned *historical* Christianity. Often associated with this charge is the further claim that in Arnold's symbolic reinterpretation of key Christian doctrines the words are stretched to the point that any common signification between the traditional words and their new use no longer obtains. These are important charges which demand attention.

First, can Arnold's symbolic reinterpretation lay claim to represent *historical* Christianity? Leslie Stephen, among others, asserted that it could not. If Arnold wished to gain for the Church of England the place in English national life that he desired, Stephen maintained he must "restore the feeling and the beliefs which were current two centuries ago"—"a task of some little difficulty," Stephen acknowledged.[15] For those who hold the position here represented by Stephen, there can be no development; Anglican Christianity must literally subscribe to the verbal formularies as commonly understood by the seventeenth-century divines. Surprisingly, this static, unhistorical form of criticism is even today frequently directed at Arnold. It appears to be implied, for example, in A. O. J. Cockshut's comment that, while Arnold's system is profoundly religious, it is "not in any acceptable historical sense, Christian."[16] But what notion of "historical sense" is at work here?

The issue can perhaps best be focused by posing the following question: Can Christian belief and practice be identified with any particular past age of the Christian church—e.g., with primitive Christianity (whatever that was), with the fifth century, the thirteenth or sixteenth centuries, with the formularies of the seventeenth-century Anglican divines? Arnold's answer is *no*. It is the answer of Alfred Loisy, of Adolf von Harnack, of Ernst Troeltsch; it is the answer of every historian of Christian origins and doctrine trained in and committed to modern historiographical work. For to refuse to answer no is to be required to select some period of the past as *the* primitive or *the* classical expression of *historical* Christianity. To do so is to "rivet" Christian belief and practice to a particular linguistic and cultural formulation expressive of a distinctive anthropology, cosmology, or world view. It is to fail to take seriously the historicity of conceptual forms or to acknowledge the fundamental hermeneutical significance of the modern revolutions in epistemology and historical consciousness. It is to fail to take seriously A. N. Whitehead's insight that one cannot claim absolute finality for a dogma without claiming commensurate finality for the sphere of thought within which it arose.

The modern difficulties with the notion of an original or classical Christianity is exemplified in the recent comments of a historian of early Christianity. "There never was," writes Robert Wilken,

> an "original Christian faith" or "a native Christian language."
> The further back one searches, the more unformed the tradition becomes. There is no moment or man or age or idea to which we can return and say: that is the Christian thing. . . .

A missionary to the Germans in the seventh century, a hermit in the Egyptian desert, a bishop in a Byzantine Court, a Span ish peasant, a Renaissance prince, an African tribesman, a twentieth-century electrical engineer, a suburban housewife in southern California—all these people have claimed the name Christian, but their style of Christian life and what they would identify as Christian would have little in common. They may all agree: "God is one, Jesus is his instrument among men, we should be faithful to Jesus." But if we try to reduce the variety of Christian experience to its common denominator we tend to speak trivialities. . . . [Christians] have managed to keep their identity amidst the most radical changes of practice, belief, thought, and institutions.[17]

Christianity is not, as Whitehead wisely remarked, a metaphysics; it is rather a community of faith and a way of life in search of a metaphysics or a coherent set of doctrines that by their nature involve ever new reconceptions.

This raises, however, another related question that is a more difficult matter. Assuming recognition of the fact of a development of doctrine and practice, what about the continuity of language and meaning between past and present formulations of belief? What, if any, are the acceptable limits of the use and reconception of Christian language in the evolution of belief? The issue is well stated by Renford Bambrough in a discussion of Arnold and reinterpretation:

It seems at least at first sight that there is an important parallel between what is done by Arnold . . . and what is done by Euripides, and there is room for the same doubt in the case of . . . Arnold as there is in the case of Euripides: a doubt as to whether what is now being affirmed is what it purports to be; a suspicion that the use of traditional words has now been carried so far away from the original and basic use that an element of deception or at least self-deception is involved in the use of old words for the expression of the new belief.[18]

Arnold played a key role in provoking this suspicion and in setting the terms of the debate over the symbolic interpretation of the Bible and the creeds that was to occupy theologians and ecclesiastics in England for decades after 1870. He was to exert a personal influence on a number of the English Modernists writing between 1880 and 1920 on the question of symbolism in doctrinal formulation and on the function of creeds.

The Church of England reached something of an official consensus on the question of symbolic interpretation with the appearance of the Report of the Commission on Doctrine in the Church of England (1938). The commission had been appointed by Archbishop Davidson in 1922 and included many eminent theologians, representing all schools of thought in the church. The Report proposed the following hermeneutical rule:

> Statements affirming particular facts may be found to have value as pictorial expressions of spiritual truths, even though the supposed facts did not actually happen. . . . It does not appear possible to delimit with finality or precision the extent to which symbolic elements of this . . . kind may enter into the historic tradition of the Christian faith. The possibility cannot be excluded that in this sense also a symbolic character may attach to the truth of articles in the Creeds. It is not therefore of necessity illegitimate to accept and affirm particular clauses of the Creeds while understanding them in this symbolic sense.[19]

What is implied in the church's position is the recognition that the ethical question of the veracity of belief is dependent on the theological interpretation of the particular belief, which in turn is subject to the judgment of criticism that frequently demands to be open-ended. Symbolic interpretation reflects the recognition of that fact. Does this mean that there are no limits, that the future development of belief is radically open-ended? The Report attempted to answer this by establishing a new interpretive fence: "In some cases the use of traditional phrases is censured as dishonest. This charge could only be sustained if the traditional phrase is being used in a sense wholly different from that originally conveyed by it. The reason for the continued use of such phrases is that *there is a core of identical meaning*.[20]

Arnold would have approved the commission's insistence on a core of identical meaning. There is ample evidence that his own reinterpretation of Christianity involved symbolic interpretations of doctrines such as the virgin birth, the resurrection, and the last judgment—in a number of instances strikingly similar to those proposed by the Anglican and Catholic Modernists. However, Arnold would have wished to go beyond the commission's Report. Many of the Anglican Modernists insisted on maintaining the formularies and creeds of the Church as long as their use was accompanied by a relaxing of subscription and a wide latitude of interpretation. In this respect Arnold's position is more radical, for, while advocating symbolic interpretation, he also calls for setting aside the creeds as liturgically *essential* and theologically *normative*. Here his position is more akin to that of the English liberals and Modernists influenced by the German historians Adolf von Harnack and Ernst Troeltsch.

Arnold believed that for the true elucidation of certain questions involving philosophic or scientific-historical criticism "time and favorable developing conditions are confessedly necessary." "Surely," he insists, "historic criticism, criticism of style, criticism of nature, no one would go to the early or middle ages of the Church for illumination on these matters." Of a true criticism of nature or history the early

> Church had no means of solving either the one problem or the other. And this from no fault at all of the Church, but for the same reason that she was unfitted to solve a difficulty in Aristotle's "Physics" or Plato's "Timaeus," and to determine the historical value of Herodotus or Livy; simply from the natural operation of the law of development, which for success in philosophy and criticism requires certain conditions, that in the early and medieval Church were not to be found (CPW 6:91).

Arnold would have agreed with Harnack's judgment that "the gospel did not enter the world as a statutory religion and can therefore have no classical and permanent manifestation in any form of intellectual or social expression, not even in the first one."[21] Harnack wrote his learned and massive 12-volume *Dogmengeschichte* to demonstrate that "the history of dogma furnishes the most suitable means for the liberation of the church from dogmatic Christianity."[22] For Harnack believed, as did Arnold, that the essence of Christianity is not coincident with either the apostolic witness or with those doctrines later hammered out in church councils. These are forms which, needless to say, have played their role in protecting and transmitting the Christian gospel, but they are not that gospel. Of these various historical forms Harnack wrote:

> Either Christianity is . . . identical with its first form (in this case, one is forced to conclude that it came and went at a certain time) or *it contains something which remains valid in historically changing forms.* Starting with the beginnings, church history shows that it was necessary for "early Christianity" to perish in order that "Christianity" might remain. So, too, there *followed,* later on, one metamorphosis upon another.[23]

Harnack concluded that a historical understanding of Christianity requires that one make an effort to separate the distinctive essence or continuum of this great historical phenomenon from the doctrinal forms in which it has been variously clothed. This he attempted in *Wesen des Christentums*, as did Arnold a quarter century earlier in *Literature and Dogma*. Both books were bold attempts at reconstruction or, better, at historical development by pruning. Both were efforts at criticism as a historical responsibility.

What sets apart the approach of Arnold, Harnack, or Troeltsch from that of either traditional Protestantism or Catholicism is the fact that for them modern experience and knowledge enter into the consideration of the development of doctrine as genuine coefficients. That is, certain presuppositions with regard to the warrants of critical judgment enter *materially* into any theological reconstruction. Hermeneutically it implies acceptance of the modern cognitional revolution in historical consciousness, Foucault's *mutation epistemologique*. Historical consciousness denies any classical normative form or doctrine for articulating the nature or essence of Christianity, namely, the gospel. Rather, it affirms that the expression of that essence always appears in forms shaped by the historical *Zeitgeist*.

Are there, then, no theological norms? If not, would it not imply such a radical accommodation to modernity that the ever-changing *Zeitgeist* (i.e., culture) becomes, in fact, the substantive norm? The worry is expressed in David De Laura's judgment about Arnold's hermeneutic: "The churches, quite literally, have no mind of their own. . . . Christianity must submit and adapt itself to the 'developing' and (presumably) changing standards of the 'philosophy and criticism' of each age for any metaphysical description of the reality that Christianity admittedly speaks to."[24]

Some clarifications are here in order. For Arnold, as for Harnack and Troeltsch, Christianity must indeed adapt in view of changes that take place in philosophy and criticism. But this, of course, is what it has done throughout its history; for, as Harnack demonstrated, early Christianity had to perish, as did the substance philosophy of the Church Fathers of Nicaea and Chalcedon and the Aristotelian categories of the Scholastics, in order that Christianity might live during new epistemic mutations. Here culture is a formative factor, but it is not the substantive norm.

Arnold recognized a tension and discontinuity that exist between culture and that continuum or essence of Christianity which remains valid in historically changing forms. The continuum or essence was what he sought to bring out in *Literature and Dogma*, although, as with Harnack, the articulation of such an essence meant the historical risk of "assuming the royal function of a judge." It involved an act of deconstruction in which the literal antique reading is seen as a debasement of the essential spiritual or metaphoric meaning, Arnold recognized that the transformations which Christianity has undergone, and will undergo in the future, may efface any obvious or homogeneous continuity with the antique doctrinal formulations; on the other hand, these transformations may make the real continuity transparent. In any case, the essence or continuum is not coextensive with or reducible to any single historical formulation. In his important essay "What Does 'Essence of Christianity' Mean?" Troeltsch speaks of the normative essence of Christianity in terms that illuminate Arnold's position:

> One of the main difficulties is the definition of this continuum itself, the connecting unity in this multiplicity of formations developing out of the original form. This continuum can of course neither simply be taken from the preaching of Jesus as being that major part of it which persists through all times, nor can it be in the generic character of that which all the formulations of Christianity have in common. Then again this continuum by no means consists in an idea which can be briefly formulated in a simple main idea, but in a spiritual power. ... The essence has to be an entity with an inner, living flexibility, and a productive power for new creation and assimilation. It cannot be characterized at all by one word or one doctrine, but only by a concept which includes from the start both flexibility and richness; *it must be a developing spiritual principle*, a germinative idea ... not a metaphysical or dogmatic idea, but a driving spiritual force.[25]

Arnold saw the essence of Christianity as such a source and such a power, a source and power capable of adapting and assimilating themselves to continuous historical change. To return to the original worry, expressed by Bambrough, Arnold would reply that in the case of symbolic interpretation it is, of course, possible to stretch words beyond their ancient use so as to court both deception and self-deception. But such reinterpretation does not, as such, involve dissembling. Arnold would argue that only if the metaphysical conceptions or historical forms of the ancient creedal statements are accepted as normative does a problem arise. The future may, however—on the grounds of historical-critical research or religious experience—controvert any notion of homogeneous continuity with these past conceptions since the substantive norm, the continuum of belief, the essence of Christianity, is not synonymous with these ancient doctrinal conceptions. On the other hand, a truly imaginative act of interpretation may disclose the original meaning of Jesus' logia, lost on the literalizing reporters and redactors. (PW 3:135-36). The gentle and tender

A further consideration, nevertheless, remains. If Arnold believed that modern critical judgment is necessary and formative, was he not guilty or at least susceptible of subsuming religion, in this case Christianity, within culture or the *Zeitgeist*? Arnold's understanding of the relations between religion and culture needs to be examined to see if this sheds additional light on these questions.

RELIGION AND CULTURE

Critics from J. C. Shairp to T. S. Eliot have asserted that Arnold does subsume religion within culture—i.e., that "literature, or Culture, tended with Arnold to usurp the place of Religion." I believe that a careful reading of Arnold's developing idea of culture and its relation to religion will demonstrate the fundamental error of these charges and will clarify his position with regard to Christianity's real autonomy and the place of theological norms.

The careless and partisan allegations of Eliot and others have done much mischief. They have focused on passages in the essays of the 1860s in which Arnold appears to be saying that religion simply subserves culture. However, as David DeLaura has shown, from 1867 onward Arnold draws back from any notion of religion as simply ministering to other more important ends. The writings reveal a growing awareness of the tension and dialectic between religion and culture.[26] Finally, in Arnold's mature writings on religion culture clearly becomes ancillary to religion, although the agency of imagination and criticism remains indispensable for the hermeneutical task of religious understanding and reconstruction.

In January 1865 Arnold wrote to his mother expressing what was by then his often-voiced dislike of "all over-preponderance of single elements," and avowing that his efforts now "are directed to enlarge and complete us" (L 1:247). This pledge was central to his purpose in the farewell lecture delivered at Oxford in June 1867, namely, to declare "culture as having its origin in the love of perfection" (CPW 5:91). In this address, entitled "Culture and Its Enemies," later revised and published as the first chapter of *Culture and Anarchy*, Arnold asserts that while religion is "the greatest and most important of the efforts by which the human race has manifested its impulse to perfect itself," nevertheless "religion comes to a conclusion identical with that which culture—culture seeking the determination of this question through *all* the voices of human experience . . . likewise reaches" (CPW 5:93-94). Here the ideal of religion coincides with that of culture. They both perceive the character of perfection as "not a having and a resting, but a growing and a becoming." Arnold goes further and predicts that "the idea of a human nature perfect on all sides, which is the dominant idea of poetry . . . is destined, adding to itself the religious idea of a devout energy, to transform *and govern* the other" (CPW 5:99-100; italics added).

Between the delivery of this, his final lecture as Professor of Poetry, and the commencement of the decade devoted to the writing of his four books on religion, several events had joined to give Arnold pause in commending his Hellenic ideal. Thus while he found many of the replies to "Culture and Its Enemies" off the mark and even amusing, some of them cut to the quick and forced him to clarify his definition of culture and its perfection. With Kierkegaardian sarcasm Frederic Harrison had mocked Arnold's culture, which "sits high aloft with pouncet-box to spare her senses ought unpleasant" while "death, sin, cruelty stalk amongst us."[27] Henry Sidgwick was even more severe. He charged Arnold with a refined and supercilious eudaemonism. Life confronts us with a fundamental conflict. "On the one hand," wrote Sidgwick, "are the claims of harmonious self-development, on the other are the cries of struggling humanity." The former, he observed, does not crush our sympathies; no, far worse, it only represses them, keeps them safely at arm's length. But what the nation requires, Sidgwick angrily admonished, is a work that "must be done as self-sacrifice, not as self-development."[28]

It was impossible, Arnold responded, "that all these remonstrances and reproofs should not affect me." In fact, they gave him the golden opportunity "to profit by the objections" (CPW 5:410) and to expand—to five succeeding articles—and to revise and clarify what he had said in "Culture and Its Enemies." The result was *Culture and Anarchy*, published in 1869.

In this book Arnold takes pains to clarify that his ideal of culture, of perfection, has nothing to do with an aloof, Paterian aestheticism or with the suppression of the social sympathies. "Perfection, as culture conceives it," he writes,

is not possible while the individual remains isolated. The individual is required, under pain of being stunted and enfeebled in his own development if he disobeys, to carry others along with him in his march towards perfection. . . . The idea of perfection as a *general* expansion of the human family is at variance with our strong individualism . . . [with] our maxim "every man for himself" (CPW 5:94-95).

The effort which Arnold makes to bring home this point accentuates the perversity of T. S. Eliot's criticism that the "thinness which Arnold's 'culture' conveys to a modern reader is partly due to the absence of social background to his picture."[29] To claim that Arnold's culture recommends a selfish personal cultivation or that society must wait upon the process of the individual's self-perfection only can be, as Raymond Williams has remarked, "a deliberate misunderstanding" if, indeed, Arnold has been read. Williams rightly places Arnold's discussion of culture in the wider context of his life: "Those who accuse him of a policy of 'cultivated inaction' forget not only his arguments but his life. . . . *Culture and Anarchy* needs to be read alongside the reports, minutes, evidence to commissions, and specifically educational essays which made up so large a part of Arnold's working life."[30]

In *Culture and Anarchy* Arnold specifically takes care to address the charges of aestheticism and a self-indulgent individualism that had been made against "Culture and Its Enemies." The book also displays a greater balance and sense of tension in Arnold's perception of the relations between culture and religion. Hellenism is now clearly balanced by Hebraism, or what Arnold calls "self-conquest, self-devotion, the following not our own individual will, but the will of God, obedience" (CPW 5:165-66)—in other words, Sidgwick's work of self-sacrifice. Moreover, Arnold's Hellenic ideal, sweetness and light, becomes more dominantly the intellectual standard of light: "Sweetness and light evidently have to do with the bent or side of humanity which we call Hellenic. Greek intelligence has obviously for its essence the instinct for what Plato calls the true, firm intelligible law of things; the law of light, of seeing things as they are." For even Greek art, "Greek beauty, have their root in the same impulse to see things as they really are, inasmuch as Greek art and beauty rest on fidelity to nature" (CPW 5:178).

Throughout *Culture and Anarchy* the tension and balance between "the scientific passion as well as the passion for doing good," between Bishop Wilson's dual reason and the will of God are essentially sustained. "Hebraism and Hellenism are, neither of them, *the* law of human development, as their admirers are prone to make them; they are, each of them, *contributions* to human development" (CPW 5:171). Different times and circumstances will, of course, mean that one ideal will become preponderant over the other and, inevitably, presume itself to be *the* law of human perfection.

> But sooner or later it becomes manifest that when the two sides of humanity proceed in this fashion of alternative preponderance, and not of mutual understanding and balance, the side which is uppermost does not really provide in a satisfactory manner for the needs of the side which is undermost. . . . The true and smooth order of humanity's development is not reached in either way. And therefore, while we willingly admit with the Christian apostle that the world by wisdom,—that is by the isolated preponderance of its intellectual impulses—knew not God, or the true order of things, it is yet necessary, also, to set up a sort of converse to this proposition, and to say likewise (what is equally true) that the world by Puritanism knew not God. And it is on this converse of the apostles' proposition that is particularly needful to insist in our own country just at present (CPW 5:177-78).

Sidgwick's demand for fire and strength rather than sweetness and light only proves to Arnold that Sidgwick has forgotten "that the world is not all of one piece, and every piece with the same needs at the same time." The Roman world in the infancy of the Christian church or French society in the eighteenth century may have needed fire and strength. "But can it be said," asks Arnold, "that the Barbarians who overran the empire needed fire and strength even more than sweetness and light; or that the Puritans needed them more; or that Mr. Murphy, the Birmingham lecturer, and his friends, need them more?" (CPW 5:180). While it is true that there is no *unum necessarium*, no one thing needful, which can free human nature, still what Sidgwick overlooks and what Arnold wished to bring home is that while Hellenism is not "always for everybody more wanted than Hebraism . . . for Mr. Murphy at this particular moment, and for the great majority of us his fellow-countrymen, it is more wanted!" (CPW 5:181).

In the years between the completion of *Culture and Anarchy* and the writing of *Literature and Dogma*, Arnold remained a believer in culture but, as in the case of his liberalism, one "tempered by experience, reflection, and renunciation." Religion and conduct now begin to emerge as the larger and more important part of life. While Hellenism remains indispensable to the flowering of whatever is to be genuinely human, the emphasis now begins to shift to its special function in the service of religion. First, it serves as the instrument of intellectual discrimination: "Culture or 'letters' is again a form of 'criticism' exhibited in 'justness of perception,' 'tact' and a 'sense' of history—in short the right method or instrument for reading religious documents."[31] Furthermore, culture serves, in the form of imagination, poetry, and emotion, as a means of "lighting up morality," of supplying the mythopoetic language, imagery, and feeling by means of which certain great religious ideas alone can properly be grasped and expressed.

The hermeneutical role of culture, in terms of both intellectual discrimination and imagination, became *the* pressing matter for Arnold in his effort after 1868 to sustain the Bible and Christian belief in an age of the apotheosis of science. In November 1870 he writes to his mother lamenting how little the English Bible-reading public derived from their study, and "how much more profit they would get from this Bible reading if they combined it with other things, and other things with it" (L 2:41-42). Arnold's challenge to the Dissenters in *St. Paul and Protestantism* diverts attention from his chief concern, which was to show how their cultural provinciality and their false reading of St. Paul and the Bible were inextricably connected. The relationship is fully elaborated in the preface to *Literature and Dogma*.

There he shows that the received theology had failed in its efforts to bring the Bible to the people because the construction which it placed on the Scriptures was "rigid, fixed, and scientific." It was a false construction that could not be put right without the aid of culture, for it was this very absence of culture—i.e., criticism and imagination—which disposed men "to conclude at once, from any imperfection or fallibility in the Bible, that it was a priestly imposture" (CPW 6:151).*

By culture Arnold here means intellectual breadth, "the acquainting ourselves with the best that has been known and said in the world, and thus with the history of the human spirit" (CPW 6:151). Such an acquaintance involves, of course, knowledge of how men have thought and expressed themselves, but it includes also "not only knowledge but right tact and justness of judgment," which turns out to be "in relation to the Bible, getting the power, through reading, to estimate the proportion and rela-

---

* Many of Arnold's judgments about biblical interpretation sound like echoes of his father's writings. Thomas Arnold had written of the young man who "is taught that all its [the Bible's] parts are of equal authority . . . and begins to read it, like the Koran, all composed at one time, and addressed to persons similarly situated." When the young man finds this not to be the case, he rebels. ("On the Right Interpretation and Understanding of Scripture," *Sermons* [London, 1832], 2:428-31.)

tion in what we read." For "if we read but a very little, we naturally want to press it all; if we read a great deal, we will be willing not to press the whole of what we read, and we learn what ought to be pressed and what not" (CPW 6:153).

It is not, then, simply reading a great deal that Arnold counsels and that ensures a just criticism, for culture implies breadth of learning and experience. A specialist such as D. F. Strauss may skillfully apply negative criticism to the Bible, but, Arnold insists, the reality of the Bible requires a richer, deeper, more imaginative mind. It requires the quality of mind that Arnold calls "justness of perception" and for the possession of which no mere specialist training is a guarantee. Arnold insists that true culture and a genuine criticism include both a knowledge of the facts and a justness of perception that come only from wide and sympathetic experience.

Literature and Dogma is witness to the fact that for Arnold religion in no sense merely subserves culture. What Arnold is insistent to maintain is that any sane and true reading of the Bible, and thus any authentic as well as relevant religious interpretation, requires the hermeneutical interdependence of religious text and "critical tact" and that the latter can come only from a wide experience of how men have thought and expressed themselves. Here Arnold is fully his father's son. In the introduction to the third of the three volumes of his *Sermons*, Thomas Arnold had written at length on the importance of a wide cultural experience as essential to a real understanding of the Bible. He insisted that interpretation requires "a lively knowledge of Scripture on the one hand and the master works of human wisdom on the other. Both are alike necessary." The elder Arnold was not, he emphasized, "speaking of moral improvement but of the understanding's perception of truth . . . to save us from viewing the Scriptures themselves through the medium of ignorance and prejudice, and lowering them by our perverse interpretations in order to make them countenance our errors."[32]

Matthew Arnold insisted that putting a right construction on the Bible, like the development of human perfection, requires culture. The key to his understanding of the interdependence of religion and culture is therefore to be found in the tension, counterpoise, and harmony of "all the voices of human experience" which can save us from that narrow, rigid, and, finally, false understanding that comes from imagining that we are in possession of the "one thing needful."

Attention to this point will result in a more accurate reading of that *locus classicus* referred to so often by critics who insist that Arnold's culture usurps the place of religion. This passage in "Culture and Its Enemies," which has already been referred to, speaks of perfection as "the harmonious expansion of *all* the powers which make the beauty and worth of human nature," an expansion "not consistent with the overdevelopment of any one power at the expense of the rest." Arnold concludes that "here culture goes beyond religion, as religion is generally conceived by us" (CPW 5:94). If read with due attention to the two critical qualifiers, even this seemingly damning passage cannot be interpreted as proposing culture's usurpation of religion. Arnold is saying that the overdevelopment of any one power is not consistent with culture's love of perfection only when it is accomplished *at the expense of the rest*. Hebraism may well have been in need of overdevelopment in Leo X's court at the time of the Reformation; but this is certainly not the case in Edward Miall's editorial room in the Dissenting Midlands of Victorian England. In the case of Miall, such an overdevelopment is at the expense of beauty and a sense of history. The religion, then, that culture—as the harmonious expansion of all our powers—"goes beyond" is the religion "as *is generally conceived by us*," that is to say, the religion of the Dissenters, the religion that crushes or denies the operation of historical knowledge, imagination, or beauty in the religious life.

True religion, which, Arnold maintains, is "the greater part of life," will always remain dependent on these Hellenic ideals. In *Literature and Dogma*, for instance, Arnold claims much more for religion—"six-eighths of life, while art and science are only two-eighths." And yet, he adds, "the world cannot do without art and science" (CPW 6:388). Arnold did not believe that culture would or should usurp the place of religion or that religion simply subserves culture. Their true relationship and interdependence is indicated in his preface to *Last Essays on Church and Religion*:

> Christianity will find the ways for its own future. What is certain is that it will not disappear. Whatever progress may be made in science, art, and literary culture—however much higher, more general, and more effective than at present the value for them may become—Christianity will still be there as what these rest against and imply; as the indispensable background, the *three-fourths of life*. It is true, while the remaining fourth is ill-cared for, the three-fourths themselves must also suffer with it. But this does but bring us to the old and true Socratic thesis of the interdependence of virtue and knowledge (CPW 8:162).

Arnold's position is perhaps best expressed in an address delivered at St. Jude's Church, Whitechapel, in the East End of London, on 29 November 1884. Arnold was honoring the church's vicar, Canon Barnett, known for his work among the poor. The occasion of special notice was the recent unveiling on the church's façade of a mosaic copy of the painting *Time, Death, and Judgment*, by G. F. Watts. Arnold praised Barnett for his efforts to alleviate the terrible conditions of the poor. But beyond these labors, Barnett sought to bring the influence of beauty into the lives of his people, signified by the commissioned mosaic. Arnold warmly commended the vicar for his work on behalf of art and beauty, but then continued: "Nevertheless, that saying remains true—'Whosoever drinketh of this water shall thirst again.' No doubt the social sympathies, the feeling for beauty, the pleasure of art, if left merely by themselves, if untouched by what is the deepest thing in human life—religion—are apt to become ineffectual and superficial" (CPW 10:252). Indeed, Arnold concludes that art and beauty reach their highest achievement, give the human spirit what it can rest upon, what can give it joy, only when they have "a deep and powerful connection with religion." These are not the words or the sentiments of an aesthete, of a man proposing culture's usurpation of religion.

If Arnold were to be placed in a comparative typology of positions regarding the relations between Christianity and culture—for example, as delineated in the work of Ernst Troeltsch and H. R. Niebuhr—he would stand with those mediating thinkers who reject both the positions of those who see Christianity in sharp antithesis to culture and those who call for a radical accommodation of Christianity to culture. Like Arnold, the mediating thinkers recognize both the incommensurability of Christianity and culture and, at the same time, their critical interdependence. They see Christ as "the fulfillment of cultural aspirations and the restorer of the institutions of a true society. Yet there is in him something that neither arises out of culture nor contributes directly to it. He is discontinuous as well as continuous with social life and its culture."[33]

It is in this tradition, which recognizes the unique and inescapable authority of both religion and culture and yet their essential interdependence, that Arnold must be placed. Modern critical judgment must be engaged in the interpretive task, but that is not to confuse it with the substantive norm, the essence of Christianity. The relation of religion to culture brings us to Arnold's understanding of poetic language and imagination and their relation to religious discourse and religious truth.

NOTES

1. For a full study of Arnold's use of the term *Zeitgeist*, see Fraser Neiman, "The *Zeitgeist* of Matthew Arnold," *PMLA* 72 (Dec. 1957). For Arnold's indebtedness to Carlyle, see David DeLaura, "Arnold and Carlyle," *PMLA* 59 (Mar. 1964) and Kathleen Tillotson, "Matthew Arnold and Carlyle," *Mid-Victorian Studies* (London, 1965).

2. Arthur Stanley, *Sermons on Special Occasions* (London, 1882) 46. For an account of the Liberal Anglicans, see Duncan Forbes, *The Liberal Anglican Idea of History* (London, 1952).

3. Thomas Arnold, *Miscellaneous Works* (London, 1845) 116.

4. T. E. Hulme, *Speculations* (London, 1949) 50-51.

5. Keith Thomas, *Religion and the Decline of Magic* (London, 1971) 639-40.

6. Thomas 647.

7. Thomas Kuhn, *The Structure of Scientific Revolutions* (Chicago, 1962) x.

8. Michel Foucault, *The Archeology of Knowledge*, trans. A. M. Sheridan Smith (London, 1972).

9. Bernard Lonergan, *Divinarum Personarum Conceptio Analogica* (Rome, 1959).

10. George Tyrrell, *Essays on Faith and Immortality*, ed. M. D. Petre (London, 1914); cited B. M. G. Reardon, *Roman Catholic Modernism* (London, 1970) 149.

11. Tyrrell 148.

12. Alfred Loisy, *The Gospel and the Church*, trans. Christopher Home (New York, 1912) 217-18, 210.

13. Nicholas Lash, *Change in Focus: A Study of Doctrinal Change and Continuity* (London, 1973) 133. This book is an excellent study of doctrinal development in the modern period.

14. Maurice Bevenot, "Primacy and Development," *Heythrop Journal* 4 (1963): 408.

15. Stephen, "Mr. Matthew Arnold and the Church of England" 424-25.

16. A. O. J. Cockshut, *The Unbelievers* (London, 1964) 62.

17. Robert L. Wilken, *The Myth of Christian Beginnings* (New York, 1971) 170, 184-85.

18. Renford Bambrough, *Reason, Truth and God* (London, 1969) 36.

19. *Doctrine in the Church of England* (London, 1938) 37-38.

20. *Doctrine in the Church of England* 34-35.

21. Adolf von Harnack, *Wesen des Christentums* (Berlin, 1900) 113.

22. Adolf von Harnack, *Grundriss der Dogmengeschichte*, 9th ed. (Berlin, 1921) 5.

23. Harnack, *Wesen des Christentums* xix (italics added).

24. David J. DeLaura, *Hebrew and Hellene in Victorian England: Newman, Arnold, and Pater* (Austin, 1969) 87.

25. *Ernst Troeltsch: Writings on Theology and Religion*, trans. and ed. Robert Morgan and Michael Pye (London, 1977) 153, 151.

26. David DeLaura, "Arnold and Literary Criticism," *Matthew Arnold*, ed. Kenneth Allott (London, 1975) 135-36. I am indebted to DeLaura for his many insights in this essay.

27. Frederic Harrison, "Culture: A Dialogue," *The Fortnightly Review* ns 2 (1867): 610.

28. Henry Sidgwick, "The Prophet of Culture," *Macmillan's Magazine* 16 (1867): 273-74.

29. T. S. Eliot, *Notes toward the Definition of Culture* (London, 1948) 22.

30. Raymond Williams, *Culture and Society 1780-1950* (London, 1958) 118-19.

31. DeLaura, "Arnold and Literary Criticism" 139. I am particularly indebted to DeLaura for his discussion of the developing relations between culture and religion in Arnold's work—although I draw conclusions from his essay with which he would not necessarily concur.

32. Thomas Arnold, *Sermons* (London, 1834) 3:xvii-xviii.

33. H. R. Niebuhr, *Christ and Culture* (New York, 1951) 42.

3 "All the Grandeur of a Natural Law": Arnold on the Status of Religious Language and Experience

> The language of figure and feeling will satisfy us better, will cover more of what we seek to express, than the language of literal fact and science. The language of science about it will be *below* what we feel to be the truth.
>
> *Literature and Dogma*

> Here again it is experience that we invoke: . . . and to this end, take a course of the Bible first and then a course of Benjamin Franklin, Horace Greeley, Jeremy Bentham, and Mr. Herbert Spencer; see which has most effect, which satisfies you more!
>
> *Literature and Dogma*

RELIGION AND POETRY

In commenting on the renewed interest in the literary imagination among theologians today, Nathan Scott remarks that "in its effort to become a truly 'foundational' discipline, it is not surprising that recent theology should be rediscovering . . . the peculiar talent of the poetic imagination for being an agency of primary truth." In this rediscovery Scott sees Martin Heidegger as the most recent influential guide. Yet, he adds, "before this great sage . . . Matthew Arnold in the 1870s was undertaking . . . with even greater audacity to suggest how inevitably and inseverably religion is grounded in the poetic imagination."[1] It is Arnold's appreciation of this very inseverability of religion and poetry that has often caused theologians to demur from following him as a guide, and that has led literary critics to declare, far too peremptorily, that poetry becomes for Arnold "a surrogate for a defunct religion."[2] It is in this context that, before examining Arnold's seasoned reflections on language, poetry, and religious discourse and their application to the task of interpretation, it is necessary to give some extended attention to Arnold's developing theory of poetry. This may help to clarify Arnold's often misunderstood view of the relations between poetry and religion.

Arnold worked out some of his enduring ideas concerning poetry through his early correspondence with Arthur Clough, between 1849 and 1853. The letters clearly demonstrate that by his late twenties Arnold already possessed a "high" doctrine of poetry and its work. "Critics," he complains, "still think that the object of poetry is to produce exquisite bits and images—such as Shelley's *clouds shepherded by the slow unwilling wind*, and Keats passim: whereas modern poetry can only subsist by its *contents*" (CL 124). By *contents* Arnold meant that the poet, unlike Keats and Browning, "must begin with an Idea of the world in order not to be prevailed over by the world's multitudinousness" (CL 97). Poetry must become "a complete magister vitae as the poetry of the ancients did: by including as theirs did, religion with poetry, instead of existing as poetry only, and leaving religious wants to be supplied by the Christian religion, *as a power existing independent of the poetical power*" (CL 124; italics added). A poetry charged with such an immense task must possess a language and style "very plain direct and severe"; "not lose itself in parts and episodes and ornamental work"; it "must press forwards to the whole" (CL 124).

Arnold's recurring stress on beginning with an idea, "pressing forwards to the whole," on poetry as "a complete magister vitae," has readily led critics to complain of the excessive didacticism, the accentuation on edification in Arnold's poetic theory. The undeniable centrality that Arnold gives to the content of poetry should not, however, minimize the essential place and attention that he also gives to poetry's formal aspects. After all, it was in Clough's poetry that he found wanting what he called the lack of naturalness, by which he meant "an absolute propriety—of form, as the sole *necessary* of Poetry as such: whereas the greatest wealth and depth of matter is merely a superfluity in the Poet *as such*" (CL 98-99). Of course, in poetry form and content are indivisible. This is professed in Arnold's letter to Clough of 1 March 1849. There he speaks of the "*two* offices of Poetry": one being "to add to one's store of thoughts and feelings" while the other is called upon "to compose and elevate the mind by a sustained tone, numerous allusions, and a grand style" (CL 100). The grand style is poetic form marked not principally by felicitous expression or rich imagery but by severity and simplicity and by what Arnold found in the Greeks, "where . . . reason, measure, sanity, also count for so much . . . and the *architectonicé* which . . . comes only after a steady, deep-searching survey, a firm conception of the facts of human life" (CPW 3:345). In the 1 March 1849 letter to Clough, Arnold identifies the grand style with Sophocles, in whom style is but the expression of life: "The style is the expression of the nobility of the poet's character, as the matter is the expression of the richness of his mind" (CL 101). And it is the style that produces as great, if not greater, effect on men's character than does the power of the poet's mind.

The poet's task, Arnold was more and more to insist, is not only to edify and interpret but to fortify, ennoble, animate. Clough thought highly of Arnold's "The Scholar-Gipsy," but Arnold, in self-reproach, replied to his friend: "But what does it *do* for you? Homer *animates*—Shakespeare *animates.* . . . The Gipsy Scholar at best awakens a pleasing melancholy." What people want "is something to *animate* and *ennoble* them—not merely to add zest to their melancholy or grace to their dreams" (CL 146).

That Arnold's high doctrine of poetry, as enunciated piecemeal in his correspondence with Clough, was closely associated in his mind with the warmth and joy and animation found in religion is transparent, even at this early stage. It is at this time that Arnold speaks of "the objection which really wounds and perplexes" him religiously; namely, "that the service of reason is freezing to feeling, chilling to the religious mood" (P 277). He confesses to Clough that if one "loved what was beautiful and interesting in itself *passionately* enough," one could produce great works "without troubling oneself with religious dogmas." But, he owns up, "as it is, we are *warm* only when dealing with these last—and what is frigid is always bad" (CL 143).

At this juncture, at least, the religious qualities of the grand style, the noble moral animation "left by a great action treated as a whole," Arnold found in the Greek spirit as perfected in Sophocles, and not in Christian literature.

The Sophoclean grand style and its "modernity" Arnold found in the "adequate and consummate representation of human life," which he associated with the portrayal of "human nature developed in a number of directions, politically, socially, religiously, morally . . . in its completest and most harmonious development" (CPW 1:28). This ideal of Hellenic measure becomes, of course, the great theme of Arnold's social and educational criticism of the 1860s, but it remains at this time central to his poetic theory as well. This is manifest in "Pagan and Mediaeval Religious Sentiment" (1864), where he observes that "the main element of the modern spirit's life is neither the senses and understanding, nor the heart and imagination," but rather "the imaginative reason." And no poets other than the Greek poets from Pindar to Sophocles "have lived so much by the imaginative reason; no other poets have made their work so balanced,

... have so well-satisfied the thinking-power, have so well-satisfied the religious sense" (CPW 3:230-31).

For Arnold the power of great poetry is "its interpretive power," "the noble and profound application of ideas to life." But this power resides in the poet's style, in the "absolute propriety" of form, which is "the power of so dealing with things as to awaken in us a wonderfully full, new, and intimate sense of them, and of our relations with them" (CPW 3:12-13).

Some may judge this to be a too intellective and moral view of poetry's function, but it is not one that is unmindful that poetry's "criticism of life" is accomplished only "under the conditions immutably fixed by the laws of poetic beauty and poetic truth" (CPW 9:44)—a truth, that is, which remains undisclosed by abstract doctrine. It is the intimate and creative conjunction of "the poetical gift" and "the one moral impression left by a great action" which constitutes for Arnold the perfect union of poetry and religion.

While the two powers of poetry remain conjoined "by having *natural magic*" and "by having *moral profundity*" (CPW 3:33), Arnold's sense of what constitutes poetry's essential "profoundness of moral impression" depends upon another quality which emerges explicitly in the 1860s but which, in retrospect, can already be found in the letters to Clough and the prefaces and essays of the 1850s: the sense of joy. In the 1853 preface Arnold reminded his readers of the Muses' lesson: "It is not enough that the poet should add to the knowledge of men, it is required of him also that he should add to their happiness. 'All art,' says Schiller, 'is dedicated to Joy'" (CPW 1:2). Arnold did not consider a work of poetry as justified either by its wealth of imagery or its accuracy of representation alone; "It has to be shown," he insists, "that it is a representation from which men can derive enjoyment" (CPW 1:2). A poem gives no joy when, as in the case of "Empedocles on Etna," "there is everything to be endured, nothing to be done." Therefore Arnold withdrew the poem from the 1853 edition.

For the same reason he judged Lucretius to be inadequate. In Lucretius one finds "no peace, no cheerfulness . . . either in the world from which he comes or the solitude to which he goes." He is "gloom-weighted, morbid" and therefore "is no adequate interpreter of his age" (CPW 1:33-34). So too, Arnold finds the "sweet, touching sadness" of "the most beautiful" Virgil. The sadness is "a source of charm" in his poem, but it is also "a testimony of its incompleteness" (CPW 1:35).

The animation and joy which Arnold finds wanting in Lucretius and Virgil, and in "The Scholar-Gipsy" and "Empedocles on Etna," derive from a particular experience of "moral profundity": the sense of consolation and exaltation that comes only when the self finds itself in perfect submission and accord with an eternal law or will. This theme distinctly emerges in the touchstones which Arnold selects for use in the literary essays—"Maurice de Guerin," "Marcus Aurelius," "Pagan and Mediaeval Religious Sentiment"—of the early 1860s. He perceives it in Shakespeare, in Hamlet's lines

> There's a divinity that shapes our ends,
> Rough-hew them as we will.

Lines such as these give one "a satisfying sense of reality"; they "reconcile him with himself and the universe" (CPW 3:33). Arnold finds the same satisfaction in Sophocles's speech: "Oh! that my lot may lead me in the path of holy innocence of word and deed, the path which august laws ordain, laws that in the highest empyrean had their birth, of which Heaven is the father alone, neither did the race of mortal men beget them, nor shall oblivion ever put them to sleep. The power of God is mighty in them, and groweth not old" (CPW 3:231).

It is in the Bible, however, that Arnold discovers the experience of moral profundity in "unexampled splendour":

> "Unto you that fear my name shall the sun of righteousness arise with healing in his wings" says the Old Testament. . . . "Whatsoever is born of God, overcometh the world," says the New.
> In such passages as these one encounters the glow of a divine warmth;—the austerity of the sage melts away [and] "he who is vivified by it renews his strength" . . . "He is a new creature" (CPW 3:135).

Moral rules presented in the form of abstract ideas only leave us cold and paralyzed, whereas the noblest souls, whether the pagan Empedocles or the Christian Paul, "have insisted on the necessity of an inspiration, a joyful emotion, to make moral action perfect" (CPW 3:134).

Herein lies Arnold's perception of the interdependence of poetry and religion. The virtue of religion is "that it has *lighted up* morality," that it has provided the emotion and inspiration needed to engage the affections in their relation to those morally profound experiences which issue in our ideas of man and his place in the universe. But when religion is subsequently reduced to creeds, to metaphysics and abstract ideas, it merely perplexes the mind and numbs the will. Only poetry can translate these ideas into sensible images and dramatic stories that engage our emotions and thereby disclose new dimensions of reality, cover more of what we experience and seek to express than does the language of literal fact and science. Arnold quotes Joubert to the point: "The true science of metaphysics consists not in rendering abstract that which is sensible, but in rendering sensible that which is abstract . . . and intelligible, finally, that which an ordinary attention fails to seize" (CPW 3:194).

In his religious books of the 1870s the religious touchstones from the Bible are Arnold's principal means of demonstrating how poetry engages the emotions as that poetry touches on the profound matters of moral governance and spiritual aspiration. It is a conception of poetry and its function in the service of religion that is evident as well in such important later essays of the 1880s as "The Study of Poetry" and "Literature and Science." In the former essay Arnold reverts to his old comparative method, using one of his favorite religious touchstones from Dante to underscore Chaucer's poetic limits. What is wanting in Chaucer is suggested by such a verse as *In la sua volontade è nostra pace*, which "is altogether beyond Chaucer's reach" (CPW 9:176-77), since his poetry lacks a comparable "high seriousness and truth." Arnold believed that it was chiefly this high seriousness "which gives our spirits what they can rest upon" and "with the increasing demands of our modern ages upon poetry, this virtue of giving us what we can rest upon will be more and more highly esteemed" (CPW 9:176-77).

This high destiny that Arnold predicts for the future of poetry was first the subject of Arnold's essay "On Poetry," which served as the brief preface to Dr. Wallace Wood's *Hundred Greatest Men*, published in 1879, the year before "The Study of Poetry." Arnold found the closing paragraph of the preface so pleasing that he used it for the opening of "The Study of Poetry," and it is in the latter, much better known, essay that critics have found what they consider to be Arnold's liberation of poetry from the Christian religion and the transfiguration of religion into a pure aesthetic experience. It was his reading of the 1880 essay that provoked T. S. Eliot to assert that "for Arnold the best poetry supersedes both religion and philosophy,"[3] and William Madden to argue that the terminus ad quem to which the movement of Arnold's criticism carried him was "a new religion of the imaginative reason."[4] The opening paragraph of "The Study of Poetry" has proven critical to Arnold interpretation. However, it is misleading when taken out of the context of the larger discussion of the matter in the 1879 preface.

In "On Poetry" Arnold had spoken of poetry's superiority over history as consisting "in its possessing a higher truth and a higher seriousness."

He then proceeded to compare poetry "with other efforts of the human spirit besides history":

> Compare it with art. It is more intellectual than art, more interpretive. . . . Poetry thinks and the arts do not. But it thinks emotionally, and herein it differs from science. . . . Poetry gives us the idea, but it gives it touched with beauty, heightened by emotion. This is what we feel to be interpretative for us, to satisfy us—thought but thought invested with beauty, with emotion. Science thinks, but not emotionally. It adds thought to thought, accumulates the elements of a synthesis which will never be complete until it is touched with beauty and emotion; and when it is touched with these, it has passed out of the sphere of science.
>
> Poetry, then, is more of a stay to us than art or science. It is more explicative than art, and it has the emotion which to science is wanting.

What of religion, for it is poetry's relation to religion that is here the matter under discussion? "The reign of religion as morality touched with emotion is indeed indestructible," Arnold declared. "But," he continued,

> religion as men commonly conceive it—religion depending on the historicalness of certain supposed facts, on the authority of certain received traditions, on the validity of certain accredited dogmas—how much of *this* religion can be deemed unalterably secure? Not a dogma that does not threaten to dissolve, not a tradition that is not shaken, not a fact which has its historical character free from question. . . . Our religion has materialized itself in the fact—the supposed fact; it has attached its emotion to the fact. For poetry the idea is everything, the rest is its world of illusion; divine illusion; it attaches its emotion to the idea, the idea *is* the fact. The strongest part of our religion today is its unconscious poetry.

Arnold concluded the passage with his celebrated prophecy that "the future of poetry is immense, because in conscious poetry, where it is worthy of its high destinies, our race, as time goes on, will find an ever surer and surer stay" (CPW 9:62).

These brief paragraphs are freighted with terms and judgments that demand a careful unpacking in view of the context in which Arnold was writing. Comments will be confined to the passage on religion, except to observe that Arnold does not regard poetry as superseding the functions of either art or science; rather, poetry *supplements* their work—in the one instance by means of its interpretive faculty, in the other through its emotional power. It is because of these gifts that poetry "is more of a stay to us," better serves our moral and imaginative nature.

When Arnold turns to religion, he immediately prefaces his comments with the assertion that "religion as morality touched with emotion is indestructible." It is evident that he regards religion, truly and adequately conceived, to be enduring. Moreover, it is just this religion which over the previous decade Arnold had repeatedly described as "a yet more important manifestation of human nature than poetry" (CPW 5:99) and as "that voice of the deepest human experience" (CPW 5:93). It was this religion which he had toiled through the writing of four books to defend and acquit.

What religion, then, is Arnold speaking of as insecure? The passage is transparent. It is *"religion as men commonly conceive it"*—i.e., the religion of the literal-minded Noncomformist, of Lord Shaftesbury, and the Bishops of Winchester and Gloucester. It is religion depending on the supposed historical facticity of certain narratives long understood as legend and myth by pious scholars familiar with ancient Semitic literature; it is traditionary religion, such as the stony doctrine passed on in the Thirty-nine Articles by "a number of second or third-rate men who lived in Queen Elizabeth's time"; it is religion as accredited dogma, the learned metaphysical science of the Nicene Creed. This is the side of religion that has "materialized itself in the supposed fact" and is finding that the foundations are no longer secure. The safe and strong "part of our religion today is its unconscious poetry"—*unconscious* because it is that which edifies and fortifies us instinctively and naturally, without our being aware of its work. But because it is unconscious, we have failed to recognize its indispensable connection with religion, and have confused religion with abstract thought, pseudo-science, and literal statement. Because this is so profoundly true, with such disastrous consequences, Arnold was committed to making explicit and *conscious* the work of literature on behalf of religion. Two years before writing "On Poetry," and upon his returning from religious criticism to literature "more strictly so-called," Arnold wrote that he was "returning, after all, to a field where work of the most important kind was now to be done, though indirectly, for religion." For, he continues, "I am persuaded that the transformation of religion, *which is essential for its perpetuance*, can be accomplished only by carrying the qualities of flexibility, perceptiveness, and judgment, which are the best fruits of letters, to whole classes of the community . . . and by procuring the application of those qualities to matters where they are never applied now" (CPW 8:148; italics added).

It is in the context of his efforts at religious reconstruction in the 1870s and his carefully stated resolution in the preface to *Last Essays* that one must read Arnold's concluding prophecy in "On Poetry" (1879): "The future of poetry is immense because in *conscious* poetry . . . our race, as time goes on, will find an ever and ever surer stay." The *conscious* poetry of this prediction is not a different kind of poetry from the *unconscious* poetry of the Bible and the Christian religion. It is poetry's function, its own high destiny, and in its indispensable role in the life of religion, to be made explicit, to serve its "higher uses" by application of the "best fruits of letters" to the interpretation of religion, where it has never been applied before.

This is also how Arnold's comment in "The Study of Poetry" (1880) should be read: "More and more of mankind will discover that we have to turn to poetry to interpret life for us, to console us, to sustain us. Without poetry, our science will appear incomplete; and most of what now passes with us for religion and philosophy will be replaced by poetry" (CPW 9:161-62). What Eliot and others have failed to attend to in this passage is the word *now* in "what now passes with us for religion." As George Watson has noted, "It is the sham religion of dogmatic assertion which will be replaced by poetry, not the true religion of Christian humanism."[5]

And so it is with the religion referred to in "On Poetry"—"the religion as men commonly conceive it," the pseudo-scientific fundamentalism of Exeter Hall. It is this traditional religion, and not the Christianity which will "find the ways for its own future" because of its natural truth, that will dissolve.* It must be remembered that Arnold continued to revere much of the old biblical language and imagery which, he predicts, will not disappear but "will survive as poetry." And, Arnold perceives in poetry a unique means to unveil and convey profound truths.

The true interdependence and dialectic of poetry and religion in Arnold's criticism is recognized by Basil Willey: "The highest art, [Arnold] says, the art of Phidias, of Dante, of Michelangelo, is an art 'which by its

---

* In 1885, several years after penning his famous predictions concerning the future of poetry, Arnold wrote the following: "The way, truth, and life have been found in Christianity, *and will not be found outside it. Instead of making vain and pedantic endeavors to invent them outside of it, what we have to do is to help, so far as we can, towards their continuing to be found inside of it*" (CPW 10:232; italics added). This is evidence enough that in the last decade of his life Arnold was not searching for some surrogate for Christianity in poetry or aesthetic experience.

height, depth and gravity possesses religiousness.' Poetry passes into religion on its highest level, and religion must pass into poetry in order to penetrate and transform 'that poor inattentive and immoral creature man.' "[6]

For Arnold there is no poetic supersession of religion, as Eliot would have it; nor has Arnold "aestheticized religion" by bringing it "down to poetry." It is not a question of the autonomy of poetry or its dominance over religion or of religion over poetry. Their relation is reciprocal and interdependent. In its highest form poetry "possesses religiousness," and if religion is to remain secure and efficacious it must "pass into poetry," where alone it is not only "touched with beauty, heightened by emotion" but finds its adequate medium for unveiling its truth. With regard to Arnold's prediction about the future of poetry, John Coulson rightly concludes: "It does not assert that religion should become poetry by evaporating, as it were, into metaphor. . . . What is asserted here is that a religion that turns its back on poetry and the imagination is under a sentence of death since it is peculiarly within the experiences it shares with poetry and literature that religion lives most strongly."[7]

The relation of poetry and religion as envisaged by Arnold is, in the words of W. M. Urban, to be

> seen in a certain community of language. The cry of the psalmist, "All flesh is grass" is equally poetic and religious. . . . It is immediately clear what it is that constitutes the similarity. Both are in the first instance at least, highly emotive forms of language, and both have the characters of intuitive and metaphorical representation which we found to be intrinsic to poetic language. The *vis poetica* is present in all genuine religious language, only in the case of religious language it is heightened and deepened in a peculiar way. It is, so to speak, poetry transposed to another scale. . . . The description of religion as poetry in no wise militates against the former's ontological character and implications.[8]

It is, then, to Arnold's understanding of the nature and status of religious language and its claims to truth that we now must turn.

THE NATURE OF RELIGIOUS LANGUAGE

Sometime in the year 1867 Arnold entered the following in his notebook: "We can *use* any language of established religion, but at certain epochs the effort of *translation* thus necessary, the partialness of the language's hold on the facts, strikes us forcibly. The language is then drawing near to the time when it must undergo a change" (NB 66).

Arnold was not yet aware of how intensely he would be involved for the next 10 years in "the effort of *translation*" which the time demanded of religion and its language. While he touches on many other issues, the question of language, its use and status in religion, is the common thread that runs from *St. Paul and Protestantism* through *Literature and Dogma*, *God and the Bible*, and *Last Essays on Church and Religion*. Commenting on *Literature and Dogma*, John Holloway has remarked how the subject of language dominates the book and how truly Arnold suggests that "those who are insensitive to poetry in particular are likely to be insensitive to language as a general means of expression, and to fall into error about it."[9]

To fall into error about language was, for Arnold, a matter that extended far beyond linguistic concerns. Arnold saw in language, as did Marx, the outward expression of implicit values, attitudes, and beliefs deeply held and of profound social significance. He saw in the hard and literal language exemplified in William Murphy's *British Banner* the similitude of those philistine values that Carlyle associated with the Gospel of Mammonism: "Laissez-faire, Supply-and-Demand, Cash-payment the one nexus of man to man, and the Devil take the hindmost."[10]

Arnold's sensitivity to language, to its use and its power in communicating and inculcating feelings and beliefs, is of course to be expected of one whose devotion to poetry and literary criticism was lifelong. However, his special concern to distinguish the poetic and symbolic language of religion from scientific and explicative language may well be traced not only to his religious inheritance but to the influence of several writers who expressed similar views and who attracted him. The Cambridge Platonists, the Oriel Noetics, Spinoza, and Coleridge are writers in whose work on the Bible Arnold obviously found ideas opposed to a religion of scientific dogma and philosophical system-making. His appreciation of the peculiar work of the poetic imagination in serving the religious wants of modern man also owes something to his hearing and his reading of Newman.[11]

In "Prospects of the Anglican Church," which appears in *Essays Critical and Historical*—a book frequently referred to in *Literature and Dogma*—Newman observed that

> the taste for poetry of a religious kind has in modern times in
> a certain sense taken the place of the deep contemplative spirit

of the early Church. At any rate it is a curious circumstance considering how much our active and businesslike habits take us the other way, that the taste for poetry should have been developed so much more strongly amongst ourselves than it seems to have been in the earlier times of the Church; as if our character required such an element to counter-balance the firmer and more dominant properties in it. . . . Poetry then is our mysticism, and so far as any two characters of mind tend to penetrate below the surface of things, and to draw men away from the material to the invisible world, so far they may certainly be said to answer the same end; and that too a religious one.[12]

Arnold's first sustained published reflections on the Bible, language, and interpretation were prompted by the appearance of Bishop Colenso's *The Pentateuch and the Book of Joshua Critically Examined* (1862). Indeed, it was the controversy over Colenso's book that impelled Arnold to write "The Function of Criticism at the Present Time" in an effort to clarify his idea of criticism and the high office which he assigned to it. In November 1862 he mentioned to his mother that he was thinking of doing an article "contrasting Colenso and Colenso's jejune and technical manner of dealing with Biblical controversy with that of Spinoza . . . with a view to showing how Spinoza broaches his in that edifying and pious spirit by which alone the treatment of such matters can be made fruitful" (L 1:176).

Colenso's "jejune and technical manner" of treating the Bible had to do with a failure of "critical tact," which Arnold associated with Colenso's insensitivity to language and literary expression—particularly with his confusion of much of the biblical narrative with scientific and literal statement.*

This concern, which lay at the heart of Arnold's quarrel with Colenso, occupied him between 1862 and the publication of *Essays in Criticism* in 1865. It did not, however, diminish with the appearance of those essays of the early 1860s. The matter is taken up again in *Culture and Anarchy*, but this time it is not the rationalists and liberal churchmen who are the object of Arnold's literary measure, but the Puritans and Dissenters. The mechanical treatment of biblical language which Arnold opposed is illustrated in the Dissenters' pedantic interpretation of Paul's Epistle to the Romans. How difficult it is, Arnold remarks, to seize another writer's

* Fuller attention will be given to Colenso in the discussion of the functions of religious criticism in chapter 4.

expression, and especially when the writer is separated from us "by such differences of race, training, time and circumstance as St. Paul." Yet one can come near to getting at the meaning of someone like Paul of Tarsus. When he does so, how profoundly he feels that terms which St. Paul employs,

> some of the most delicate, intricate, obscure, and contradictory workings and states of the human spirit, are detached and employed by Puritanism, not in the connected and fluid way in which St. Paul employs them . . . but in an isolated, fixed, mechanical way, as if they were talismans. . . . Who, I say, has watched Puritanism . . . handle such terms as *grace, faith, election, righteousness,* but must feel, not only that these terms have for the mind of Puritanism a sense false and misleading, but also that this sense is the most monstrous and grotesque caricature of the sense of St. Paul (CPW 5:182).

Because, as he confessed to his mother, the Dissenters' employment of the Bible was the instrument most responsible for keeping them narrow and intolerant, and for preventing their progress, Arnold was compelled to continue his discussion of language and biblical interpretation in *St. Paul and Protestantism* and *Literature and Dogma.* The Dissenters' mechanical and materialized theology was, Arnold believed, the result of "the poverty and inanition of our minds." Hence the first step toward a right understanding of the Bible is "to understand that the language of the Bible is fluid, passing, and literary, not rigid, fixed, and scientific." But to take this first step requires "some experience of how men have thought and expressed themselves" (CPW 6:152), which means *"getting the power, through reading, to estimate the proportion and relation in what we read.* If we read but a very little, we naturally want to press it all" (CPW 6:152-53).

The language of the Bible is, in Arnold's celebrated phrase, "language *thrown out* at an object of consciousness not fully grasped, which inspired emotion." If the object of the Bible—God, human nature and destiny, or a vision of the new creation—eludes scientific statement and yet profoundly gives shape to and animates our lives, then "the language of figure and feeling," of poetry, "will satisfy us better, will cover more of what we seek to express, than the language of literal fact and science. The language of science about it will be *below* what we feel to be the truth" (CPW 6:189). The language of poetry will be the most adequate vehicle for disclosing these truths. When Wordsworth calls the earth the mighty mother of mankind and the geographers call her an oblate spheroid,

Wordsworth's expression, Arnold insists, is unquestionably "more proper and adequate to convey what men feel about the earth but it is not therefore the more scientifically exact" (CPW 6:190).

There are, as Wittgenstein has shown, different modes of discourse appropriate to particular types of experience and forms of life. To apply the logic of one universe of discourse to a very different one is to engage in a "category mistake." Wittgenstein gives the example of the use of the image or picture "God's eye sees everything." The religious believer is quite prepared to discuss the question of providence that is implied in the picture. But as Wittgenstein asks rhetorically: "Are eyebrows to be talked of in connection with the Eye of God?" Obviously not. That is not the way theists use the picture.[13]

Again and again, Arnold makes his case for the poetic, symbolic language of religion simply by juxtaposition—for example, the language of the Nicene Creed with that of the Psalms, or the words of the Calvinist Dissenter purporting to convey St. Paul's teaching with the words of St. Paul himself. This kind of contrast between the adequacy of the language of image and metaphor and the inadequacy of the prosaic and literal is brought out vividly in Arnold's comparison of morality and religion:

> "By the dispensation of Providence to mankind," says Quintilian, "goodness gives men most satisfaction." That is morality. "The path of the just is as the shining light which shineth more and more unto the perfect day." That is morality touched with emotion, or religion. . . . "We all want to live honestly, but cannot," says the Greek maxim-maker. That is morality. "O wretched man that I am, who shall deliver me from the body of this death!" says St. Paul. That is religion (CPW 6: 177-78).

The peculiar adequacy of figurative and metaphorical language in pointing to the objects of religious experience is especially evident in the words used for God. Here Arnold is one with the contemporary biblical scholarship that agrees with New Testament scholar George Caird that "all, or almost all, of the language used by the Bible to refer to God is metaphor."[14] Arnold recognized that the ancient Israelites possessed a rare poetic or metaphoric genius. "The spirit and tongue of Israel," he writes, "kept a propriety, a reserve, a sense of the inadequacy of language in conveying man's ideas of God, which contrast strongly with the license of affirmation in our Western theology" (CPW 6:18). Arnold acknowledged that even the phrase he formerly used for God—that for science God is simply "the stream of tendency by which all things seek to fulfill the law of their being"—"is inadequate, certainly it is a less proper phrase than, for instance: 'Clouds and darkness are round about him, righteousness and judgment are the habitation of his seat'" (CPW 6:189).

The reviews of *Literature and Dogma* disclosed how many of Arnold's critics quite misunderstood his attack on the theologians' "license of affirmation." Many reviews interpreted the book as a prohibition on figurative or analogical language about God, comparable to Herbert Spencer's call for the reduction of all God-talk to the minimalism of the agnostic Unknowable. Nothing could have been further from Arnold's intent. "We know," Arnold responded, "that men inevitably use anthropomorphic language about whatever makes them feel deeply, and the biblical language about God we may therefore truly use." He continues:

> To seek to discard, like some philosophers, the name of God and to substitute for it such a name as the Unknowable, will seem to a plain man, surely, ridiculous. For *Unknowable* is a name merely negative, and no man could ever have cared anything about God in so far as he is simply unknowable. It adds, indeed, to our awe of God that although we are able to know of him what so greatly concerns us, we know of him nothing more; but simply to know nothing of him could beget in us no awe whatever (CPW 7:396).

Biblical God-language can be freely used as long as it is understood for what it is, "approximative and poetical," and that such language is always "essentially concrete." "The moment one perceives," Arnold adds, "that the religious language of the human race is in truth poetry, which it mistakes for science, one cannot make it an objection to this language that it is concrete" (CPW 7:396).

Having said this so emphatically, did Arnold adequately allow in his own writings for the concrete and anthropomorphic language concerning God's personality which is central not only to Christian theology but to its devotion as well? Was it not exactly their concrete talk of God as a person that brought down on the heads of the Bishops of Winchester and Gloucester Arnold's recurrent derision? The question was put to Arnold by the sympathetic critic Llewelyn Davies: "If Israel, then, might with propriety call God 'the high and holy one that inhabiteth eternity,' why [Davies asks] may not the Bishop of Gloucester with propriety talk of 'the blessed truth that the God of the universe is a person?' Neither one expression nor the other is adequate; both are approximate." Arnold replied:

> Let it be understood then, that when the Bishop of Gloucester, or others, talk of the blessed truth that the God of the universe is a person, they mean to talk, not science, but rhetoric and poetry. In that case our only criticism on their language will be that it is bad rhetoric and poetry, whereas the rhetoric and poetry of Israel is good. But the truth is, they mean it for science . . . and it is false science because it assumes what it cannot verify (CPW 7:156).

It is difficult to believe that the bishops were so naïve as to use the word "person" of God in a wholly literal, univocal sense. But giving Arnold the benefit of the doubt on that point, he undoubtedly reveals a crucial theological blind side in his persistent failure to appreciate the central role that the concrete language of personal relations plays in the biblical vision of man's encounter with God. Of this odd prejudice of Arnold's more will be said in chapter 5. Here the matter of moment is the nature of religious language, and on this Arnold was right in insisting on its poetic form. The language of biblical theology, the symbols used for God—such as shepherd, potter, physician, judge, king, warrior, or even father—are obviously approximate and provisional symbols, terms "thrown out at an object of consciousness not fully grasped," "the language of figure and feeling."

It was Arnold's conviction, nevertheless, that the language of poetry better satisfies the religious sense of reserve, the experience of awe and wonder before the great objects of our religious experience (CPW 6:200). When properly qualified, poetic language also more adequately discloses the reality of those very objects of human belief and devotion. The power of poetry is not, as in the case of philosophy or science, "a power of drawing out in black and white an explanation of the mystery of the universe"; rather, it is a power of "so dealing with things as to awaken in us a wonderfully full, new and intimate sense of them and of our relations with them" (CPW 3:12-13). To claim for poetry such a power to awaken an intimate sense of things, "to be in contact with the essential nature of those objects," is to attribute to poetry an epistemological status and function. In his 1862 Guerin Lecture Arnold refrains from judging whether or not poetry's awakening power can be proved to be or not to be illusive. In later essays—for example, "On Poetry," where he says the "idea *is* the fact"—he is no longer noncommittal about the awakening power of poetry to put us in touch with reality and truth.

Various contemporary writers have spoken of the unique way in which religious language, in its effort to point to and unveil aspects of reality, must use images and metaphors that distort perceptible reality in a certain way or stretch language beyond "observables" or its ordinary use.[15] Ian Ramsey did pioneer service in this regard. For Ramsey religious discourse is language about situations that bear striking affinities with situations that are ordinary and perceptual and yet "with a difference." Religious language has to do with experiences that are "perceptual and more . . . i.e., object language which has been given very special qualifications."[16]

Theistic discourse is logically odd for the very reason that it is talk about what is perceptual and yet about what is also "more than observable." However, Ramsey notes, such language about transcendence is not unique to God-talk. It is characteristic, for example, of our language about persons. Our knowledge of persons is not independent of their public behavior, but neither is it exhausted by such descriptions. "So, if we wish to speak of everything which, for each of us, this 'I' refers to, we shall have to use phrases which—while beginning with and having some foothold in observational language—are somehow or other qualified to make it plain that their reference is in part beyond such language as well."[17]

Religious, even theological language, while stretched in such a way as to exhibit its logically odd and paradoxical character, nevertheless remains anchored in human, perceptual experience. With Arnold, Ramsey resists any severing of the natural and the revealed or any talk about two worlds. Nevertheless, religious discernment or revelation occurs in those empirical experiences which push us beyond percepts so that we discern something "more" in the situation. Ramsey suggests, among numerous examples, our experience of gestalt patterns as exhibiting our experience of disclosure situations, or revelations in which mere bundles of data are, in different situations, seen as recognizable images. An example of Ramsey's appropriation of Wittgenstein's concept of "seeing as" is the ambiguous duck/rabbit drawing. Images, like metaphors, can assist us in seeing things in new ways.

The point to be emphasized here is Ramsey's attention to the oddness of language and the need to revert to metaphorical words and phrases—in religious disclosures to the use of such metaphors as depth, father, perfect, not ourselves—in order to remind our imaginations that we are stretching language, pointing in certain directions, but are neither being wholly adequate nor entirely effacing the mystery.

Ramsey insists, nevertheless, that some disclosure situations strike us as more adequate, more revealing or better able to fit and explain the empirical circumstances. Such a revelatory occasion is better able "to match a wide range of phenomena, by its overall success in meeting a variety of needs. Here is what I call the method of empirical fit."[18]

In a similar discussion of the metaphorical or, in Kantian parlance, the "limit" use of religious language, Paul Van Buren makes explicit use of Arnold's metaphor, the "not ourselves." Theological language often is metaphysical or aesthetic or, in this case, moral discourse pushed to the very edges of language. The "pointing" of this particular metaphor may be paradoxical or even logically incoherent, but it is not loosened from real experience. It is, for Arnold, his most adequate way of expressing the meaning of a certain form of religious experience. Van Buren writes:

> We may say, indeed, that the most important part of what we do is not our doing. We might even speak of a "not our-selves that makes for righteousness." We should have arrived at the point which I have been calling the edge of language. . . . The use of this expression is one way of behaving when we long to say the most that could possibly be said about religious conduct because it matters to us so much, and we feel our words are inadequate. . . . On this interpretation of Arnold's thesis, the "not ourselves" is . . . an example of a specific aspect of human life in this world. . . . To say "not ourselves," then, is another way of saying that we want to say the very most that could be said on this subject, but are not sure what that would be.[19]

We must ask, of course, the critical question: Is Arnold's "not ourselves" merely a desperate effort to express a feeling? Arnold would deny that in using the metaphor "not ourselves" he is asserting no more than a subjective emotion. For him the metaphor points to a reality common to human experience. The metaphor, however, is "tensive"; the referent is indirect, not literal. Furthermore, the reality pointed to is "discovered" and, in a certain sense, "created" by the very work of the metaphor, since the function of such a metaphor is not the picturing of an object but the interpreting of an odd structure of relationships which press to the edges of language.[20] These terms, of course, are not Arnold's; but the realist view of metaphor—i.e., its power of indirect reference—is tacit in what Arnold says about the poetic language of the Bible.

In *Metaphor and Reality*, Philip Wheelwright has worked out a theory of the poetic imagination that perhaps best illuminates Arnold's understanding of the experiential and epistemological status of the poetic language of religion. Wheelwright speaks of poetic language as "partly creating and partly disclosing certain hitherto unknown, unguessed aspects of what is."[21] For Wheelwright, as for Arnold, poetry partly "creates" aspects of what is. By this seemingly contradictory statement Wheelwright means that poetic language possesses an evocative power which can bring to consciousness new aspects of reality by the way if affects the reader subjectively or existentially. However, this does not mean that the work of the poetic imagination is subjective in the sense of being purely psychological, without objective, cognitive significance. Rather, it is subjective in the voluntarist sense of engaging the will as a cognitive desideratum. For, as Wheelwright further insists, poetry also discloses, unveils, reveals "hitherto unknown, unguessed aspects of what is." Poetry is, then, both emotive and referential, and the two are interdependent. The fallacy of the positivist literary critic—e.g., the early I. A. Richards—is to assume that poetry must simply be either one or the other. As Wheelwright reminds us, "An utterance can be more or less either of them without thereby having to be less or more of the other. For the negative of *referential* is not emotive but *nonreferential*, and the negative of emotive is not referential but *nonemotive*."[22]

Poetry is what Wheelwright calls "expressive discourse," a form of language that is referential and emotive at once, and

> not by incidental conjunction . . . but in the more organic sense that the referential function, the full proper meaning, takes at least some of its essential character from the precise emotivity of the language and changes therefore as the emotivity changes. . . . Truly expressive symbolism . . . means, refers, awakens insight, *in and through* the emotions it engenders and where an appropriate emotion is not aroused the full insight is not awakened."[23]

The interdependence of the emotive and the referential is implicit in what Arnold writes about the poetic language of religion. If we place Arnold once again along a spectrum of positions, this time relative to the status of the poetic language of religion, his position can best be characterized as a form of *critical realism*. He rejects both naïve realism (the language of Dissent) and positivism (the language of natural science), which, in their different ways, require literal statement in religious assertion.[24] On the other hand, Arnold is not an instrumentalist—one who holds that the language of religious metaphor is neither true nor false but only useful, i.e., serves a psychological function. Critical realists, as Sallie McFague points out, hold that all perception and interpretation is metaphorical—i.e., indirect, a "seeing as" or "interpreting as." Furthermore, they insist that their constructions are not merely heuristic fictions but disclosures of some aspect of reality. A critical realist, like Arnold, will claim that his metaphors are not simply a matter of personal preference but that they are more adequate than the alternatives.[25]

Two points may well summarize Arnold's understanding of the nature of religious language. First, religious language is, as Arnold defined it, "language *thrown out* at an object of consciousness not fully grasped, which inspired emotion," and, paradoxically, often this "language of figure and feeling will . . . cover more of what we seek to express than the language of literal fact and science." Second, this language is not only a more adequate mode of expression, it is grounded in and refers to objects of our common human experience; it is referential and cognitive as well as evocative. It gives us knowledge of crucial aspects of human existence in the world.

This discussion of poetry and religion and the distinctive nature of religious language will serve as background for a better appreciation of Arnold's understanding of the relationship between religious language, experience, and religious truth.

RELIGIOUS LANGUAGE, EXPERIENCE, AND THE TRUTH OF CHRISTIANITY

Arnold was foresighted in recognizing that a critical problem facing a world increasingly dominated by science and technology was the nature and status of language. The issues at stake are, finally, the questions of meaning and truth, and Arnold recognized that the truth of religion was doomed if it made claims for its language that were of the same logical order as those appropriate to the natural sciences. He therefore sought to show that religious language, the language of the Bible, could be understood, and properly so, in such a way as to demonstrate its compatibility with science as well as its unique role as a vehicle for disclosing truth.

It is on this issue of the cognitive status of the poetic language of religion that critics often assert that Arnold reduced religion, and Christianity in particular, to its subjective effects, to what is useful but not "true." The key to sorting out the differences between Arnold and his modern critics is to be found in the different notions of experience that are assumed and the implications of these discrepant views for a theory of knowledge and truth. Arnold believed that the truth of Christianity is verified in experience and that such an experiential test is in accord with the scientific temper of the age. He found his notion of experience consistent, for example, with the kind of scientific attitude expressed by his friend 1. H. Huxley when he asserted that "the gravitation of sin to sorrow is as certain as that of the earth to the sun, and more so—for experimental proof of the fact is within reach of us all—nay, it is before us all in our own lives, if we had but the eyes to see it."[26]

Consistent with his educational and cultural ideal, Arnold believed that the widest and deepest experience of the human spirit would more and more show the weakness of what he called a "notional work," or religion defended on abstract principles rather than by an "experimental work." The more we know of "the history of the human spirit and its deliverances," the more we become disabused and skeptical of purely rational arguments. Arnold is confident, on the other hand, that "the great thing, as we believe, in favour of such a construction as we put upon the Bible is, that experience, as it increases, constantly confirms it; and that, though it cannot *command* assent, it will be found to *win* assent more and more" (CPW 6:378).

Arnold illustrates his experimental,—i.e., his experiential—approach as it applies to our apprehension and knowledge of God, of the Bible, and of Jesus Christ. The greatness of Israel's vision of God is in "the extraordinary force and vividness" with which she perceived the great power of the "not ourselves" and thus was able to "communicate it irresistibly because she feels it irresistibly."

> But if they ask: "How are we to verify that there rules an enduring Power not ourselves, which makes for righteousness?"—we answer at once: "How? Why as you verify that fire burns—by experience! It *is* so; try it! . . . Disbelieve it, and you will find out your mistake as surely as if you disbelieve that fire burns and put your hand into the fire, you will find out your mistake! Believe it, and you will find the benefit of it!" (CPW 6:370).

Assuming, for the moment, that there is a God that makes for righteousness, "why should we study the *Bible* that we may learn to obey him?—will not other teachers and books do as well?" Arnold replies, "Here again it is experience that we invoke: *try it!* Having convinced yourself that there is an enduring Power, not ourselves, that makes for righteousness, set yourself next to try to learn more about this Power, and to feel an enthusiasm for it" (CPW 6:371). To this end Arnold calls upon his readers to compare their encounter with the Bible with a reading of Jeremy Bentham or Herbert Spencer, and to see which satisfies the most. The God and the religion of the Bible are revealed in Israel's experience in a plain, artless, but infinitely more vivid, powerful, and real way than in other teachers or books. And so it is, Arnold maintains, with the method and secret of Jesus. More and more people will discover in their own experience and in the experience of the race that in Jesus "is the righteousness which is salvation. . . . No proof can be so solid as this experimental proof" (CPW 6:402).

Arnold's stress on the experiential grounds of Christian belief was not, of course, new in English theology. He drew upon and was conscious of standing in a great tradition that ran from the Cambridge Platonists in the seventeenth century through Butler to Coleridge. As noted earlier, in "A Psychological Parallel" Arnold suggests the striking analogy between the theological interpretation of St. Paul and that of the Cambridge Platonist John Smith—a lesson in what today is called demythologization, namely, the interpreting of religious texts in radically experiential or existential terms. What Arnold admires in Smith's *Select Discourses* is their insistence "on the profound *natural truth* of Christianity . . . [basing] it upon a ground which will not crumble under our feet" (CPW 8:123).

Arnold found much to fault in Butler's religious probabilism and in his faculty psychology, yet warmly commended his natural, experiential approach to Christianity, his "conviction that religion and Chritianity do somehow, 'in themselves entirely fall in with the natural sense of things'" (CPW 8:59). In "A Comment on Christmas," written in 1885, Arnold once again speaks of the "'great Coleridgian position,' that apart from all question of evidence for miracles and of the historical quality of the Gospel narratives, the essential matters of Christianity are necessary and eternal facts of nature or truths of reason." Henceforth this will be "the key to the whole defense of Christianity" (CPW 10:227). By Christianity's natural truth Arnold means that

> things must stand, not by people's wishes and asservations about them. *Omnium Deus est, cujus, velimus aut nolimus, omnes sumus,* says Tertullian. "The God of all of us is the God that we all belong to whether we will or no." The Eternal that makes for righteousness is such a God; and he is the God of Christianity. Jesus explains what this God would have of us; and the strength of Jesus is that he explains it right. The natural experimental truth of his explanations is their one claim upon us; but this is claim enough. Does the thing, being admittedly most impor-

tant, turn out to be as he says? If it does, then "we belong to him whether we will or no" (CPW 8:159).

There is another aspect of the experiential test. Arnold believed—and here, at least, he stands with Augustine—that geniune knowledge will not be forthcoming unless the will is engaged in the act of cognition. Knowledge depends on certain predispositions, perspectives, and experience. This is not to say that we do not all observe the same world of nature and human experience; rather, that due to certain predispositions or from the vantage point of certain perspectives, aspects of reality, or what counts for evidence, are left in the shade, unobserved, while other features are given prominence. Therefore, one must get oneself in the proper position if certain latent qualities or aspects of experience are to be disclosed. As in the case of Coleridge and Newman before him, Arnold lays great stress on the cumulative evidence of a great tradition which can be put to the test of Coleridge's "Try it." "Everyone is aware how those, who want to cultivate any sense or endowment in themselves, must be habitually conversant with the works of the people who have been eminent for that sense, must study them, catch inspiration from them" (CPW 6:198-99).

It is the Hebrews who, according to Arnold, have proven themselves eminent for their moral and religious profundity. One therefore should "take their fact of experience, to keep it steadily for our basis in using their language, and to see whether from using their language with the ground of this real and firm sense to it, as they themselves did, somewhat of their feeling, too, may not grow upon us" (CPW 6:200). For Arnold the act of knowing is always dialectical and intersubjective. The self is never *in vacuo* since it is engaged by an objective, given reality, often in the form of the testimony of a great tradition or a common form of life. But knowledge involves *both* testimony and experience, the discovery of analogies between the givenness of the experience of others and our own. Knowledge in this sense is the discovery that there is a resonance, an aptness or appropriateness, between what we observe and what we deeply feel. The "penny drops, the light dawns." Arnold speaks of the appeal to experience *and* testimony: "His own experience may in the end be the surest teacher for every man; but meanwhile, to confirm or deny his instinctive anticipations and to start him on his way, testimony as to the experience of others, general experience, is the most serious weight and value" (CPW 10:227).

One consequence of Arnold's experiential grounding of belief is that he cannot accept the common antithesis between the natural and the revealed. After discoursing at length on the experiential grounds of Christianity, he feels obliged to anticipate the criticism that the Christianity of which he speaks "is but natural religion." He points out

> the falseness of the common antithesis between *natural* and *revealed*. For that in us which is really natural is, in truth, *revealed*. We awake to the consciousness of it, we are aware of its coming forth in our mind; but we feel that we did not make it, that it is discovered to us, that it is what it is whether we will or no. If we are little concerned about it, we say it is *natural*; if much, we say it is *revealed*. But the difference between the two is not one of kind, only of degree (CPW 6:194-95).

It is difficult to comprehend how a revelation that had no point of contact, no analogies with our ordinary language and experience could be known—not to say how it could commend itself to belief—unless, Arnold owns, it were believed on purely external grounds, such as the proof of miracle or the inerrancy of the scriptural text, grounds he knew would not long hold.

Arnold's position has often been compared with that taken more recently by the British empiricist R. B. Braithwaite. Indeed, Braithwaite saw Arnold as the patron saint of his own conative interpretation of religious language and belief. However, despite considerable similarity in their approaches, there remains the crucial difference that Arnold believes that Christianity does make assertions of fact that can be experientially verified. Braithwaite, on the other hand, remains committed to the classical British empiricists' conception of what constitutes facts, and thus he finds it impossible that religious statements convey knowledge of the world. Arnold's conception of religious language, experience, and verification therefore can be compared more fruitfully with the approach of another British empiricist of considerable eminence, H. H. Price, who is not happy with Braithwaite's indifference to the truth of theistic assertions. "A Theist," Price maintains, "would say that it matters very much whether these assertions [about God and his actions] are true or false, indeed, nothing matters more; and he claims that they are in fact true."[27]

According to Price, the theist can rightly claim that it is possible to obtain empirical evidence for his assertions. "But the Theist also says that this evidence is not accessible to every normal human being as the existence of Saturn's rings is."[28] That is, there may be latent capacities in all of us, which only if developed might "enable us to obtain evidence relevant to the truth or falsity of the Theist assertions."[29] Such experience, Price contends, is accessible only to those whose spiritual senses have been, as

Arnold similarly maintained, developed to a certain degree. "'Seek and ye shall find' is the traditional way of putting this."[30] Such a requirement is frequently demanded when, for example, a system of physical exercises is recommended to us. The thing required is: put yourself in the *position* to test it empirically. Christian theists have long recommended such a procedure to test their assertions. "The procedure is difficult to carry out; but though difficult it is not," Price concludes, "in principle impracticable. It is open to anyone to try it and see for himself whether it does produce the effects it is alleged to produce. . . . 'Try it and see for yourself' is one way of formulating the empiricist principle."[31]

Arnold resorts to this empiricist rule in his own apologetic, most programmatically in the tenth chapter of *Literature and Dogma*, in "A Psychological Parallel," and in the important preface to *Last Essays*. According to Arnold, experience may not only test the veracity of our moral intentions but also give us evidence, though not demonstration, relevant to the determination, what he called a "maintainable thesis," of the truth and falsity of our theological assertions. Obviously such evidence is different from that obtained in science, but it is evidence of a radically empirical kind.

Arnold's writings must, I believe, be seen as a percursor of this type of empiricism, which is different from that of either the British classical or linguistic types. It is a form of empiricism we now associate with the American philosophers William James, C. S. Peirce, John Dewey, and H. N. Wieman, and which more recently is to be found in the work of the philosopher John E. Smith. Smith has taken the psychological and epistemological insights of radical empiricism and applied them to an understanding of religious language, experience, and truth. His position has certain affinities with Arnold's empiricism, and because he presents his case with a theoretical interest and philosophical clarity sorely lacking in Arnold, his work can illuminate the rather inchoate and unmethodical ideas that underlie Arnold's similar understanding of religious language and experience.

Smith begins by calling attention to the tyrannical hold that scientific positivism—rooted as it is in the tradition of British empiricism from Hume to Russell—has had on other modes of experience: aesthetic, moral, religious. According to the classical empiricist view, "experience is coextensive with the domain of what can be sensed, and as a consequence the material of experience was analyzed into the qualities—colors, sounds, odors, tastes and tactile sensations—that correspond to man's sensory apparatus." Smith notes the implications of such a circumscribed doctrine:

> Experience so understood . . . when it is made to serve as a touchstone for testing our complex beliefs, [means] that any reference to these beliefs, to God, to the intentional center of a person, to freedom or to obligation must mean reference to what goes beyond experience. For having identified experience with the deliverances of the standard senses . . . we cannot think of the concepts previously mentioned and many others, as referring to objects analyzable into sensible data, [and] are left with the conclusion that what we mean to talk about when we use these concepts is entirely beyond experience.[32]

Arnold would agree with Smith that classical empiricism suffers from the prejudice that experience is merely "a sort of private showing on an interior, mental screen." On the contrary, a radically empirical theory of experience rejects the notion that genuine experience is confined to sense qualities and objects or that it represents a private mental content. It recognizes experience in its real variety, including moral, aesthetic, and religious dimensions which give meaning and purpose to life. Smith illustrates this point and draws out its implications:

> The same content of experience can be taken, as William James put it, many times over: The tree standing on a gently sloping hillside will be considered by the lumberman as yielding so many board feet for the sawmill, whereas the poet may see it as a lonely sentinel standing guard over the meadow rolling beneath. The man of faith, experiencing the same tree, will see it as a creature and as a part of the order of creation brought forth by God. . . . The sensory content remains invariant for all three persons and yet the meaning is very different for each. If, however, experience is no more than the sensory content they share, the different dimensions of meaning which are undeniably present for each individual must be banished from the world or confined entirely to the mind of the one who has the experience. On the latter alternative the world itself is deprived of the full depth of meaning which it reveals—moral, aesthetic, religious—and it is supposed instead that man simply "adds" this meaning through his own mind and feeling. . . . [But] to say that the sensory contents are "really there" while the meaning patterns are all supplied by the mind is to falsify experience as we have it. The content and the meaning are always together and while we can distin-

guish the two elements we cannot separate them without distortion.[33]

If we can assume the epistemological propriety of distinguishing yet not sundering percept and meaning, sense data and intuition, how, nevertheless, are we to be assured that our experience of the tree is not in fact only a tissue of subjective impressions, lacking objective reference? The radical empiricist answer, and Arnold's answer, is that experience is not a private affair; it is intersubjective, and issues in "a funded result of many encounters . . . in the form of qualities, relations, events, objects, purposes, meanings" disclosing the real world. Our experience of the world has a shared character that "gives to it an objective or public form reaching beyond the limits of what is encountered by any one individual. . . . Two persons, for example, are able to share their experiences and witness to their mutual understanding because they start with the belief that experience is continuous. And wherever they are mistaken in this belief, the fact itself can be discovered only by continuing the process of sharing and comparing reports of what we have encountered."[34]

Smith, like Arnold, illustrates this point by reference to the rich experiences and intuitions of the world's religious prophets and sages, such as the holy awe which struck Isaiah, the defiant despair experienced by Job, the peace which passes understanding hymned by St. Paul, the grace that saved the tortured Luther, or the affection of spiritual joy experienced by Augustine and Isaac Barrow. These are not private experiences confined to the rare individual. They are experiences shared by the human family, by hosts of witnesses throughout time, experiences that continuously testify to their pervasive character. They are, Smith argues, experiences "which disclose structures of human existence, structures of life in the world."[35] They have, in Arnold's words, "all the grandeur of a natural law."

This public, intersubjective nature of experience is testable, though not scientifically demonstrable, according to both Smith and Arnold, through the shared yet critically conscious life of a historical community. The test is not an immediate one, nor does it require preternatural explanation. Rather, as Arnold insists, the test of experience "proceeds on a large scale, and therefore slowly" (CPW 10:235). It also leads beyond the borders of any one tradition or community to the discovery of analogies and homogeneities in experience across time and cultures—for example, as Arnold perceived it, in "the holy innocence" of Sophocles and St. Francis, the fruit of their common submission to divine law. This is not to deny the heterogeneities; rather, only to point to the genuinely public, inter-subjective nature of religious experience.

The indifference shown toward the older natural theology as well as the reaction against a purely revelational theology, such as neo-orthodoxy, is a notable feature of theology during the past quarter century. This same period has witnessed a return to an inductive, empirical approach to religion which reveals a kinship with both Arnold's method and intentions. In support of such an experiential turn the sociologist Peter Berger urges that "theological thought seek out what might be called *signals of transcendence* within the empirically given human situation." He suggests "that there are *prototypical human gestures* that may constitute such signals, . . . reiterated acts and experiences that appear to express essential aspects of man's being," and that can be found in the life of every man.[36]

The recent linguistic turn of philosophy also has helped to free experience from the tyrannical hold of the earlier scientific positivism and its pride of place in the realm of truth. This change is reflected in the 1970 edition of I. A. Richards's essay *Science and Poetry*. In the revised essay Richards takes pains to dissociate himself from the position of those critics who interpreted him as holding "that poetry and literature, whatever they purport to refer to, are in fact referring solely to the author's feelings."[37] One such critic was Owen Barfield, who commented that "Richards's opponents have pointed out that unfortunately the 'emotive' power of a poetic statement depends precisely on our interpreting it as an objective reference to something other than emotion itself."[38] This evoked Richards's protestation that he had to accustom himself "to being accused of the views he was attacking."[39]

While it is clear that in the 1970 edition Richards has repudiated the hegemony of scientific empiricism in matters of fact, verification, belief, and truth, the positivist ring of many sections of the 1926 edition are unmistakable. For example, he then wrote: "Science cannot tell us what we are or what this world is; not because these are in any sense unsolvable questions but because they are not questions at all. And if science cannot answer these pseudo-questions, no more can philosophy and religion."[40] But in the new edition Richards adds the qualification that science cannot answer these questions because "they do not belong to its province." He then changes the original passage to read: "Nor can philosophy or religion answer them in the sense in which *science has taught us to expect answers for its questions. As the senses of 'question' shift, so do those of 'answer' and those of 'fact,' 'truth,' 'belief,' and 'knowledge' with them"* [italics added].[41]

A pseudo-statement, Richards now makes clear, "is not necessarily false *in any sense*. It is merely a form of words whose scientific truth or falsity is irrelevant to the purpose at hand" [italics added].[42] What to believe has given place to "with what different kinds of believings must we order the different ranks of our myths."[43] Richards now writes in good Arnoldian fashion:

> There are many feelings and attitudes which, though in the past supported by beliefs now untenable, can survive their removal because they have other moral, natural supports and spring directly from the necessities of existence. . . . Our protection, as Matthew Arnold insisted, is in poetry. . . . The poetic function is the source and the tradition of poetry is the guardian *of the supra-scientific myths* [italics added].[44]

The changed situation reflected in Richards's new edition of *Science and Poetry* is traceable in large measure to the influence of the later Wittgenstein and the philosophical analysts who have come to recognize in the language of religion a logic and a meaning of its own. Yet long before Wittgenstein, Arnold perceived that the language of religion had a peculiar function to perform alongside that of scientific, moral, and aesthetic language; and that while part of that function is regulatory, another aspect is referential—to disclose and to refer to qualities and dimensions of existence in the world, to facts that entail theological claims wanting verification, albeit by a method of verification calling for different logical requirements than those employed by scientific positivism.

As I have argued, what Arnold meant by the experimental basis of Christianity is not a groundwork that is competent to pass muster by the application of the critical evidence of scientific positivism. After all, Arnold goes to great lengths—indeed, it is the justification of *Literature and Dogma*—to attempt to show that the claims of the religion of the Bible and of Christianity are not to be confused with the claims and warrants appropriate to the natural sciences. The "scientific" basis of religion is found in the fact that it rests upon the foundations of radically empirical experience—forms of evidence that will not conform to the perceptual grids and the descriptive capabilities of the natural sciences. It is Arnold's contention, however, that this experimental or "scientific basis" of Christianity makes both cognitive and ontological assertions about the human world and its theological ground and is, therefore, a maintainable thesis.

William Robbins, a critic who has done justice to Arnold's epistemology, rightly points out that "what the imagination seizes on as poetically true, what conduct accepts as morally true, has for [Arnold] a practical and experiential truth superior to that of a logically verifiable proposition. . . . Nor is this experiential verification merely an emotional response akin to wishful thinking. Arnold believes that Christianity has, in Spinozist idiom, 'all the grandeur of a natural law.'"[45]

The question as to whether or not Arnold's religious objectivism and truth-claims include and entail belief in a transcendent God will be explored further in chapter 5, where his substantive beliefs will be examined. What can be said at this point is that the claim that Arnold's religion is a pure subjectivism or emotivism cannot be sustained upon a careful reading of his religious prose. Arnold's work has been readily appropriated by others from Pater to Richards and Braithwaite, all of whom have felt free to use him for their own purposes. But it is a great error, as David DeLaura has remarked, "to nail Arnold's thought . . . to the mast of Richardian psychologism and positivism."[46]

NOTES

1. Scott, "Arnold's Vision of Transcendence" 274.

2. Krieger, *The New Apologists for Poetry* 183.

3. T. S. Eliot, *The Use of Poetry and the Use of Criticism* (London, 1933) 113.

4. Madden, *Matthew Arnold* 193, 187. For similar judgments see Krieger, 183-85 and Dale, *The Victorian Critic* 167.

5. George Watson, *The Literary Critics* (London, 1957) 157.

6. Basil Willey, *Nineteenth Century Studies* (London, 1949) 253-54.

7. Ian Gregor and Walter Stern, eds., *The Prose of God* (London, 1973) 42.

8. W. M. Urban, *Language and Reality* (London, 1939) 572, 578. Scott (275) writes: "Nor is [Arnold] intending to offer poetry as a surrogate for the old religion of the prophets and the apostles. He wants, rather, to assign the poetic imagination merely a Virgilian function, as that which brings us into the precincts of the not-ourselves—by (if the neologism may be permitted) deconcealing it, in the way that anything is made manifest when it is addressed by a language appropriate to its nature; and he assumes—as in varying ways Coleridge and Keble and Newman had done before him—that it is, indeed, in the language of the poetic imagination that the religious consciousness finds its primary vehicle."

9. John Holloway, *The Chartered Mirror* (London, 1960) 153.

10. Thomas Carlyle, *Past and Present* (London, 1843) 228.

11. Both Denis Butts (*Notes and Queries* ns 5 [June, 1958]: 255-56) and David DeLaura (*Hebrew and Hellene in Victorian England* 139ff.) see Newman's influence at this point, particularly Newman's "Prospects of the Anglican Church."

12. John Henry Newman, *Essays Critical and Historical* (London, 1897) 1:290-91.

13. Ludwig Wittgenstein, *Lectures and Conversations on Aesthetics, Psychology and Religious Belief* (Oxford, 1966) 71, 59.

14. George B. Caird, *The Language and Imagery of the Bible* (Philadelphia, 1980) 18.

15. See, e.g., Urban, *Language and Reality*; Ian Ramsey, *Religious Language* (London, 1957); Paul Van Buren, *The Edges of Language* (London, 1972); Sallie McFague, *Metaphorical Theology* (Philadelphia, 1982).

16. Ramsey 38.

17. Ramsey 38.

18. Ian Ramsey, *Models and Mystery* (Oxford, 1964) 17.

19. Van Buren 120-21.

20. For a recent discussion of the truth-claims or referential character of metaphor, see Paul Ricoeur, *The Rule of Metaphor: Multi-Disciplinary Studies of the Creation of Meaning in Language* (Toronto, 1977) and McFague, *Metaphorical Theology*.

21. Philip Wheelwright, *Metaphor and Reality* (Bloomington, 1967) 51.

22. Philip Wheelwright, *The Burning Fountain* (Bloomington, 1968) 68-69.

23. Wheelwright, *Fountain* 70.

24. For this perspective on the epistemological status of models and metaphors I am dependent on Ian G. Barbour, *Myths, Models, and Paradigms* (New York, 1974) chap. 3.

25. McFague 132.

26. L. Huxley, ed., *Life and Letters of Thomas Henry Huxley* 3:272.

27. H. H. Price, *Belief* (London, 1969) 480.

28. Price 480.

29. Price 479.

30. Price 480.

31. Price 488.

32. John E. Smith, *The Analogy of Experience* (New York, 1973) 34.

33. Smith 35-36.

34. Smith 40-41.

35. Smith 41.

36. Peter Berger, *A Rumour of Angels* (London, 1970) 70.

37. I. A. Richards, *Science and Poetry* (London, 1970) 91-92.

38. Richards 91-92.

39. Richards 53-54.

40. Richards 53-54.

41. Richards 60.

42. Richards 77.

43. Richards 75-76, 78.

44. Richards 78.

45. William Robbins, *The Ethical Idealism of Matthew Arnold* (London, 1959) 80. Dorothea Krook also has rightly understood Arnold here. She writes: "God is the Eternal 'not ourselves': the word 'not ourselves' is intended to draw attention to our experience of the *obligatory force* of those most permanent and indestructible values that make for righteousness. Our most intimate experience of them is that thay are not created by ourselves; that they are not merely subjective. . . . They are experienced, says Arnold, as given, not created, as absolute, not relative, as objective, not subjective. They are so experienced because they prove themselves in experience to be the *only* values by which we can enjoy peace, power, joy; and it is for this decisive reason that they oblige our assent and our obedience." (*Three Traditions of Moral Thought* [Cambridge, 1959] 212-13). However, Krook speaks of the values Arnold believed to be verified by reason and experience as values "transcendent within the human order alone" but having redemptive power akin to the Christian. She concludes that "there is no question of their [Arnold's humanistic values] being acceptable to the Christian; if they were acceptable to him, he would cease to be a Christian" (225). This is another example of the either-or Arnold was opposing. Either the older supernaturalism or Christianity must be given up. Krook's concept of values transcendent within the human order might well have theological meaning not only to Arnold but to modern theologians, since they entail a transcendent ground and power within the radically immanent.

46. David DeLaura, "What, Then, Does Matthew Arnold Mean?" *Modern Philology* 66 (1968-69):354.

4 The Functions of Religious Criticism: Arnold's Hermeneutics

> The less he can deal with his object simply, the more things he has to take into account in dealing with it,—the more, in short, he has to encumber himself—so much the greater force of spirit he needs to retain his elasticity.
> "On Translating Homer: Last Words"

> What criticism continually endeavors to exorcise is the *logos* of the *mythos*.
> Paul Ricoeur

At least since the appearance of Hegel's *Phenomenology*, Western consciousness has approached its spiritual heritage in a new critical key—one that has involved either an unmasking or a reconception of what previously was thought straightforward, realistic, or literal. Paul Ricoeur has identified these two directions of modern criticism as the hermeneutics of suspicion and the hermeneutics of restoration.[1] The former, as seen in the work of Feuerbach, Nietzsche, Marx, and Freud, has been driven by the urge to demystify religion, to expose those hidden sources and meanings which, in their view, better explain the persistent and pervasive power of religious belief and practice. The hermeneutics of restoration, the effort at positive restatement, is evident in the work of the right-wing Idealists—Biedermann, the Cairds, Royce—in the Catholic Modernists, and, more recently, in such theologians as Tillich and Bultmann. It may appear that Arnold's radical yet conservative effort can be located in both traditions. However, when his religious prose is read in its totality, it is clear that Arnold's is essentially a hermeneutic of restoration, despite the fact that his effort at reconception is repudiated—as is that of the forenamed—by those who would simply repristinate an earlier orthodoxy. Basil Willey is correct when he remarks that "like a good surgeon [Arnold] destroyed only for preservation's sake."[2]

Arnold's feeling for the pathos of modernity is traceable to his profound sense that our modern consciousness exhibits a hiatus, what he called "a want of correspondence," between the forms in which our cultural and religious heritage comes to us and our own modern ethos. In his Oxford lecture on Heinrich Heine (1863), he spoke directly about this dissociation and its effect:

> Modern times find themselves with an immense system of institutions, established facts, accredited dogmas, customs, rules, which have come to them from times not modern. In this system their life has to be carried forward; yet they have a sense that this system is not of their own creation, that it by no means corresponds exactly with the wants of their actual life, that, for them, it is customary, not rational. The awakening of this sense is the awakening of the modern spirit (CPW 3:109).

It is, he continues, "the settled endeavor of most persons of good sense" to attempt "to remove this want of correspondence." What Arnold feared was that such an effort would produce only "acrid dissolvents" of "the old European system of dominant ideas and facts" (CPW 3:109-110). This is what he observed happening on the Continent. As an example he cites Angelo de Gubernatis, distinguished and liberal professor of Sanskrit at Florence, who had dismissed Arnold's endeavor in *Literature and Dogma*. The learned professor could understand how the Bible might appear to lovers of literature as a fine specimen of Oriental poetic eloquence, or to scholars as a valuable, though suspect, collection of Semitic historical documents. It would, of course, equally strike unbelievers as a book laden with superstition and moral obscenities. De Gubernatis could not conceive its being taken seriously "as a fruitful inspirer of men's daily life." How wonderful, he wrote "that any one should wish to make it so, and should raise intellectual and literary discussions having this for their object." "What," he asks, "would the author of *Literature and Dogma* say if Plato had based his republic upon a text of Hesiod?" (CPW 8:150-51).

In de Gubernatis, Arnold saw the intellectual surfeit of the European Enlightenment and what had become "the genuine opinion of Continental liberalism concerning the religion of the Bible and its future." It was not a climate of mind that had yet taken hold in England or America, but Arnold could not doubt that unless "the want of correspondence" was overcome, "the mere barriers of tradition and convention will finally give way" in these lands as well. He was troubled by the complacency of the partisans of orthodoxy who, "dream of patching up things unmendable," for what they do not see is that the tide of liberal thinking, while rejecting "the obsolete religion of tradition," rejects also, and on like grounds, "all concern for the Bible and Christianity." And so for Arnold the real question to be asked is "whether this conclusion, too, of modern liberalism is to be admitted, like the conclusion that traditionary religion is unsound and obsolete" (CPW 8:151-52).

Arnold had learned from his father and Spinoza—and from a host of other liberal but pious thinkers—that rejecting unsound tradition did not entail rejecting the Bible and Christianity as well. The question posed by Spinoza is this: So "there are errors and contradictions in the Bible, What then? What follows from this? What change is it, if true, to produce in the relation of mankind to the Christian religion? What is the new Christianity to be like?" (CPW 2:170). Arnold was convinced that neither the philosopher nor the scientist, neither the learned Hebraist nor the physicist, could answer these questions and make progress toward removing the want of correspondence. That, he believed, is the function of criticism. Arnold perceived criticism as occupying a middle position between literature (the imagination) and science (understanding); it serves as broker between abstract thought and poetry. "The main element of the modern spirit's life," he observed, is "neither the senses and understanding, nor the heart and imagination; it is the imaginative reason" (CPW 3:230), which alone can heal the split and remove the want of correspondence between tradition and the modern. It can do this, for, unlike science and philosophy, which appeal to a limited faculty, criticism engages the whole man in a dialectical process: sense and idea, beauty and moral insight.

EDIFICATION AND INSTRUCTION

One of the functions of criticism is "to try books as to the influence which they were calculated to have upon the general culture." By this Arnold meant the testing of what effect the work of a learned Hebraist and critic, such as T. K. Cheyne, or a popular journalist, such as Miall, would have on the general public and its understanding of religion and the Bible. Are such works negative and reductive? Do they reinforce crude ideas and provincial attitudes? In the instance of either a Professor Cheyne or a Mr. Miall, the ideas and sensibilities conveyed in their writings have an influence beyond religion. They prepare persons to approach other matters with similar suppositions. Thus religious books come within the jurisdiction of literary criticism, for they have a profound effect on the general culture. "They affect it," writes Arnold, "whether they appeal to the reason, or to the heart and feelings only" (CPW 3:41).

Arnold was fond of Goethe's remark that *Der Engländer ist eigenlich ohne intelligenz*, by which he meant that the Englishman approaches things in isolation, that he fails to perceive opinions in relation to other ideas, their "due place in the general world of thought." In short, Englishmen are uncritical. In Arnold's mind there was no better instance of this than the case of Bishop Colenso. The wide interest in the bishop's *The Pentateuch and the Book of Joshua Critically Examined*, "which all England is reading," persuaded Arnold that, whatever its theological faults or merits, it was necessary that the book be called up for judgment "before the Republic of Letters"; "to try it in respect to the influence which it is naturally calculated to exercise on the culture of England or Europe." Criticism must ask of Colenso: "Does this book tend to advance that culture, either by edifying the little-instructed, or by further informing the much-instructed?" (CPW 3:43). Here Arnold lays down one of his most important hermeneutical canons.

The good bishop was acutely conscious of his book's largely negative and unedifying effect. He speaks of "the sharp pangs" which he felt in destroying forever "the ordinary view of the Mosaic story" and how he "trembles" at the results of his inquiries, which show the "groundlessness of that notion of Scripture Inspiration which so many have long regarded as the very foundation of their faith and hope." He is aware, he admits, of his failure "to supply the loss," "*to fill up the aching void*" (CPW 3:45). It is this failure, Arnold is convinced, which is the root of the book's miscarriage. The *Pentateuch* presents intellectual demonstrations, but in such a way as to have nothing about them at all edifying. Like Voltaire's *Sermon of the Fifty*, Colenso's arithmetical calculations from the Bible can only elicit mockery and disgust from the reader. Each demonstration serves as a reductio ad absurdum of one or another of the Pentateuchal books. Colenso appears driven to pile problem upon problem. His approach can be illustrated by his characteristic rhetorical question regarding the provisions for priests in Leviticus: "If three priests have to eat 264 pigeons a day, how many must each priest eat?" And so Colenso proceeds, on and on in his pedantic, rationalistic, unedifying way.

Neither, are the bishop's researches instructive. For generations scholars had been keenly aware of the incongruities and the exaggerated legends present in many of the biblical narratives. But Arnold insists that what the culture of Europe wants is an answer to Spinoza's question: "What then? What follows from all this?" It is just "these questions which the Bishop of Natal never touches with one of his fingers" (CPW 3:49). What is needed, and what Arnold calls for, is an effort of imagination, what

Paul Ricoeur refers to as a "second naïveté," which is a work of literary criticism. It is a going "beyond criticism, by criticism that is no longer reductive but restorative."[3]

While Arnold's contemporaries were surprised, and many were perplexed, at "a liberal attacking a liberal," Arnold showed an increasing dislike of and alarm over the work of the radical biblical scholars—men like Strauss, the Tübingen critics, and the author of the popular *Supernatural Religion*, published anonymously in 1874. A letter of Arnold's to Walter Cassels, the author of this book, is instructive. "I look with disquietude," Arnold writes,

> on all merely negative criticism of the Bible. . . . Perhaps it is here that we differ. I should prefer to begin by saying to them: "Yes the Bible is as grand a tome as you can imagine but not in your sense, in this other sense; and then when one had succeeded in giving them some inkling of this other sense, I should go on to show how in their old sense the Bible could not stand upright any longer" (28 April 1875; the Robert H. Taylor Collection, Princeton University Library).

Arnold believed that it was the responsibility of the biblical scholar who genuinely instructs the learned to publish his findings, but to do so in the proper scholarly places and preferably in a language not normally accessible to the little-instructed. Such, Arnold pointed out, was the method of Spinoza, whose *Tractatus Theologico-Politicus* could not unsettle the unprepared believer since it was written in Latin. But this was not the way taken by Voltaire and Colenso or numerous German critics. They wrote for wider audiences, yet began and ended by showing how the traditional view of the Bible simply could not stand. They failed to instruct their peers, but, worse, they failed to edify their general audience. Arnold contends that scholars writing for the untutored have first to succeed in "giving them some inkling of this other sense," "the putting of a new construction" on the old texts. *Only then* should they "go on to show how in their old sense the Bible could not stand." This was the way followed by Spinoza and, in Arnold's day, by the historian, Arthur Stanley in his *Lectures on the History of the Jewish Church* (1863).

A comparison of Stanley's method with that of Colenso sets Arnold's point in relief. Arnold points out that Stanley proceeds with perfect freedom, using the most recent critical theory available to him. For example, in handling the deliverance of the Israelites out of Egypt, he faces the difficulty of "conceiving the migration of a whole nation under such circumstances" and acknowledges the scholarly judgment that it is appropriate "to reduce the numbers of the text from 600,000 to 600 armed men." He mentions as well "the difficulty of determining the exact place of the passage of the Red Sea." None of these scholarly matters are shunned. Yet Stanley immediately fixes the mind of the reader "on the essential features of this great deliverance." Unlike Colenso, Stanley does not dilate on all the difficulties of understanding how the event could have taken place; rather, he points out how the Israelites "are the only nation in ancient or modern times which, throwing off the yoke of slavery, claims no merit, no victory of its own. . . . All is from above, nothing from themselves" (CPW 3:70). Here, of course, is the true religious import of the marvelous story.

The proper question for the critic is one of proportion and fitness. Arnold acknowledged that the precise time when the Book of Deuteronomy assumed its present form is not an inconsiderable question, but is it to be given pride of place, as the goal of a true science of the Bible, over that which helps men to follow the cardinal injunctions of the Bible? Stanley did not think so, and Arnold agreed. Men need to be edified, not only informed. This is as true of the scholar as it is of the simple believer. The *religious* voice which needs speak to all men "must have the tone of the spiritual world." The critics' role, particularly in a time of cultural dissociation, is one of synthesis or, in Leon Festinger's term, the role of reducing "cognitive dissonance." But this is not always possible for the critic, and in such cases Arnold suggests a less ambitious but fitting response:

> The religious life maintains its indefensible claims, and *in its own sphere* inexorably refuses to be satisfied with the new thought, to admit it to be of any truth and significance, until it has harmonized it with itself, until it has imparted to it its own divine power of refreshing souls. Some day the religious life will have harmonized all the new thought with itself, will be able to use it freely; but it cannot use it yet. And who has not rejoiced to be able, between the old idea, tenable no longer, which once connected itself with certain religious words, and the new idea, which has not yet connected itself with them, to rest for awhile in the healing virtue and beauty of the words themselves? (CPW 3:81).

Arnold's concern for edification, by which he meant bringing out the text's religious meaning or significance as well as its "healing virtue," is apparent in his handling of the questions of biblical revision and the language of the Prayer Book. On both questions he sought a proper balance between historical accuracy, or instruction, and edification. That the former has its proper place is incontestable. The issue was joined in the Forster Education Bill debate on the question of whether and how the Bible should be used in the school curriculum. Arnold saw the time coming when the study of the Bible would be removed from the schools altogether. No longer would it be a force at work in forming and moving the minds and wills of English youth. This eventuality prompted him to prepare a new version of Isaiah 40-66 for schools, which he hoped would make this grand text more accessible to children than was the Authorized Version.

A Bible-Reading for Schools, published in May 1872, is prefaced by a long introduction in which Arnold enunciates his principles of biblical translation and editing and fully sets out his concern for a proper historical instruction. On the thorny questions that gather around the messianic passages in Isaiah 53, for example, Arnold acknowledges that it would be a bad critic indeed who thought the literary and historical base of these verses was unimportant. He agrees with Goethe that "without this historical and literary substructure the full religious significance of the Bible can never build itself up for our minds" (CPW 7:68).

Arnold insists, then, that any serviceable version of scripture must, in its critical apparatus, illuminate the historical and literary *Sitz im Leben* of the text. However, when it comes to revision and translation, he urges the greatest caution. In general, alterations should be restricted "to those cases where in the authorized version there is unintelligibility or ambiguity baffling the reader." He acknowledges that a purely scientific critic, such as T. K. Cheyne, must have more latitude in order to ensure that he renders the original with perfect accuracy. But his audience is different from the one that listens to the Authorized Version in church or reads it for its religious teaching. Scholars undertaking revision by public authority, such as those at Westminster preparing the Revised Version of the New (1881) and Old (1885) Testaments, have less latitude in Arnold's view, though they must correct "the old version not only where it is unintelligible, but also where they think it in error."

Arnold's own object in *A Bible-Reading for Schools* is "to retain as far as possible" the Authorized Version, since it is, as a whole, a matchless literary monument which, moreover, "has created certain sentiments in the reader's mind" that there is no reason to disturb. He judges that most revisers, including those at Westminster, fail to apply the proper restraint; they alter passages needlessly. For example, Arnold maintains that it is doubtful that any corrector should, merely for the sake of being more exactly literal, change "Her iniquity is pardoned" to "Her sin-offering is accepted."

Arnold was disappointed that his *Bible-Reading* had little effect, but this did not deter him from preparing a version of the first 39 chapters of Isaiah, which he published in 1883 as *Isaiah of Jerusalem*. Here he again enunciates a series of critical principles, which amount essentially to a reiteration of those set forth in 1872. The Authorized Version, he argues, should be departed from only of necessity, only when real mistakes require alteration, and then as gently as possible. What appeared to have become a translator's rule—"He succeeds best who renders the original most literally and exactly"—should be resisted. Arnold now expresses his belief more insistently that the translations of the experts, of Cheyne and Robertson Smith, while exact, seriously impair the religious feeling and effect of the great texts. He argues that if the general sense of the old version can be preserved, it should in no wise be tampered with. The first requisite of biblical translation "is to amend the authorized translation without destroying its effect." Arnold now is even more worried that the critics are in fact losing themselves in the details, "in the preliminaries," and thereby "missing the main design" (CPW 10:103, 106).

Arnold's concern for religious edification as crucial to the critical task, as long as it is kept in balance with instruction, was commended by many scholars, including the exacting T. K. Cheyne, who wrote reviews of each of Arnold's versions of Isaiah. Cheyne thought that *Bible-Reading* was "amply justified" and wished that his fellow revisers at Westminster would "take to heart Mr. Arnold's exposition of his principles."[4] However, there was another side of the matter which showed that the problem was more complex than Arnold recognized. The critic must, as Arnold knew, make judgments as to when "consecrated expressions" must be given up and when they should be retained. To retain them, Cheyne points out, sometimes is "entirely wrong, and commonly among the chief obstacles to understanding the Scriptures."[5] But to make that judgment one cannot simply fall back on the notion of a general sense of the original, unless of course one is thoroughly conversant in the technical points of Hebrew scholarship. Cheyne desired a "gentle revision" as much as did Arnold, but he feared that "Bible students might imagine that it represented the ripest and the best scholarship, and that the rhythmical and rhetorical effect of the Authorized Isaiah corresponded to that of the Hebrew."[6] Maintaining a proper tension between instruction and edification was a greater problem for the professional biblical scholar than Arnold, the amateur Hebraist, was either able or willing to acknowledge.

Nevertheless, Arnold's concern to seize on the *religious* function of edification was highly salutary, in view of the negative hermeneutics fostered by the likes of Colenso and the vast apparatus of learning which in the new biblical scholarship was about to eclipse the religious intention and significance of the biblical literature. Arnold wisely observed that biblical scholars, like literary critics, often allow textual and historical-critical matters to gain too exclusive attention and importance. These critics are eternally "reading the theories of their colleagues," and "their personal reputation is made by emitting, on the much-canvassed subject, a new theory of their own." As in the case of the Tübingen critics, this theorizing often leads to the temptation "of introducing into the arrangement of facts a system and symmetry of one's own, for which there are no sufficient data." Arnold also believed that scholarly myopia is often the result of a "want of variety and balance in [the critic's] own life and occupation." The critic's technical interests and investments may well intoxicate him, and judgment is thereby impaired. A truth which never must be lost sight of is that "in the domain of religion, as in the domain of poetry, the whole apparatus of learning is but secondary, and that we always go wrong with our learning when we suffer ourselves to forget this" (CPW 8:243-44).

Criticism, Arnold insisted, requires a "justness of perception" that no specialist can claim to derive solely from the knowledge of his particular science. Discerning the meaning and significance of the Bible involves something that critics such as Colenso and Strauss are wanting. Arnold called it "critical tact."

CRITICAL TACT

Arnold observed that a new breed of biblical critics talks a great deal about knowing the truth but, lamentably, seems to equate knowing the truth about the Bible with knowing "that much of it is legendary and much of it of uncertain authorship." On the contrary, he contended that "no one knows the truth about the Bible who does not know how to enjoy the Bible." Such a person may imagine that Moses or Paul or John wrote books that in fact they did not write, but, more importantly, he "knows how to enjoy the Bible deeply, is nearer the truth about the Bible than the man who can pick it all to pieces but cannot enjoy it" (CPW 7:148).

A shortcoming of much radical criticism was what Arnold called rationalism, by which he specifically meant a certain failure of historical perspective, the fallacy of present-mindedness. That is, rationalism aims to explain away certain supernatural events by giving those events natural explanations which, it is hoped, will make them historically reasonable and approvable. The effort to see Jesus' death as a swoon and his resurrection as a recovery from a swoon is a classic example. Arnold considered it to Strauss's credit, despite his other shortcomings, that he exploded this method of interpretation and recognized myth and legend for what they are.

Arnold has been called a rationalist critic; but if the term is to be used for Arnold it must be defined with some care, since a rationalist in the above sense he was not. Indeed, it was his critical tact that made him aware that this kind of rationalist interpretation "rests on too narrow a conception of the history of the human mind, and of its diversities of operation and production." Rationalism puts "us ourselves in the original disciples' place, imagines the original disciples to have been men rational in our sense and way, and then explains their record as it might be made explicable if it were ours" (CPW 6:269). Arnold's approach to interpretation is both more conservative and, paradoxically in the eyes of many, far more radical.

What Arnold found depressing in much of the criticism of the Bible was a scientific erudition which often had the effect of encumbering the critic so as to throw him off balance, particularly when faced with matters of literary judgment. As early as 1861 Arnold had addressed the question of critical tact in responding to Francis Newman's *Reply* to Arnold's lectures *On Translating Homer*. The subject was the poetry of Homer, not the Bible, but for Arnold the issue was basically the same. What Newman's handling of Homer needed was a certain critical poise, which his erudition had destroyed. "To press to the sense of the thing itself with which one is dealing," Arnold writes, and "not to go off on some collateral issue about the thing, is the hardest matter in the world." What Arnold means by the thing itself is "the critical perception of poetic truth," which is of all things the most "elusive and evanescent." "The critic of poetry," Arnold insists, and he is soon to apply the same standard to the critic of biblical literature, "should have the finest tact, the nicest moderation, the most free, flexible, and elastic spirit imaginable; he should be indeed the '*ondoyant et divers*,' the *undulating and diverse* being of Montaigne" (CPW 1:174). It is here that culture becomes the indispensable servant of the biblical interpreter.

This Arnoldian cultural prerequisite has been ridiculed, and it clearly leaves itself open to caricature as a critical desideratum. But reflective consideration will, I think, acknowledge that it is a sine qua non of any sane criticism, for which all the philological and textual learning in the world cannot serve as a substitute. The lack of a wide acquaintance with the history of the human spirit disposes the reader, whether scholar or not, to treat the books of the Bible as would a pedant—"all alike, and to press every word."

A person who lacks this wide experience is not prepared "to read between the lines, to discern where he ought to rest with his whole weight and where he ought to pass lightly." On the contrary, he is prone to take what he reads too straightforwardly or prosaically, "amplifying certain data which he finds in the Bible, whether they ought to be so dealt with or no." Experience with history and literature gives one the power "to estimate the proportion and relation in what we read" (CPW 6:151-53). It was the absence of critical tact that Arnold found so widespread in the England of his day and which made possible, for example, the watchword of the British and Foreign School Society: *The Bible, the whole Bible, and nothing but the Bible!* (CPW 6:159-60). It also made possible and explains the popularity of the work of Colenso, W. R. Greg, and Walter Cassel's *Supernatural Religion.*

Arnold recognized that there is something inexplicable about critical judgment or tact. It cannot simply be called forth or assured. If one is lucky, he wrote, one can *hope* to attain it. Arnold insisted that critical tact "comes almost of itself." Like Coleridge's reason, it involves an intuition which is more than the sum of its parts and cannot be sundered and analyzed in terms of its component elements. In this it has affinities with Newman's illative sense or with the judgment of the Shakespearean savant or the art connoisseur, persons who are able to pronounce judgment of authenticity unhesitatingly on the basis of innumerable factors which alone may seen inconsequential and which taken together may elude simple formulation.

Critical tact thus often works imperceptibly. "What it displaces," Arnold writes, "it displaces easily and naturally." The object of inquiry simply comes to look different to us. The old understanding is not beaten off by logical argument; we are not even driven off our ground. Rather, "our ground itself changes with us" (CPW 6:168). Through letters, then, one can hope to "gain some hold on sound judgment," a hold which neither logic nor learned science alone can achieve.

Arnold wished to insist that humane letters not only can refresh and delight us but, as he says in "Literature and Science," can have that "evaluating" and "suggestive power, capable of wonderfully helping us to relate the results of modern science to our need for conduct, our need for beauty" (CPW 10:68). Humane letters does this by helping us to perceive and to weigh relations and values of human import that cannot otherwise be so forcefully and yet so subtly grasped. Thus it is that critical tact involves a fully human way of judging and of knowing—distinct, perhaps, but not arcane or esoteric.

PREUNDERSTANDING, ACCOMMODATION, AND RESERVE

The critic possessing the requisite tact will appreciate that interpretation entails complex epistemological considerations as well. C. G. Lichtenberg put the matter humorously but sagely: "A book is a mirror: if an ass peers into it, you can't expect an apostle to look out."[7] Or, to put it in other terms, understanding always involves certain predispositions that are born of long habituation. Therefore, if we go to the Bible looking for morally outrageous behavior, we shall doubtless find it. If we go looking for historical contradictions and errors, we will discover them in abundance. If we are searching for divine wisdom and succor, again we shall not go away disappointed. Arnold would have agreed with Karl Barth's shrewd observation that "the Bible gives to every man and to every era such answers to their questions as they deserve."[8]

Joubert's brilliance as a critic is traceable in part, Arnold believed, to his ability to grasp that temper or those predispositions which lay behind and yet unveil the heart and mind of a movement or a man. This Joubert does with genius in his comparison of the Jesuits and Jansenists, for example. In each case a certain disposition of mind and moral temper conduce them to concentrate on certain notions in the Bible and the tradition and to allow others to fall into the shade. A great defect in the Jansenists, Joubert finds, is to be observed in what they leave out in their reading of Scripture. Rather than laying stress on what is clear, serene, and satisfying to our minds, the Jansenists appear to find in the Bible only what puzzles, troubles, and checks our reason. "They lay stress upon what is uncertain, obscure, and afflicting" and "eclipse the luminous and consoling truths of Scripture . . . truths that are full of clearness, mildness, serenity, light." Arnold agrees with Joubert that the Jansenists are not "to be condemned for what they say, because what they say is true." But they are "to be condemned for what they fail to say, for that is true, too—truer, even, than the other" (CPW 3:200).

Relevant to Arnold's point is Frank Kermode's discussion of the hermeneutical supersession of traditional meanings and the discovery of latent meanings in sacred texts. This is often due to new, tacit forms of knowledge which allow the texts to "cast shadows important to the perceiving eye, emitted signals intelligible to the understanding ear." Kermode comments that "sometimes it appears that the history of interpretation may be thought of as a history of exclusions, which enable us to seize upon this issue rather than on some other as central." Often our divinatory powers increase as the primary or literal reading—"the one most obvious to the first readers—loses its compelling force, its obviousness."[9]

The point is that all interpretation involves a certain preunderstanding. That is, the reader, whether he be critic or simple believer, does not approach the text as a tabula rasa but rather brings to the text, consciously or not, certain metainterpretive presuppositions, preconditions, and values that limit what he is looking for and frame what he sees. Unless certain questions are put to the text, it will remain mute, but the very nature of the questions implies a particular interest on the part of the reader. Arnold was acutely aware that the issue facing biblical interpretation was not whether one comes to the Bible with certain interpretive presuppositions, but rather what kind of interpretive stance is appropriate for reading the particular body of literature that constitutes the biblical canon. Some questions and interpretive preconceptions are more appropriate than others to certain types of texts. One does not, for example, put geological questions to an analysis of *Pilgrim's Progress*.

Arnold stands in that hermeneutical tradition which runs from Bishop Butler through Coleridge to Newman. It goes back much further, of course, for it has its roots in Augustine's insistence that knowing is inextricably bound to a certain engagement of the will and affections. Arnold reverts again and again to Butler's statement that the object of religion is to bring us to a certain temper of mind and behavior. And he agrees with Butler that before this can be accomplished, "our affections must be engaged" (CPW 10:100). That is, the true object of the Bible will remain opaque unless we come to the Bible properly engaged to ask the right questions and seek the answers it is prepared to reveal. This involves a certain predisposition born of what Butler called "general habits of life and conduct." Arnold was deeply impressed by the function of habit, not only in accustoming us to certain modes of action but in our very acts of knowing.

It is to Coleridge, however, that we turn to find the epistemological prerequisites of Arnold's own biblical hermeneutics most fully advanced. In the *Confessions of an Inquiring Spirit*, Coleridge proposes that the Bible is revealing only when it is read "in faith." The Bible, he acknowledges, is full of folly, error and the simply profane. But we would not think of rejecting Shakespeare because his work includes *Titus Andronicus*. The truth and value of the Bible are not dependent on its collective purity or inerrancy. Quite the contrary, it is only in the real humanity of the biblical texts that its spiritual truth and power are discerned. Because contradictions, errors, and moral weakness are found in the Bible, are we, asks Coleridge, to say that "the Ten Commandments are not to be obeyed, the clauses of the Lord's Prayer not to be desired, or the Sermon on the Mount not to be practised?"[10] The logic is foolish, of course, and is based on the specious conjunction of two different statements. To say that "the Bible contains the religion revealed by God" is not the same as saying, "Whatever is contained in the Bible is religion and was revealed by God." One can hold the former while rejecting the latter. Thus, for Coleridge the Bible is the *source* of the Christian religion, but it does not constitute the Christian religion. It follows that if the Bible is the source, then one needs some interpretive key to discern the indispensable message of the Christian faith from that in which it is enveloped. Coleridge holds that this key is found in the richness that constitutes the Christian tradition itself. For Coleridge, both a knowledge of and belief in the Christian religion should precede the study of the Hebrew canon. "Indeed," he writes, "with regard to both Testaments, I consider oral and catechismal instruction as the preparative provided by Christ himself in the establishment of a visible Church."[11] So it is that Coleridge counsels that it is only where one sees faith, a desire to believe, that one should then say

> there are likewise sacred Writings which taken in connection with the institution and perpetuity of a visible Church, all believers revere as the most precious boon of God, next to Christianity itself.... In them you will find all the revealed truths which have been set forth and offered to you.... In all of which you will recognize the influence of the Holy Spirit, with a conviction increasing with the growth of your own faith and spiritual experience.[12]

Arnold is one with Coleridge in holding that unless a person comes to the Bible openly in faith and is receptive to its message, one will be prone to lay hold of an isolated text here or there and say "of what use is this," which, Coleridge remarks, only proves "that nothing can be so trifling as to supply an evil heart with a pretext for unbelief."[13]

Similar epistemological preconditions were worked out by Newman, especially in the series of *Sermons on the Theory of Religious Belief* and *The Grammar of Assent*. Newman held that our judgments and beliefs are always under the sway of what he called "antecedent considerations," by which he meant that our judgments are "influenced by previous notices, prepossessions, and (in the good sense of the word) prejudices." Thus it is that "a good man and a bad man will think very different things probable. In the judgment of a highly disposed mind, objects are desirable and obtainable, which irreligious men will consider to be fancies."[14] Arnold found highly congenial Newman's acute perception of how the mind actually moves and forms judgments—that is, not by logical reasoning but by those concrete instances and moral experiences which alone are too numerous, fine, and circuitous to avail, but which together converge to produce a judgment. Newman's comment, in "The Tamworth Reading Room," that "instances and patterns, not logical reasonings, are the living conclusions which alone can have a hold over the affections or can form character," unmistakably touched a sympathetic chord in Arnold, for he entered the lines in his notebooks on four occasions (NB 326, 335, 350, 515).

If it is true that mind can speak only to a mind receptive to hear, that what we are open to see and receive is dependent on prepossessions— what today hermeneutics calls preunderstanding—then the teacher or the interpreter must take into account whether the listener or the reader is in a position to receive strong meat or should be offered only milk. Arnold's practice as religious critic and reformer embodies two principles that were dominant in the writing of both the Tractarians and the Oriel Noetics: the ideas of reserve and of accommodation.

The principle of reserve, the process of withholding the fullness of truth and dispensing it gradually, and only as the context requires, was a cardinal doctrine of the Tractarians. It was rooted in their profound sense of divine mystery, of the hiddenness and otherness of God, and in their belief that the sublimity of religious truth can only be approached in humility, in wonder, and reserve. The Tractarians found support for this view in the *disciplina arcana* of the Church Fathers, especially in Clement of Alexandria and Origen. The need for reserve in communicating religious knowledge is especially pronounced in the writings of John Keble, Arnold's godfather, and in the poetry of Isaac Williams. However, it was Newman's work on the Arians and his controversy with Charles Kingsley and the subsequent publication of the *Apologia pro Vita Sua* that perhaps more than anything else brought the teaching to wider attention.

Newman's defense of the use of reserve and accommodation drew from Kingsley charges of a disingenuous evasion of truth very similar to the charge leveled against Arnold by W. R. Greg in his influential attack occasioned by Arnold's essay on Colenso.[15] Newman's suspicion of rationalist proof and metaphysical dialectics was as deep, if not deeper, than Arnold's. Both men were called skeptics because they publicly acknowledged that the purely rational grounds for atheism were as compelling as those for theism. Both men were sensitive to the need for discrimination in the use of religious words and to the limits of the finite mind in comprehending and adequately communicating sacred realities. Newman used the words "reserve" and "economy" to convey his sense of the care and prudence necessary in communicating sacred truth. In the *Apologia*, Newman spoke of the Christian mysteries as "but the expressions in human language of truths to which the human mind is unequal"; therefore it is incumbent upon all Christians to show due caution in instructing others in the faith: "As Almighty God did not all at once introduce the Gospel to the world, and thereby gradually prepared men for its profitable reception, so, according to the doctrine of the early Church, it was a duty, for the sake of the heathen among whom they lived, to observe a great reserve and caution in communicating to them the knowledge of 'the whole counsel of God.'"[16] Newman describes the working of the principle of reserve or economy: "Out of various courses in religious conduct or statement, all and each allowable antecedently and in themselves, that ought to be taken which is most expedient and most suitable at the time for the object in hand."[17] By this means God has gradually imparted to the world the knowledge of his will, having "winked at the times of ignorance among the heathen."

In recalling Newman's influence on his brother Matt, Tom Arnold assigned it to Newman's "perfect handling of words, joined to the delicate presentation of ideas."[18] This Newmanian "disposition of mind" included the sense of the importance of tone, of the need for a delicate handling of words and ideas and the requisite moderation, prudence, and reserve in conveying religious ideas. Among other devices, Arnold was also to adopt the use of economy and accommodation as rhetorical means of persuading his audiences.

Arnold saw the error of the rationalist critic as, in part, the failure to see the need for accommodation and reserve. Does he not see, Arnold writes,

> that he is even bound to take account of the circumstances of his hearers, and that information which is only fruitless to the religious life of some of his hearers, may be worse than fruitless, confounding to the religious life of others of them? Cer-

tainly, Christianity has not two doctrines, one for the few, another for the many; but certainly, Christ adapted His teaching to the different stages of growth in His hearers, and for all of them adapted it to the needs of the religious life (CPW 3:80-81).

Arnold was convinced that the intellectual revolution of the nineteenth century would inevitably force painful and profound changes in the received religion. "In no country," he warns, "will it be more felt than in England." All the more reason, Arnold urges, that "there is incumbent on every one the utmost duty of considerateness and caution," for

> there can be no surer proof of a narrow and ill-instructed mind, than to think and uphold that what a man takes to be the truth on religious matters is always to be proclaimed. Our truth on these matters, and likewise the error of others, is something so relative, that the good or harm likely to be done by speaking ought always to be taken into account. . . . The man who believes that his truth on religious matters is so absolutely the truth, that say it when, and where, and to whom he will, he cannot but do good with it, is in our day almost always a man whose truth is half blunder, and wholly useless.
>
> To be convinced, therefore, that our current theology is false, is not necessarily a reason for publishing that conviction. . . . To judge rightly the time and its conditions is the great thing; there is a time, as the Preacher says, to speak, and a time to keep silence (CPW 6:147-48).

Arnold believed that the time was right to speak and that he was justified in speaking out because the task he had set for himself in *Literature and Dogma* was a hermeneutics, not of suspicion and reduction, but of retrieval and restoration.

The use of reserve and prudence in communicating religious truths involves, of course, the formidable problem of how these truths are best to be presented. And so the other side of reserve is what the Church Fathers and Newman called economy* and what Arnold spoke of as ac-

---

* In his work on the Arians, Newman spoke of economy in terms of the providential working of God. He wrote that "all those so-called Economies or dispensations, which display his character in action, are but condescensions to the infirmity and peculiarity of our minds" (*The Arians of the Fourth Century* [London, 1876], 75). In the sermon on "Developments in Religious Doctrine," Newman mentions how, by accommodation, the teacher instructs children in the most perfect truth, "that is, the nearest approach to truth, compatible with their condition" (*Fifteen Sermons Preached before the University of Oxford* [London, 1872], 341. This sermon, preached on 2 February 1843, could well have been heard by Arnold while he was at Balliol.

commodation. Arnold's theory of accommodation owes much as well to Thomas Arnold, whose sermons "On the Right Interpretation and Understanding of Scripture" were highly praised by his son (L 2:28).

Thomas Arnold assumed as a principle of biblical interpretation that, due to the imperfections of the human mind and changes of historical and cultural circumstance, *"accommodation* must exist in every revelation from God to man." Since our minds are indeed finite and limited by our cultural horizons, it is essential that the revelations of God to man should be gradual, "and adapted to his state at the several periods when they were successively made." In consideration of imperfection, "perhaps we do not enough consider how in the very message itself, there must be a mixture of accommodation to our ignorance." And so it is that "in the case of our Lord Jesus Christ, the necessity of this accommodation becomes more evident." That is, Christ adapted his message to the notions of his hearers, and so "we cannot, therefore, argue that all the opinions which Christ did not contradict be sanctioned with Divine Authority."[19] The implication here is that much in the language and worldview which Christ was required to use to convey his message was, in fact, time-bound and passing, the historically conditioned husks, so to speak, in which the essential kernel of his message was necessarily enveloped. As time and conditions change, the message can be freed from its antique husks and couched in a language and in forms more congruent with our own present experience.

Thomas Arnold's theory of accommodation had deeper hermeneutical implications, however, than simply maintaining "abiding truths in changing categories." For it made reasonable and sanctioned a theory of revelation that allowed for adaptation and change in the substance of belief as well as its form. The laws of early Israel, Arnold pointed out, were adapted to the condition of the Israelites at a particular time in their experience. God's revelations are gradual and adaptive to "the several periods when they were successively made." On this principle Arnold can say that some divine commands "were given at one time which were not given at another; and which, according to God's method of dealing with mankind, not only were not, but *could not have been given.*"[20]

Matthew Arnold frequently used the term "accommodation," especially when referring to Jesus' presentation of his message and what the form of that message implied for the present work of interpretation. In this he is clearly following his father's hermeneutical lead. He speaks, for example, of Jesus' talk "of drinking wine and sitting on thrones in the kingdom of God" as "using the language of accommodation to the ideas current

amongst his hearers" (CPW 6:145). Similarly, he considers all the eschatological passages that have to do with miraculous, supernatural interven-
tions, future messianic comings, a future kingdom of God, and so on, as
exemplifying Jesus' accommodation to his Jewish followers. The reports
of Jesus have him announcing that this generation shall not pass away till
they see "the Son of man coming on the clouds with great power and
glory, and then shall he send his angels and gather his elect from the four
winds" (Matthew 24:30-31,34), and popular theology puts a plain, literal
sense upon the passage. Arnold insists that "a more plausible theology
will say that the words are an accommodation; that the speaker lends
himself to the fancies and expectations of his hearers" (CPW 6:259).

Arnold sees Jesus as accommodating the futuristic and otherwordly
eschatology of first-century Judaism to his own realized eschatology—the
one "the ideal of popular *Aberglaube*" and the other his own ideal: "And
this is why the phrases of the popular *Aberglaube* come so often from his
lips. He was forever translating it into the sense of the higher ideal, the
only sense in which it had truth and grandeur" (CPW 6:305).

Despite the ongoing failure to grasp the new meaning that Jesus conveys in the ancient modes of thought, Arnold commends an accommodation to their continued use as a contemporary hermeneutical rule. He
gives the following justification:

> The great reason for continuing to use the familiar lan-
> guage of the religion around us as approximative language,
> and as poetry, although we cannot take it literally, is that such
> was also the practice of Jesus. . . . But if Jesus used this way of
> speaking in spite of its plainly leading to . . . misapprehension,
> it must have been because it was the best way and the only one.
> For it was not by introducing a brand-new religious language,
> and by parting with all the old and cherished images, that
> popular religion could be transformed; but by keeping the old
> language and images, and as far as possible conveying into
> them the soul of the new Christian ideal (CPW 8:137).

Arnold believed that, while much of popular religion still holds that
Jesus spoke literally of a Son of man coming on the clouds of heaven,
"very many religious people, even now, suppose that Jesus was but using
the figures of Messianic judgment familiar to his hearers, in order to impress upon them his main point" (CPW 8:137).

The question remains, of course, whether Jesus was, in fact, accommodating his listeners or was using "this language because he himself

shared the materialistic notions of his disciples about the kingdom of God . . . and was mistaken in thinking so." Arnold's response to the question is emphatic: "There are plain signs that . . . Jesus did not really share the beliefs of his disciples or conceive the kingdom of God as they did," since "they report him describing the kingdom of God as an inward change requiring to be spread over an immense time, and coming about by natural means and gradual growth" (CPW 8:137-38). Arnold only can urge that, since Jesus does actually use the materializing language and imagery of his disciples, "it cannot have been because he shared their illusions." Rather, it was solely for the purpose of accommodation.

Arnold was wise not to underestimate the central place of eschatology in the Gospel accounts of the teaching of Jesus. He also showed himself advanced in not rejecting the old eschatological language and imagery out of hand—as did many liberal critics—but in calling for a radical reinterpretation. He was, nevertheless, very much the liberal critic of his day in his tortured efforts to distance Jesus from the worldview and apocalyptical beliefs of first-century Palestinian Judaism. It is this effort that makes aspects of Arnold's interpretation of Jesus' message so very dated both historically and theologically. Modern scholarship generally is agreed that Jesus shared the Jewish apocalyptical worldview of first-century Palestine and that it was absolutely central to his eschatological message. But modern historical theology, from Harnack to C. H. Dodd and Bultmann, also has insisted that there is a tension in Jesus' preaching between a thoroughgoing or consistent eschatology, advanced by scholars such as Johannes Weiss and Albert Schweitzer, and a realized eschatology that cannot simply be subsumed within first-century Jewish apocalyptic. Furthermore, biblical scholarship has demonstrated that there is a movement toward reinterpretation, toward demythologization of the apocalyptic eschatology, within the New Testament itself and that this is particularly evident in the later Pauline and the Johannine writings.

Although certainly wrong in denying that the historical Jesus shared the Jewish apocalyptical vision of an imminent, catastrophic end of the present age, Arnold was quite justified in seeing more in Jesus' eschatological preaching than this, and in taking the theological responsibility to reinterpret that eschatological message for his own day. That is to say, in his own context Arnold was justified in reinterpreting first-century *Aberglaube*, and especially its apocalyptical eschatology, as an *accommodation*, since that message was bound up with the historical circumstances and the prescientific cosmology of first-century Palestine and therefore couched in a cultural form which does not have the same claim upon a later age.

DEMYTHOLOGIZATION

Nathan Scott has observed that Arnold "may rightly be claimed to be the first major specialist of the modern period of 'demythologization.'"[21] If one limits Scott's claim to Anglo-American theological writing, the judgment certainly can stand. It is also true, as Scott indicates, that the contemporary theological avant-garde has hardly consulted Arnold's work, though it preceded Bultmann's program of demythologizing the New Testament by 70 years. While there are important differences in the theological contexts, assumptions, and languages used by Arnold the Victorian moralist and the German Lutheran existentialist, and while Bultmann is incontestably the superior biblical scholar and theologian, nevertheless there are striking similarities in the programs of the two men. A comparison with Bultmann can illuminate important aspects of Arnold's hermeneutics.

The work of both Bultmann and Arnold is impelled by the conviction that the Christian message must be freed from its antique form which, taken in a literal and scientific sense, has become a scandal and stumbling block for modern, scientific man. The real stone of stumbling lies elsewhere—for Bultmann in the unique claim of the kerygma, for Arnold in the spiritual claim and promise of *necrosis*. What modern man finds incredible in the Bible is its prescientific view of the world and its attendant picture of God acting in a mythological way—that is, as an otherworldly being intervening supernaturally, and yet all too anthropomorphically, in the course of worldly events. Bultmann has summarized the nature of this mythical worldview in a classic passage:

> The cosmology of the New Testament is essentially mythical in character. The world is a three-storied structure, with the earth in the center, the heaven above, and the underworld beneath. Heaven is the abode of God and of celestial beings— the angels. The underworld is hell, the place of torment. Even the earth is more than the scene of natural, everyday events. . . . It is the scene of the supernatural activity of God and his angels on the one hand and of Satan and his daemons on the other. This aeon is held in bondage by Satan, sin, and death (for "powers" is precisely what they are) and hastens toward its end. That end will come very soon, and will take the form of a cosmic catastrophe. It will be inaugurated by the woes of the last time. Then the judge will come from heaven, the dead

will rise, and last judgment will take place, and men will enter into eternal salvation or damnation.

This, then, is the mythical view of the world which the New Testament presupposes when it presents the event of redemption. . . . It proclaims in the language of mythology that the last time has now come. "In the fullness of time" God sent forth his Son, a pre-existent divine Being, who appears on earth as a man. He died the death of a sinner on the cross and makes atonement for the sins of men. His resurrection marks the beginning of the cosmic catastrophe. Death, the consequence of Adam's sin, is abolished, and the daemonic forces are deprived of their power. The risen Christ is exalted to the right hand of God in heaven and made "Lord and King." He will come again on the clouds of heaven to complete the work of redemption and the resurrection and judgment of men will follow. Sin, suffering, and death will then be finally abolished. All this will happen very soon; indeed, St. Paul thinks that he himself will live to see it.[22]

Bultmann indicates the problem which such a prescientific worldview presents to the modern reader and gives his solution:

All this is the language of mythology, and the origin of the various themes can easily be traced in the contemporary mythology of Jewish Apocalyptic and the redemption myths of Gnosticism. To this extent the kerygma is incredible to modern man, for he is convinced that the mythical view of the world is obsolete. We are therefore bound to ask whether when we preach the Gospel today, we expect our converts to accept not only the Gospel message but also the mythical view of the world in which it is set. If not, does the New Testament embody a truth which is quite independent of its mythical setting? If it does, theology must understand the task of stripping the kerygma from its mythical framework, of "demythologizing" it.[23]

The problem of belief that Bultmann here identifies is strikingly similar to what Arnold observed as early as his years in Oxford. Among the educated class there is, Arnold felt, the growing sense of a dissociation between the antique forms in which Christianity is preserved and its genuine spirit.

In addressing this problem, he did not use the term "myth" in the sense in which it is currently used by theologians, literary critics, and historians of religion. Nevertheless, what he called *Aberglaube*, or "extra-belief," is analogous to what these contemporary critics call myth. He confronts the issue in the opening pages of his first extended work on religion, *St. Paul and Protestantism*. The permanent worth and power of a religious teacher or book depend on "its correspondence with important facts and the light it throws on them." He writes: "Never was the truth of this so evident as now. The scientific sense in man never asserted its claims so strongly; the propensity of religion to neglect those claims, and the peril and loss to it from neglecting them, never were so manifest" (CPW 6:8).

The peril is that in attempting to meet the demand of a scientific age, the apologists for the Bible and Christianity have laid claim for the scientific character of the biblical language and its story of redemption, as if this dramatic and visionary God-talk were equivalent to scientific discourse about publicly verifiable events of the past and future. The difficulty with this kind of "licence of affirmation" about God and his proceedings is that more and more it will be met by the demand for proof and verification. Scientific assertions, modern man insists, call for scientific warrants. But such a religious claim to scientific statement and verification is, Arnold knew, impossible in our day, and to call upon men to accept this form and warrant of Christian belief is either to demand a *sacrificium intellectus* or to touch these spiritual realities with the finger of death. Arnold would have agreed with Bultmann that such a demand is neither possible nor necessary. It is not necessary because the Christian message is *not* inextricably tied either to Hellenistic cosmology or to the language and spirit of sixteenth-century Calvinism and capitalism. Behind both the apocalyptic and gnostic imagery of the New Testament and the juridical and commercial language of the Westminster divines lies a deeper and more enduring message.

What then is called for is not the elimination of these mythical forms of expression but a reinterpretation, or demythologizing, of these forms in order to unveil their real religious significance or intention. In *Literature and Dogma* Arnold distinguishes between the apocalyptical and dogmatical *Aberglaube* of primitive and popular Christianity and what he perceives to be the true essence of the religion of Israel and Christianity—and calls for the demythologizing of the *Aberglaube* in order to disclose that true essence in terms consonant with the language and experience of modern man.

It is worth noting that, unlike a number of radical critics, neither Arnold nor Bultmann calls for an elimination of the mythological *Aberglaube*. Both recognize what the philosopher W. M. Urban call "indispensable myth," myth as an indispensable form of religious expression.[24] Arnold refers to *Aberglaube* as "the poetry of life," and he was certain that humanity does not live without its poetic myths—that by which "we hope, augur, imagine."

This is why for the *Aberglaube* "of religion one has, or ought to have, an infinite tenderness." It is "the spontaneous work of nature." It is "the travail of the human mind to adopt to its grasp and employment great ideas of which it feels the attraction;" *Aberglaube* being the means by which these great ideas are clothed and vividly made present to our minds and affections. It is this fact that impels Arnold, despite his scorn of creedal "learned science," to acknowledge that the Apostles' Creed

> was the only vehicle by which, to generation after generation of men, the method and secret of Jesus could gain any access; and in this sense we may even call it . . . *providential*. And this rude criticism is full of poetry, and in this poetry we have been all nursed. To call it, as many of our philosophical Liberal friends are fond of calling it, "a degrading superstition," is as untrue, as it is a poor compliment to human nature. . . . It is an *Aberglaube* . . . produced by taking certain great names and great promises too literally and materially; but it is *not* a degrading superstition (CPW 6:358).

It is in the context of responses such as this that we can appreciate Arnold's conviction that ordinary people are not wrong in turning away from the brilliant "philosophical Liberal" W. K. Clifford, for "compared with Professor Clifford, Messrs. Moody and Sankey are masters of the philosophy of history" (CPW 7:381). This, of course, is not all that must be said.

Myth, or *Aberglaube*, may be a providential accommodation, but it should never be confused with the essential message, or kerygma, of Christianity itself. Arnold knew, however, that "human nature is such, that the mind easily dwells on an anticipation [an *Aberglaube*] . . . until we forget the order in which it arose, place it first when it is by rights second, and make it support that by which it is in truth supported." It is by this process that *Aberglaube* comes "to surpass the original conviction itself in attractiveness and seeming certitude," and so it is that Christians have "more and more rested the proof of Christianity, not on its internal evidence, but on prophecy and miracle" (CPW 6:230-31). There is, of course, a "drawback to a man's advantage in thus treating . . . what is extra-belief and not certain as if it were a matter of certainty. . . . *He pays for it.* The time comes when he discovers that it is *not* certain; and then the whole certainty of religion seems discredited" (CPW 6:232).

Of the great eschatological myths of Israel and primitive Christianity, Arnold writes: "Now most of this has poetical value, some of it has a moral value. All of it is, in truth, *a testimony to the strength of Israel's idea of righteousness.*" Here we have the clue to Arnold's understanding of the function of religious myth and his demand for reinterpretation. As Bultmann expresses it, in a more contemporary idiom, "The real purpose of myth is not to present an objective picture of the world as it is, but to express man's understanding of himself in the world in which he lives. Myth should be interpreted not cosmologically, but anthropologically, or better still, existentially."[25]

The function of demythologization is to interpret the biblical mythology in such a way as to disclose the essential truth of the Bible. This demands that the moral or existential intention to which the myth testifies be identified and restated in non-mythological terms. The process can be observed within the New Testament itself in the Synoptic Gospels but more especially in the writings of St. Paul and, most decisively, in St. John. We can see the eschatological imagery interpreted in terms of its moral and existential significance when, for example, St. John writes that "he who believes in the Son *has* eternal life," or that "*this* is the judgment, that the light has come into the world, and men loved darkness rather than light, because their deeds were evil" (John 3:36,19).

Arnold writes at length on St. Paul's interpretation of the primitive Christian *mythos* and how, in later popular Christianity, Paul's interpretation of the resurrection and eschatology is ignored. "They use it," he writes, "to mean a rising again after the physical death of the body. Now it is quite true that St. Paul speaks of resurrection in this sense. . . . But it is true also, that in nine cases out of ten where St. Paul thinks and speaks of resurrection, he thinks and speaks of it in a sense different from this;— in the sense of a rising to a new life before the physical death of the body" (CPW 5:182-83).

Arnold is confident that if the reader carefully follows St. Paul's line of thought in his later epistles, he will acknowledge that it is not "the physical and miraculous aspect of the resurrection which holds the first place in [Paul's] mind," for the simple reason that it "does not fit in with the ideas he is developing." What is original in the mature Paul is the effort "to find a moral side and significance for all the processes, however mystical, of the religious life, with a view of strengthening, in this way, their hold upon us and their command over our natures" (CPW 6:51). This, Arnold insists, is what lies behind St. Paul's thinking about resurrection, as well as behind his adaptation of the conventional Jewish ideas and language respecting the Messiah, his kingdom, the end of the age, the parousia, and the glory. There can be no doubt that these ideas, couched in their "materialized" mythological imagery, were a reality for St. Paul. Nevertheless, as to Paul's *use* of these ideas and imagery, Arnold offers two comments:

> One is, that in him these Jewish ideas,—as any one will feel who calls to mind a genuine display of them like that in the Apocalypse,—are spiritualized; and as he advances in his course they are spiritualized increasingly. The other remark is, that important as the ideas are in Paul, of them, too, the importance is only secondary, compared with that of the great central matter of his thoughts: *the righteousness of God, the non-fulfillment of it by man, the fulfillment of it by Christ* (CPW 6:41-42).

Arnold readily acknowledges that St. Paul's spiritualized doctrines do not, in most instances, exclude a materialized sense, and that this latter sense dominates Victorian popular Protestantism. But he is aware that the modern scientific mind reverses the entire process. "For science, the spiritual notion is the real one, the material notion is figurative." St. Paul's greatness is that he grasped the spiritual notion, "if not exclusively and fully, yet firmly and predominantly" (CPW 6:55).

When Arnold turns from St. Paul to the Gospels, he observes the same process of spiritual interpretation at work in the accounts of Jesus' teaching. While Jesus appears to take over the entire Jewish *Aberglaube*, he nevertheless adapts it to his own message. For example, the meaning of Christ's death and resurrection in the Gospels is by no means wholly subsumed by the event on Golgotha or the appearances on the third day. Scholars rightly speak of St. Mark's Gospel as an extended passion narrative. "Long before his signal Crucifixion," writes Arnold, "Jesus had died, by taking up daily that cross which his disciples, after his daily example, were to take up also." Again, Jesus had "risen to life long before his crowning Resurrection, risen to life in what he calls 'my joy,' which he desired to see fulfilled in his disciples also;—'my joy to have kept my Father's commandments and abide in his love.'"

Arnold renders Jesus' message as follows: "He that has believed on me and had my secret, . . . though his body die to the life of this world, still lives; for such an one had died to the life of this world already, and found true life, life out of himself, life in the Eternal that loveth righteousness, by doing so" (CPW 6:320-21). He thus interprets Jesus' own resurrection as "the victory of his cause after his death and at the price of his death," and the disciples' hope of resurrection as summed up in Jesus' words: "If a man keep my word he shall never see death" (John 8:51).

Arnold's critical demythologization of the Jewish and Hellenistic *mythos* must, as in the case of Bultmann, be seen as a radical theological interpretation which has its beginnings within the New Testament itself. The "materialized facts" of, for instance, the birth stories, or the resurrection accounts, or the eschatological prophecies are, as Arnold insists, not the foundation, not what is first, but are rather the vehicles by which more fundamental moral and theological beliefs and religious experiences are envisioned and communicated. But the myths, or *Aberglaube*, are invariably made to support that by which in truth they are supported, when in fact they are born out of and subsequent to theological and existential reflection and experience. Arnold's sense of the relation of the materialized fact to the spiritual or existential fact may be clarified by an observation of a contemporary Modernist theologian, Don Cupitt, concerning belief in the Immaculate Conception:

> It's no accident that Catholics have visions of Mary and Buddists have visions of Buddha, and not the other way round. Bernadette's vision in the Grotto at Lourdes crystallized and expressed beliefs she already entertained, already perhaps held, but which now in the moment of experience came to flower and took full possession of her soul. The vision is not the logical ground of the doctrine. No Catholic theologian would use the vision as a reason for believing the doctrine. The doctrine is prior to the vision, and indeed is a necessary condition for its occurrence.[26]

With regard to the resurrection, Cupitt asserts that

> so far from the Easter Event creating the Easter faith as is commonly said, it was rather the Easter faith which made the Easter Event possible. For the Easter Event was presumably an apprehension by men of the risen and exalted Jesus. But for men to be able to cognize Jesus in a religious experience they must already have and know how to use the concepts by means of which they are to interpret that experience. The possibility of a recognition of the living Christ in Christian

experience *presupposes* good independent theological grounds for believing him risen.[27]

According to Cupitt the apostles put together their experience of the facts of Jesus' life, his teachings, and his passion and death alongside their reading of the Old Testament and, in the convergence of these disclosures, it was manifest to them that this man must be the Christ.

> Thus when the apostles said that in the risen Lord they recognized the same Jesus, the identity here is not the identity of a thing which persists unchanged through a period of time, but the identity predicated when we assent that Edward Heath is the same man as the Prime Minister. To see Jesus as risen Lord was to see someone who had been an acquaintance as nothing less than Lord and Christ, living and exalted. The myth of a posthumous apparition plays no essential part in this.[28]

It is important to add that Cupitt does not deny that faith in the living and exalted Christ may have given rise to genuine realistic visions or other remarkable resurrection experiences, and then finally to the ex post facto physical accounts. But these visions and materialized accounts are not, Arnold would agree, the logical grounds or reasons for believing in the resurrection. They are, rather, expressions, however interpreted, of that belief. Therefore, an attempted scientifc-historiographic proof of the birth or resurrection narratives is not crucial, indeed may well be a false stone of stumbling. For, as Arnold insists, the time may come when one discovers they are *not* true grounds, and one's belief is then discredited.

What must be kept in mind is that the Gospel writers did not sharply distinguish myth and legend and history. The modern critic and believer is, however, in a quite different position. He cannot go back to a precritical naïveté rather, he must aim, in Paul Ricoeur's words, "at a second naïveté in and through criticism."[29] Arnold's understanding of the interpreter's task is similar. He would agree that "the dissolution of the myth as explanation is the necessary way to the restoration of the myth as symbol" and that we are, as Ricoeur reminds us, "in every way children of criticism" who must "seek to go beyond criticism by means of criticism," a criticism albeit "no longer reductive but restorative."[30]

Arnold was certain that as time passed, the Christmas story, the Easter narratives, and the eschatological visions, clothed in mythical and legendary *Aberglaube*, would be understood more and more for their symbolic meaning. These narratives will continue to be read, recited, and loved, but as poetry—"as poetry endeared by the associations of some two thousand years." And religious belief "will rest upon that which the legend symbolizes" (CPW 10:231). Arnold regards demythologization as the critical work of disclosing "*that which the legend symbolizes*," or what he elsewhere refers to as "the spiritual notion" (CPW 6:55) and "the idea which is the fact" (CPW 9:63,161). It is the responsibility of the modern religious critic to demonstrate that the myth and the legend are the poetic or symbolic representations of, and *not* the grounds of, religious experience and belief. The birth story, the resurrection narratives, and the eschatological prophecies are born out of and subsequent to theological and existential reflection, subsequent to the theological idea which is the fact, which alone is the ground of authentic religious experience and belief.

Arnold's focus on the spiritual notion has raised the question in the mind of some critics whether he is guilty of an extreme Idealism whereby, for example, the connection between the historical Jesus and the "idea" of Christ in the Gospels is regarded as largely, if not purely, external and accidental. Such was the position taken by the left-wing Hegelians in Germany, including D. F. Strauss. It was a view that also gained a certain acceptance in Britain during the period of Arnold's later years through the writings of the British Hegelians—men such as the theologian John Caird. Caird's Idealism permitted him to assert that "it is not the facts of His [Christ's] individual history, but the ideas that underlie it, that constitute the true value of his life." Caird thus was able to insist that "even if many of the details of Christ's life and teachings should fail to stand the test of scientific criticism . . . still the ideas and doctrines . . . which had their historic origin in that life, would be recognized as true in themselves, and as having an indestructible evidence in the reason and conscience of man."[31]

Now there is much in this position that Arnold would find congenial, and his own essays reveal semblances to what one finds in the writings of John and Edward Caird and T. H. Green in the last years of the nineteenth century. However, there is no evidence that Arnold read or was influenced by the British Idealists, and in many respects—their interest in metaphysics, for example—he differed from them profoundly. But neither is Arnold's understanding of the relationship between history and interpretation, between fact and idea, as sophisticated or as radical as that of the British Idealists. He does not, in fact, sever the "idea" of Christ from the so-called historical Jesus, for the simple reason that he erroneously assumed many of the Gospel traditions about Jesus to be historically sound. If Arnold can be faulted here, it is for his uncritical assumption of the historicity of some of the Gospel traditions concerning Jesus and his message and, most notoriously, his recourse to those traditions found in the Gospel of John. The narratives which Arnold treats, and with considerable critical justification, as mythic and legendary expressions of the meaning of Jesus' life, message, and death are those that lie outside the bounds of history—the birth stories, the resurrection appearances, and the eschatological prophecies. Whatever faults one may find in his handling of the question of history and interpretation, it should not simply be equated with the radical Idealistic reduction that one finds in Strauss or even to a lesser degree in the Cairds or Green.

Arnold's appeal to the "idea which is the fact" has, however, received sharp criticism from quite another quarter. Stephen Prickett views Arnold's commitment to demythologization as the substitution of a deadly moral and rational abstraction for the life of the poetic imagination. Prickett contends that while "the title of Arnold's best-known theological work, *Literature and Dogma*, sounds as if it is about the superiority of literature over dogma . . . it turns out to be about the superiority of dogma over literature."[32] Prickett argues that Arnold's attempt to reconcile the German critical tradition of demythologization with the poetic-theological tradition of Wordsworth and Coleridge is the source of his failure as both religious and literary critic. For Wordsworth and Coleridge "form and content were essentially indivisible." "A poetic or religious symbol could not, they believed, be paraphrased or adequately expressed in philosophical or abstract language," which is exactly what Arnold attempts. The Coleridgeans, Prickett continues, insist that "the human mind works not primarily in terms of rational argument, but in myth and symbol as its basic mode." Now it is this very notion of poetry as a unique, imaginative mode of knowing, with its implicit doctrine of the indivisibility of poetic content and form, that Arnold, according to Prickett, is committed to opposing. Therefore, Arnold "constantly finds himself in the position of surreptitiously attributing to poetry an importance and a 'life' that his theory demands should be attached to abstract concepts themselves."[33]

And thus, Prickett argues, Arnold finds that poetry and truth are divisible and must be separated. The kernel must be extracted from the husk. Of course the husk has its function—"it protects the seed, carries it safely to its destination, and provides for its safe arrival and acceptance. . . . But in order that the seed of truth may grow, the husk," Prickett insists, "must be dispensed with," since for modern man "it can be a source of confusion, misunderstanding, 'delusion and error.'"[34] Prickett concludes that the upshot of Arnold's demythologization is that he finds himself between the worlds of poetry (now dead) and philosophy (which lacks the power to give life). And what is crucial for both literary and religious criticism is that Arnold's "attempt to substitute reconciliation for polarity has drastically altered and weakened the value of poetry itself."[35] According to Prickett, in Arnold's hands poetry and myth remain only a husk, a vehicle, a mode of expression.

This is a severe indictment, for if Prickett is correct, Arnold's program of demythologization undermines his hermeneutical effort to rehabilitate the poetic imagination for the life of religion. There are, however, two objections that must be raised against Prickett's analysis. First, poetic images, symbols, and myths cannot remain "unbroken," as Tillich has insisted.[36] They must be *interpreted* unless they are merely to serve as Zen rafts, as vehicles to transport us to realms of solitary, ineffable spiritual experience. The dominate feature of Western religious literature—i.e., the literature of the Bible—is its association with narrative, with a story about the corporate life of a people, their God, and their history. However, this story is not a mere temporal series; it always has a *telos*, or meaning. An *idea* is embodied in the narrative. We are always trying to catch in our net of successive moments something that is not successive—an enduring meaning or truth. But to insist on this in no way implies that the meaning or truth is detachable from its literary form. The idea and the story are interdependent, but they can be distinguished.

The point that must be insisted on is that the story embodies a meaning which interpretation seeks to unveil and communicate. The poetic imagination, or "the symbol," as Ricoeur puts it, "gives rise to thought."[37] This is imperatively so for modern man, since we no longer live in a precritical state of primitive naïveté, in the immediacy of myth as explanation, or if we do, we are living precariously. Criticism *has* intervened, whether we will it or not, and so if there is to be a "second naïveté," it must, as Ricoeur says, be in and through interpretation or criticism itself: "What criticism continually endeavors to exorcize is the *logos* of the *mythos*."[38] Prickett is simply wrong if he thinks that religious belief today, in contrast to a purely imaginative fancy, can remain in a state of immediacy; that there exist religious texts, couched in the language and imagery of their antique time, that today can be appropriated without interpretation. "We can believe," Ricoeur properly insists, "only by interpreting."[39] For Arnold, interpretation does not, however, entail a reduction of myth and poetry to abstract ratiocination.

In his often-cited prediction of the future of poetry, Arnold asserts that "poetry gives us the idea," but it is the idea "touched with beauty, heightened by emotion." And it is only when it is so touched and so heightened that we feel the idea to be interpretive for us, to satisfy us" (CPW 9:62). The great objects of our religious consciousness, being objects that elude literal statement, require "the language of figure and feeling," for it not only satisfies us better but, more importantly, "will cover more of what we seek to express, than the language of literal fact and science. The language of science about it will be *below* what we feel to be the truth" (CPW 6:189).

Demythologization does not entail the supersession of myth or antique imagery, but it does involve the necessary task of interpretation. Interpretation is not the simple reduction or substitution of the language of poetry into or for abstract concepts. This is the very thing that Arnold, in *Literature and Dogma*, is anxious to resist, whether it be by the Bishop of Gloucester, the Wesleyan minister, Rev. Cattle, or Frederic Harrison. The old images and languages are "not extinguished by the growth of a truer conception of their essential contents." Text and interpreter remain, for Arnold, interdependent, for through poetry alone can we come to *know*, to be awakened to the "wonderfully full, new, and intimate sense" of things. Therefore, Arnold insists that we begin with the testimony of the biblical writers. "Matters are not all mended by taking their language of approximate figure and turning it into the language of scientific definition." It would be better "to take their fact of experience, to keep it steadily for our basis in using their language, and to see whether from using their language with the ground of this real and firm sense to it, as they themselves did, somewhat of their feeling, too, may not grow upon us" (CPW 6:200).

It is quite wrong to assert that Arnold the hermeneut undercuts Arnold the guardian of poetic truth. As Nathan Scott observes, "On the contrary, so paramount is the role that [Arnold] accords the poetic imagination in the religious enterprise that it may, indeed, be said to be for him the very means of transcendence, the vital agent whereby men first 'hail' the numinous, the mysterium tremendum, the not ourselves."[40]

For Arnold, the task of demythologization is simply the work of unveiling those moral imperatives or spiritual meanings which may now lie hidden or only dimly glimpsed. It is the helpmate in disclosing the moral or spiritual intention and message of the biblical text. If, finally, it is admitted that demythologization is not all that is involved in the interpreter's task, it remains nevertheless a crucial function of modern biblical interpretation in the Judeo-Christian tradition. This leads to one additional and critical feature of Arnold's hermeneutics, the essentially moral purpose of criticism. While out of favor in recent years, it is a sine qua non of any interpreter who makes claim to the title of humanist.

THE MORAL FUNCTION OF CRITICISM

At the center of Arnold's theory and practice of criticism is the perception of a moral function, what he called "a criticism of life." As he made plain, literature interprets by expressing imaginatively and with a unique felicity the form and the movement of the outer world. But Arnold believed that literature's indispensable and most urgent function is to interpret "with inspired conviction the ideas and laws of the inward world of man's moral and spiritual nature"; literature must, that is, have "moral profundity" (CPW 3:33). To the very end of his life he held firmly to this high claim for literary criticism, for its service in the exercise of what Lionel Trilling has called the critical moral intelligence. He did this through his literary essays—for example in "Heinrich Heine" and "Falkland,"— and through his essays in biblical and social criticism, but perhaps most subtly and impressively in essays such as "Marcus Aurelius" and "Pagan and Mediaeval Religious Sentiment," where he is able to seek out what is central and characteristic in the great Stoic or in Isaiah, in Paul or Jesus, in St. Francis, or in Goethe, and set their moral vision in relation to the moral qualities and visions of other men and other times—Theocritus, Epictetus, Spinoza, or the Benthamites—and to make these moral insights known.

Arnold especially sought to bring out the central moral tendency or sentiment, what today we might refer to as the intentionality, which shaped and gave wholeness to the Hebraic and Christian visions and to compare these with the Platonic, the Stoic, or the modern Jacobin or Rationalist sensibility. He did this by a sagacious choice of passages that served as touchstones of those moral ideals and power which, for Arnold, defined the grand style, and which are expressive of the human condition in its true heights and depths.[41] While one can quarrel with Arnold's specific choices from Homer, Isaiah, Jesus, Sophocles, St. Paul, Dante, Virgil, or Milton, they represent, on the whole, a profound discernment of and engagement with the full range of human experience and emotion: the sense of a lost and irrecoverable happiness, the majesty of a noble personality brought down by a tragic flaw, the irreducible contingency and flux of human life. David DeLaura has remarked that "the bulk of Arnold's supreme touchstones are 'formative' and 'transforming' for human character because . . . they repudiate precisely the easier sorts of nineteenth-century consolation, whether religious or rationalistic . . . Any authentically 'religious' view of human possibility, Arnold is saying implicitly, must make its way against such a view and, in a sense, can never simply cancel this perception of the quality of human life, faced unflinchingly."[42]

At the same time, the range of religious sentiments, and of the grand style, extend for Arnold beyond the fact of human sorrow, melancholy, and tragedy. They reveal, as DeLaura has discerned, "the 'Christianization' of Arnold's thought." In the essays from the mid-1860s the biblical motifs of hope, of redemptive sacrifice, and especially of joy and regeneration experienced in spiritual *necrosis* are dominant. It is in these later works that Arnold's comparative method is most pronounced and where, with subtlety, he contrasts, for example, the cheerful, sensuous beauty of the pagan religious idyll from Theocritus with the sorrowful, yet joyful and profoundly consoling, religion of Christ and St. Francis; or the Stoic morality of Marcus Aurelius—austere and sublime—with the warmth and vivifying power of the Old and New Testaments. Of Marcus Aurelius' teaching, Arnold writes these beautiful lines: "I have said that religious emotion has the power to *light up* morality: the emotion of Marcus Aurelius does not quite light up his morality, but it suffuses it; it has not the power to melt the clouds of effort and austerity quite away, but it shines through them and glorifies them; it is a spirit not so much of gladness and elation, as of gentleness and sweetness; a delicate and tender sentiment which is less than joy and more than resignation." And yet, Arnold adds, beautiful as his character is, "there is something melancholy, circumscribed, and ineffectual" about the teaching of Marcus Aurelius, "a feeling that the burden laid upon man is well-nigh greater than he can bear." What the noblest souls, whether the pagan Empedocles or the Christian Paul, "have insisted on [is] the necessity of an inspiration, a joyful emotion, to make the moral action perfect." In the Old and New Testaments, Arnold found that joyful emotion, that "glow of a divine warmth" in which "the austerity of the sage melts away under it, the paralysis of the weak is healed"; in which "he who is vivified by it renews his strength" (CPW 3:149, 134-35).

Arnold's comparison of the religious idyll of Theocritus with St. Francis's *Canticle of the Sun* brings out in a perceptive and affecting way the unique moral vision as well as the element of intemperate excess which he finds in both the pagan and the Christian life. It is natural that a man should take pleasure in his senses, and the idyll of Theocritus "is poetry treating the world according to the demand of the senses." It is also natural that man should, with St. Francis, take refuge in the heart and imagination. Theocritus "takes the world by its outward sensible side," St. Francis "by its inward, symbolical side." The first, Arnold observes, "admits as much of the world as is pleasure-giving," but the second "admits the whole world, rough and smooth, painful and pleasure-giving, all alike, but all transfigured by the power of a spiritual emotion, all brought under a law of super-sensual love, having its seat in the soul." And yet when St. Francis says, "Praise be my Lord for *our sister, the death of the body*" we see "that we are touching upon an extreme," just as when we see Pompeii "we can put our finger upon the pagan sentiment in its extreme" (CPW 3:225). In either case we see a sign that the measure of sensualism and the measure of spiritualism have been overpassed. Human nature, Arnold says, "is neither all senses and understanding, or all heart and imagination," and in St. Francis's *Canticle* the senses and the heart are by and large beautifully joined.

It is the rare writer, such as St. Francis, in whom we sense that fullness of delight in the common material world—sun, air, earth, and water—and yet a material world spiritually transfigured. And it is this concurrence, Arnold concludes, "which made the fortune of Christianity, . . . not its assigning the spiritual world to Christ and the material world to the devil, but its drawing from the spiritual world a source of joy so abundant that it ran over upon the material world and transfigured it" (CPW 3:230).

In Arnold's skillful juxtaposing of the compelling moral visions of life embodied in classical, Christian, and modern literature we see the genius of the interpreter as moralist. Here and there, as in his later abhorrence of French "lubricity," some may find an unattractive moralism asserting itself, but for the most part Arnold exhibits an acuteness of perception, a sensitivity and rightness of judgment, and a fitness that is rare. When in the mid-1870s Arnold turned from his religious writings to literature once again, he predicted that the future of religion would be assured only by carrying those qualities of perceptiveness and judgment, "which are the best fruits of letters," to whole classes of the community. What he might have said as well is that these qualities are also essential in those whose job it is to interpret the Bible to a wider public. Today hosts of people view the Bible iconically; if they go to the Bible, they go to it talismanically and thaumaturgically, or they don't go to it at all. On the other hand, biblical scholars all too often are zealously preoccupied with the apparatus of biblical research, and this has concealed the biblical message and silenced its living voice. Arnold's concern that the critic should address that want of correspondence between those religious sources of our cultural life and the modern spirit goes largely unheeded.

There are, however, signs of hope in the current interest among some critics and biblical scholars in approaching religious texts through attention to the literary imagination, to narrative, story, parable, and myth. Here criticism of literature, including the biblical literature, could help accomplish in our secular age what neither science, nor philosophy, nor even theology can adequately do: to bring out the moral visions of those great texts in the religious tradition and to compare them with those other visions of the human condition which attract allegiance today. Literature embodies a moral vision. Wayne Booth rightly observes that "there can be no 'innocent' art, no art that can be considered free of ethical responsibility."[43] The critic as humanist will not dawdle over the trivial or remain fixed on what is preliminary; like Arnold he will engage in moral criticism. This is not an easy task. On the contrary, as John Gardner reminds us with regard to the contemporary plight of criticism, "Not everyone is capable of judging the moral maturity or emotional honesty of Günter Grass or Robert Creeley. Nevertheless, to avoid such judgments is to treat art as a plaything. It is not."[44]

Amos Wilder has spoken words which echo Arnold's humanistic advice, in this case to all religious critics and interpreters. The passage stands as a suitable Arnoldian hermeneutic conclusion: "Admitted that every art has its own refined discipline, whose independence is to be jealously guarded; admitted that literary (and biblical) criticism has its own sophisticated and scrupulous procedures; yet all such rightful aut?omy can only be penultimate. Art and letters are too important not to be referred back finally to what is at stake in the human story."[45]

NOTES

1. Paul Ricoeur, *Freud and Philosophy* (New Haven, 1970) 27-28.
2. Basil Willey, "Arnold and Religion," *Matthew Arnold*, ed. Allott 239.
3. Paul Ricoeur, *The Symbolism of Evil* (New York, 1967) 350.
4. T. K. Cheyne, *The Academy* 9 (19 Feb. 1876): 163.
5. Cheyne 163.
6. T. K. Cheyne, *The Academy* 24 (22 Dec. 1883): 410.
7. Quoted W. H. Auden, *The Dryer's Hand and Other Essays* (New York, 1962) 3.
8. Karl Barth, *The Word of God and the Word of Man* (New York, 1957) 32.
9. Frank Kermode, *The Genesis of Secrecy* (Cambridge, MA, 1979) 20, 10.
10. Samuel Taylor Coleridge, *Confessions of an Inquiring Spirit*, ed. H. St. J. Hart (Stanford, 1956) 74.

11. Coleridge 65-66.

12. Coleridge 67.

13. Coleridge 80.

14. John Henry Newman, *Sermons on the Theory of Religious Belief* (London, 1843) 179, 182-83.

15. Greg's article, "Truth *versus* Edification," appeared anonymously in the *Westminster Review*, American ed. 74 (1863): 265-72. In 1869 the article was published as a pamphlet.

16. John Henry Newman, *Apologia pro Vita Sua* (London, 1913) 432.

17. Newman, *Apologia* 432.

18. Thomas Arnold, Jr., *Passages in a Wandering Life* (London, 1900) 57.

19. Thomas Arnold, *Sermons* (London, 1832) 2: 435, 434, 436, 437.

20. Thomas Arnold 434.

21. Scott, "Arnold's Vision of Transcendence" 263.

22. Rudolf Bultmann, "New Testament and Mythology," *Kerygma and Myth*, ed. Hans Werner Bartsch (London, 1953) 1: 1-3.

23. Bultmann 3.

24. Urban, *Language and Reality* 592ff.

25. Bultmann 10.

26. Don Cupitt, "The Resurrection: A Disagreement," *Theology*, 75 (Oct. 1972), p. 509.

27. Don Cupitt, *Christ and the Hiddenness of God* (London, 1971) 164.

28. Cupitt, *Christ* 165-66.

29. Ricoeur, *Symbolism of Evil* 350.

30. Ricoeur, *Symbolism of Evil* 350.

31. John Caird, *The Fundamental Ideas of Christianity* (Glasgow 1899) 2: 241-42.

32. Stephen Prickett, *Romanticism and Religion: The Tradition of Coleridge and Wordsworth in the Victorian Church* (London, 1976) 213.

33. Prickett 219-20.

34. Prickett 221.

35. Prickett 220.

36. Paul Tillich, *The Dynamics of Faith* (New York, 1958) 50ff.

37. Ricoeur, *Symbolism of Evil* 348.

38. Ricoeur, *Symbolism of Evil* 352.

39. Ricoeur, *Symbolism of Evil* 352.

40. Scott 273-74.

41. For a study of Arnold's use of touchstones see John S. Eells, *The Touchstones of Matthew Arnold* (New Haven, 1955). However, for insights into aspects of Arnold's hermeneutics as developed in this section, I am dependent on David DeLaura's masterful essay cited below.

42. DeLaura, "Arnold and Literary Criticism" 133.

43. Wayne C. Booth, "Metaphor as Rhetoric: The Problem of Evaluation," *On Metaphor* ed. Sheldon Sacks (Chicago, 1979) 69.

44. John Gardner, *On Moral Fiction* (New York, 1978) 146.

45. Amos Wilder, "The Uses of a Theological Criticism," *Literature and Religion*, ed. Giles Gunn (New York, 1971) 42.

5 "Die and Come to Life":
Arnold's Religious Belief

This total stamp of "grace and truth," this exquisite conjunction and balance, in an element of mildness, of a method of inwardness perfectly handled and a self-renouncement perfectly kept, was found in Jesus alone.

Literature and Dogma

"Left to ourselves, we sink and perish; visited, we lift up our heads and live." And we may well give ourselves, in grateful and devout self-surrender, to that by which we are thus visited.

Thomas á Kempis, quoted in *Literature and Dogma*

"Matt is a good Christian at the bottom." So Mrs. Matthew Arnold used to say of her husband. And so indeed he was. Anyone who has read Arnold's religious prose works in conjunction with his self-revealing letters and notebooks will recognize a spirit Christian in belief as well as in feeling. He was a man who in his later years was graced by what can be called a nonchalance of faith, a man whose levity in treating religious subjects was, to those who knew him best, "but the freedom of the man who has so sure a hold on essentials that he can afford to play with accidents."[1]

However, there are critics who remain unconvinced. Matthew Arnold did not, they contend, believe in those essentials that would permit him to lay claim to the title Christian. Some critics[2] have in effect asked, in the case of Matthew Arnold, the same rhetorical question that Newman asked of Thomas Arnold: "But is *he* a Christian?"[3] And they, too, answer no. The matter, of course, entirely depends on the question of what constitutes essentials and where one thinks the line on "essentials" ought to be drawn, or how such beliefs are to be interpreted. Chapter 2 explored some of the complexities associated with these questions regarding the development of doctrine, and it would appear that some of the critics who have judged Arnold's belief as not in any acceptable historical sense Christian have not plumbed the complications involved in determining such a question. Other critics have shown a deeper appreciation of the

143

matter as well as of Arnold's personal religious beliefs. Yet some continue to label Arnold's religious position as simply rationalist or agnostic, or to call him a religious humanist or an ethical idealist. Because of the weight which such labels often carry and because of the uncertainty as to Arnold's real position prompted by the multiplication of such terms, an effort at clarification is in order. This chapter will therefore be devoted to an exposition and analysis of Arnold's substantive religious beliefs.

"THE ETERNAL NOT OURSELVES THAT MAKES FOR RIGHTEOUSNESS"

In 1848, at a time of intellectual and spiritual unrest, Arnold wrote to his friend Clough: "There is a God, but he is not well conceived of by all" (CL 87). It was such misconceptions that later caused Arnold to make great sport of Herbert Spencer's abstract and vacuous Unknowable as the name of God. "'The Unknowable is our refuge and strength, a very present help in trouble,' is what would occur to no man to think or say" (CPW 7:396). But wasn't this a case of the pot calling the kettle black? Leslie Stephen thought so. "I glanced the other day at a satirical novel, in which the writer asks whether an old Irishwoman is to say, instead of 'God bless you,' 'the stream of tendency bless you.' I then opened the Preface to Arnold's *God and the Bible* and found him making a similar criticism upon Mr. Herbert Spencer."[4] Arnold acknowledged he was much blamed for using the phrase God is "the stream of tendency by which all things seek to fulfil the law of their being." And his friend and editor, G. W. E. Russell, remarked that "'a Stream of Tendency' can never satisfy the idea of God, as ordinary humanity conceives it. It is not in human nature to love a stream of tendency, or worship it, or ask boons of it."[5] Arnold could not have agreed more. The fact is that hostile and friendly critics alike, whether Stephen or Russell, have misread Arnold at this point.

When Arnold first used this phrase, in *St. Paul and Protestantism*, he did so to demonstrate that if theologians wish to claim to use scientific language about God, they "must stand the tests of scientific examination." Figurative and anthropomorphic language about, for example, "parties—contractors," as if God were "a sort of magnified and non-natural man," will not satisfy the scientific mind. "However much more than this the heart may with propriety put into its language respecting God," it is simply a fact that "this is as much *as science can with strictness put there*" (CPW 6:10; italics added). In other words, Arnold is neither limiting the use of theological discourse to scientific exactitude nor claiming a preference for such scientific statement when speaking of God. Quite the contrary. If we are searching for a phrase that will satisfy what is, on reflection, the *scientific* basis at work in the theist's consciousness, "the stream of tendency by which all things seek to fulfil the law of their being" may, Arnold suggests, "be allowed, and may even prove useful." But certainly, he adds, "*it is inadequate*; certainly it is a less proper phrase than, for instance: 'Clouds and darkness are round about him, righteousness and judgment are the habitation of his seat'" (CPW 6:189; italics added).

Arnold never suggested or implied that the Irishwoman or even Professor Jowett, for that matter, should pray to a Stream of Tendency. Theology is not religion. Theology is the reflective and scientific statement of an original, unmediated experience of God's claim, power, and promise. It is not surprising that the existential experience of God should find expression in a great variety of vivid words and images. But theology must attempt, and rightly, to give descriptive order and precision to what is vivid yet inchoate. What Arnold considered incoherent was the theologian's scientific claims for a language of "figure and feeling." The Thomistic theologian, seeking the scientific precision of Aristotelian categories, would, on the other hand, find "the stream of tendency by which all things seek to fulfil the law of their being" not only allowable but quite useful.

Gordon Kaufman has pointed out that generally theologians have worked with two distinct models of theological transcendence which lead to quite diverse concepts of God. One model is drawn from the experience of interpersonal relations. Here, Kaufman indicates,

> God is viewed as an autonomous agent capable of genuinely free acts. Correspondingly . . . the divine reality is viewed more anthropomorphically on this model, since in our finite experience only persons enjoy this kind of fully objective transcendence. Here, then, God (in analogy with persons) is believed able to love and forgive, as well as punish and destroy, and knowledge of God results from his special act or acts of revealing himself; indeed without such self-disclosing action no knowledge of him would be possible.[6]

The second model is what Kaufman calls teleological transcendence. Theologians guided by this model—and it is the one that has been used by most philosophical theologians engaged in natural theology—are led toward a theology of *being*:

> The ultimate reality will be understood as that good "which

moves all other things but is itself unmoved."* All finite reality will be viewed as necessarily grounded in this ultimate reality, and as, in turn striving toward it. . . . It can be viewed ethically as the ultimate good, aesthetically as perfect beauty, or intellectually as being-itself or the ground of being or the absolute idea. . . . Personalistic notions of ultimate reality are, moreover, usually viewed by theologians of this perspective as somewhat embarrassing anthropomorphisms, to be tolerated primarily because of man's "religious" needs . . . rather than because the understanding of reality requires it.[7]

The model of teleological transcendence greatly attracted Arnold, especially prior to about 1865. It was the theological model of Aristotle, the Stoics, Spinoza, and Goethe. For a "scientific" theology it is indispensable, but Arnold increasingly found it religiously inadequate. "Spinoza's ideal is the intellectual life; the Christian's ideal is the religious life. Between the two conditions there is all the difference which there is between being in love, and the following, with delighted comprehension, a reasoning of Plato" (CPW 3:178). By the time Arnold wrote *Literature and Dogma*, the God of the philosophers appears relegated to a quite secondary role:

We would not allow ourselves to start with any metaphysical conception at all, not with the monotheistic idea, as it is styled, any more than with the pantheistic idea; and indeed we are quite sure that Israel himself began with nothing of the kind. The idea of *God*, as it is given us in the Bible rests, we say, not on a metaphysical conception of the necessity of certain deductions from our ideas of cause, existence, identity, and the like; but on a moral perception of a rule of conduct not of our own making, into which we are born, and which exists whether we will or no; of awe at its grandeur and necessity, and of gratitude at its beneficence. This is the great original revelation made to Israel, this is his "Eternal" (CPW 6:241-42).

This is an instructive passage. It clearly reveals Arnold's rejection of a metaphysical starting point for a theology, yet he continues to hover between a teleological and a personalistic model. It is apparent that religiously he prefers what is, in fact, Hebrew personalism: a God who reveals his will, covenants with his people; a God to whom men can pray. And yet he shies away from personalistic language and continues to speak of "a rule of conduct not of our own making into which we are born," as if

---

* Aristotle, *Metaphysics* 12:7.

God were an abstract precept, a structure of reality immanent in human experience.

Arnold never satisfactorily resolved this tension in his theological writings, and it did lead him into logical incoherences and apparent contradictions. However, better theologians than Arnold have been guilty of the same failure, and it is clear that Arnold saw both the need and the danger of using personal analogies in talking about God. He took back with his right hand what he gave up with his left. He was not able philosophically ("scientifically") to justify a personalistic theological model that at the same time became crucial to his actual religious program. Nevertheless, while it can be argued that Arnold failed to grasp the necessity of a Christian *theology* based on a model of interpersonal relations (as distinct from a *religious* use of personal analogies), his stricture against anthropomorphic God-talk was and remains salutary. Futhermore, despite the excess of his protestations against theological anthropomorphism, Arnold actually held doctrines of God's transcendence and personal agency.

It has been said that Arnold should be counted among those nineteenth-century practitioners of transformational criticism, such as Feuerbach, Marx, and, later, Freud, who put the predicate in place of the theological subject and who, by "reducing theology to anthropology, exalt anthropology into theology."[8] The claim is that Arnold transforms theology into either a naturalism or a humanism. In so doing, he empties religion of theological transcendence. False as I believe this judgment is, it perhaps is excusable when made by critics familiar only with Arnold's poetry, for there one does find evidence of a kind of Feuerbachian theological reduction. It is present most unambiguously in the sonnet "The Divinity":

> *God's wisdom and God's goodness!* Ay, but fools
> Mis-define these till God knows them no more.
> *Wisdom and goodness*, they are God! what schools
> Have yet so much as heard this simpler lore?
> This no Saint preaches, and this no Church rules;
> 'Tis in the desert, now and heretofore.   (P 530)

William Robbins considers this kind of theistic reduction as "fundamental to the whole of Arnold's religious writing" and a desideratum "for a mature formulation of the principal ideas in Arnold's religious thought."[9] However, the prose writings on religion simply will not sustain such a view. There is a possible misconception that may explain why this kind of judgment is not uncommon even among those critics, like Robbins, who are familiar with Arnold's prose. Arnold thoroughly rejected natural theology as a way to knowledge of God. He considered it both metaphysically too abstract and too pretentious. God cannot, he insisted, be known through our experience of "cruel" and "stubborn" Nature. Rather, God is known only in his moral effects upon us. Here Arnold's approach to theological knowledge has much in common with his German contemporary, the neo-Kantian Albrecht Ritschl.* Ritschl taught that the mind's knowledge consists of both causal and value judgments which occur simultaneously, both of which are indispensable to knowledge. Our so-called objective knowledge is never entirely disinterested. Ritschl agreed with Kant that as humans we do not and cannot know things in themselves (*Ding an sich*), but, on the other hand, with Lotze he asserted positively that we can know things through their qualities and effects on us and our response to them. This is true as well of our knowledge of God, who cannot be known in himself but "only in his effects upon us." According to Ritschl,

> apart from this value-judgment of faith, there exists no knowledge of God worthy of this content, so that we ought not to strive after a purely theoretical and "disinterested" knowledge of God, as an indispensable preliminary to the knowledge of faith. To be sure, people say that we must know the nature of God and Christ ere we can ascertain their worth for us. But Luther's insight perceived the incorrectness of such a view. The truth rather is that *we know the nature of God and Christ only in their worth for us.*[10]

Arnold held a similar view. He maintained that, while the real constitution of a thing may be beyond us, we nevertheless give it a substantial form; we personify it** and apply to it a figurative name that may originally have been suggested to us by the phenomenon's effect upon us.

Arnold applies the principle to our knowledge of "the Eternal not ourselves that makes for righteousness." This is, he asserts, "really a law of nature, collected from experience, just as much as the law of gravitation is; only it is a law of nature which is conceived, however confusedly, by

---

* Arnold was not influenced by Ritschl directly, since the latter's formative works, *The Christian Doctrine of Justification and Reconciliation* 3 (1874) and *Theology and Metaphysics* (1881) appeared after Arnold's religious prose was essentially completed. However, the ideas derived from Kant and Lotze were in the air. For parallels between Arnold and Ritschlianism see chapter 6.

** Here Arnold likely was influenced by Max Müller's philogical work on language and the personification of nature in archaic religion. Arnold corresponded with Max Müller on these and related issues (see, e.g., CPW 6:182).

very many more of mankind as affecting them, and much more nearly. But it has its origin in experience, it appeals to experience, and by experience it is, as we believe, verified." Nevertheless, we cannot know "the Eternal not ourselves" in itself and for itself. We cannot literally personify it as "some material agent, somebody, some gas." We cannot pretend "to know the origin and composition of the power that makes for righteousness than of the power that makes for gravitation. *All we profess to have ascertained about it is, that it has effect upon us, that it operates*" (CPW 7:191; italics added).

The fact of the matter is that from the effects which the "Eternal not ourselves" has upon us as moral agents, we can say a great deal about God or, more accurately, about our lives as determined by God. Arnold's rather Kantian agnosticism concerning God's intrinsic being and his practical approach to the knowledge of God through our moral experience should not be confused or equated with theological subjectivism or with the reduction of theology to anthropology, any more than in the case of Kant.

Arnold's practical and experiential approach to *knowledge* of God has a kinship not only with Ritschlianism but also with the views of the French Modernist Édouard LeRoy, as formulated in his *Dogme et Critique* (1907). LeRoy, too, was sensitive to the twin errors of theistic anthropomorphism and absolute agnosticism. According to LeRoy, our concepts of God function in two ways. Negatively, they serve as a protection against false beliefs—for example, against a crude and naïve anthropormorphism. More importantly, our concepts serve to guide our religious life; they are essentially prescriptive. Take, as illustrative, the dogma "God is personal." LeRoy describes its negative function as follows: "I don't see any definition of the divine personality. It tells me nothing of this personality; it doesn't reveal its nature to me; it does not furnish me with a single explicit idea of it. But I see very clearly that it says to me: 'God is not impersonal . . . not a simple law, a formal category, an abstract entity.'" The positive, prescriptive meaning of "God is personal" is: "Conduct yourselves in your relation to God as you do in your relations with a human being," that is, in a personalistic manner. LeRoy insisted, as did Arnold, that concepts of God interpreted practically as rules of conduct involve implicitly the affirmation that ultimate reality is such as to justify such conduct.

The reality of God implies the transcendence of God over the world and the human self, an objectively existing reality on which the self is radically dependent. It implies a distinctly theological valuation—the logical and ontological link—of the object of religion, i.e., conduct, by joining the object to its transcendent ground and power. Does Arnold secure that link, grounding his religion in a genuine theological transcendence? There are critics who claim that he does not. David Edwards concludes that "the one thing that [Arnold] cannot say is: God is real."[12] However, when one turns to *Literature and Dogma* and *God and the Bible*, the reality of God for Arnold is patent, an obvious essential of his religious reconstruction.

Early in *St. Paul and Protestantism*, while reprimanding the Puritans for their "license of affirmation" about God, Arnold pauses to remind his readers that, despite this license and other crudities, the Calvinists, like the evangelists Moody and Sankey, were essentially correct in their theological intuition. In rebutting the Arminians the Calvinists not only obtained a theological triumph but proved themselves to be "in accordance with historical truth and with the real march of human affairs." In what sense was this the case? The Calvinists, Arnold points out, allow "more for the great fact of the *not ourselves* in what we do and are. The Calvinists seize . . . that great fact better than the Arminians" (CPW 6:16). That is, the Calvinists better protect the great fact of divine transcendence—although their *means* of doing so is inadequate, for it involves use of the anthropomorphic language of the "magnified and non-natural man." But that is another matter. Divine transcendence is safeguarded.

So it was also protected by the ancient Israelites. Here was a people whose mind was long and deeply engaged by the question of righteousness. Since they were so deeply attentive to conduct, what was it that could not fail to strike them?

> It is this: the very great part in righteousness which belongs, we may say, to *not ourselves*. In the first place we did not make ourselves and our nature, or conduct as the object of three-fourths of that nature; we did not provide that happiness should follow conduct, as it undeniably does; that the sense of succeeding, going right, hitting the mark, in conduct, should give satisfaction. . . .
>
> All this we did not make; and in the next place, our dealing with it at all, when it is made, is not wholly, or even nearly wholly, in our power. . . . So that we may most truly say with the author of the *Imitation*: "Left to ourselves, we sink and perish; visited, we lift up our heads and live." And we may well give ourselves, in grateful and devout self-surrender, to that by which we are thus visited (CPW 6:181-82).

The context of this passage makes the meaning indisputable: the transcendence spoken of here is a *theological* transcendence. Elsewhere Arnold, characteristically Victorian, asks: "Who first amid the loose solicitation of (sexual) sense obeyed (for create it he did not) the mighty *not ourselves* which makes for moral order, the stream of tendency which was here carrying him, and our embryo race along with him toward the fulfilment of the true law of their being?—became aware of it and obeyed it?" We smile at the illustration, but for the critic who wishes to interpret Arnold's religion as a thoroughgoing naturalism or humanism, Trilling's response is apposite: "*For create it he did not*: the phrase is not a comforting one."[13] It is not comforting for Trilling because he recognizes in Arnold's "Eternal not ourselves" an objective ground and power immanent in the world but also transcendent of it.

Robbins also acknowledges that Arnold could not stay with the pantheism of Spinoza and Goethe. "He had to go on, in his objectifying of an immanent moral principle, to a non-pantheistic statement for a controlling Power outside man. . . . Arnold has added something to the Goethe 'who once for all put the standard inside every man.' It was at this point, where Arnold was carefully putting a cosmological dome on his psychological edifice, and moving the divine upstairs, that F. H. Bradley fell on it with his logical sledge-hammer."[14]

God and the world may be correlative terms, but they are not for Arnold, as they are for pantheism, interchangeable terms. Arnold, it must be kept in mind, was writing about God and the Bible, and in the Bible the God that weighed upon the mind of the Hebrew people and engaged their awe was the "Eternal *not ourselves* that makes for righteousness." "This conception," Arnold points out, "was indubitably what lay at the bottom of that remarkable change which under Moses . . . befell the Hebrew people's mode of naming God" (CPW 6:182).

It is the personalistic mode and meaning of God-talk that has remained normative in the Judeo-Christian traditions. But it is not, Arnold reminds us, the only sense or use of language about God. "The *not ourselves*, which is in us and in the world around us, has almost everywhere, as far as we can see, struck the minds of men as they awoke to consciousness, and has inspired them with awe." And so we know of what "differences of operation men's dealing with this power has in different places and times shown itself capable." In fact, Arnold suggests, "our very word *God* is, perhaps, a reminiscence of these times, when men invoked 'The Brilliant on high,' *sublime hoc candens quod invocant omnes Joven*, as the power representing to them that which transcended the limits of their narrow selves, and by which they lived and moved and had their being" (CPW 6:182).

While conduct may be for us three-fourths of life and God is for us the "Eternal not ourselves that makes for righteousness," God is also the Eternal power not ourselves "by which all things seek to fulfil the law of their being." If Arnold were writing a history of religions and not an essay on the Bible, he might well have traced out the multifarious ways in which men have represented the power which to them transcends "the limits of their narrow selves, and by which they lived and moved and had their being."

Arnold had learned from Newman and Keble, as well as from his own literary experience, that our ideas and our language are but pale expressions of those spiritual truths which they feebly attempt to approximate. And especially is this true of our conceptions and representations of God. "It would be strange indeed," wrote Newman, "if any doctrine concerning God's infinite and eternal Nature were not mysterious."[15] Arnold, too, felt this and wished to protect the awe and wonder, the sense of the holy or *mysterium tremendum* which he found in the Hebrew scriptures, expressed most profoundly in his beloved Isaiah, and which he sensed in Catholic worship. It was, he wrote, because the Hebrew "had not talent for abstruse reasoning to lead him astray" that Israel "kept a sense of propriety, a reserve, a sense of the inadequacy of language in conveying man's ideas of God," of "that vast object of consciousness, which he could not fully grasp."

> How little we know of it besides, how impenetrable is the course of its ways with us, how we are baffled in our attempts to name and describe it, how, when we personify it . . . we presently find it not to be a person as man conceives of person, nor moral as man conceives of moral. . . . Say what we can about God, say our best, we have yet, Israel knew, to add instantly: "Lo, these are *fringes* of his ways; *but how little a portion is heard of him*" (CPW 6:188).

This is the language of reserve, not the language of a man evacuating God of all positive attributes or his aseity. On the contrary, it expresses Arnold's often-repeated insistence on God's holiness and hiddenness. "Though he was often taxed with having done so," writes Nathan Scott,

> Arnold was by no means proposing, in the manner of Feuerbach, to convert "theology" without remainder into "anthropology." Indeed, the most basic reason for his impatience with

traditional theism was that its doctrine of the *ens realissimum*, of the *deus faber*, did, as he felt, inevitably promote a kind of anthropomorphism that, at the level of theos, has the effect of nullifying what is radically transcendent . . . so that we end up talking about "the Eternal not ourselves" as if it were "a man in the next street."[16]

If the evidence points to Arnold's safeguarding the transcendence of God, there remains the further question, fundamental to a Christian theism: Does Arnold conceive of God as personal? James Martineau asked if a man could pray to an abstraction, a stream of tendency, and implore, "O thou Eternal not ourselves that makes for righteousness, if it be possible, let this cup pass from me."[17] Other contemporary critics, such as R. H. Hutton[18] and J. Llewelyn Davies,[19] were equally sever with Arnold because of what they considered his obsessive strictures against speaking of God in personal terms. The conviction that Arnold did not believe in a personal God persists today.[20] The judgment is, I believe, mistaken—despite the undeniable fact that Arnold persistently refused to use language of personal agency in speaking of God's intrinsic nature. This requires explanation.

In *Literature and Dogma*, Arnold acknowledged that the Bible artlessly personifies God and that this is perfectly correct, for Israel "was strongly moved" by its encounter with the Eternal and Israel "was an orator and poet." Indeed, "in poetry and eloquence man *may and must* follow this tendency, but in science it often leads him astray" (CPW 6:184; italics added). Israel spoke of God as "the high and lofty One that inhabiteth eternity, whose name is holy," which "is far more proper and felicitous language than 'the moral and intelligent Governor of the universe,' just because it far less attempts to be precise, but keeps to the language of poetry" (CPW 6:187). The point here to be distinguished, and on which Arnold insisted, is simply that "Israel did not scientifically predicate *personality* of God" (CPW 6:184). If it had done so, Israel and the continuators of its faith would have been forced to resort to demonstration—to the kind of tortured arguments resorted to by Butler and Paley, whose philosophical limitations by now had long been exposed and the force of whose arguments, it was generally conceded, had been enfeebled by the likes of Hume and Kant.

Butler and Paley and the whole tradition of natural theology had assumed that nature necessarily implied a moral and intelligent—i.e., a *personal*—mind and agent. "It necessarily implies," writes Arnold, "an intelligent designer with a will and character, a ruler all-wise and all-powerful." But "the proposition that this world, as we see it, necessarily implies an intelligent designer with a will and a character, a quasi-human agent and governor, cannot, I think, but be felt, by anyone who is brought fairly face to face with it and has to rest everything upon it, not to be self-demonstrating, nay, to be utterly impalpable" (CPW 8:52). Arnold was convinced that the demonstrations of natural theology had been ex-ploded, and in this he has been fully vindicated by the dominant opinion among philosophical theologians of the past half-century.

Arnold acknowledged that "nothing would be easier for us than by availing ourselves of the ambiguity natural to the use of the term God," to use anthropomorphic language "as might satisfy some of our critics." But this would have been "clean contrary" to the design of *Literature and Dogma*, which was "to recommend the Bible and its religion by showing that they rest on something which can be verified." If our assertions about God are to be verified, we must use care in our choice of language; we must know when we are using language scientifically and when we are resorting to the language of poetry and feeling. When Llewelyn Davies inquires, "If Israel might with propriety call God 'the high and holy one that inhabi-teth eternity,' why may not the Bishop of Gloucester with propriety talk of 'the blessed truth that the God of the universe is a person?'" The answer is: the Bishop of Gloucester uses his assertion as scientific statement, and "it is false science because it assumes what it cannot verify" (CPW 7:156).

Arnold's critics, however, have not been satisfied to let the matter rest here. Beyond Arnold's rightful insistence on care in the use and claims we make for theological language, questions remain concerning his no-tion of what kind of assertions can and cannot be verified and whether in fact—assuming proper qualifiers—God should be understood and spo-ken of in terms of personal agency. Arnold denied that the assertion "God is a person" can be verified, and he is obviously right if he is implying what empiricists call a strong sense of demonstration. But elsewhere Arnold does assume that he can legitimately apply a "weak" or mitigated form of empirical (i.e., experiential) verification to a score of his own theological assertions. This is to say, there remains an ambiguity in Arnold's use of the terms "verification" and "scientific" that allows him to apply standards of verification to certain types of theological assertions which he does not appear in practice to apply to others. This is strikingly evident in his handling of personalistic God-talk.

An early critic, Henry Dunn, pointed out this ambiguity regarding the verification of personalistic language. It is only under human conditions,

Dunn stated, that we know what is meant by "the Eternal making for righteousness." We use human analogies—the paradigm analogy being Christ as the meeting point of the divine and the human. And yet Arnold scolds Dunn and insists that he "must not talk thus because the relation of God to man, so understood, is not *verifiable*." Dunn replied: "Quite as verifiable, I think, as the statement 'the enduring power around us makes for righteousness,' that 'Jesus is the offspring of that power,' that 'the attempt to reach righteousness by any way except that of Jesus is a mistake.' If these things can be verified by experience—[if] they can *prove themselves*—so can many other things relating to God."[21]

Arnold was chided for not recognizing that when he spoke of God as making for righteousness, the language implied consciousness and will, what Albert Réville spoke of as "Spirit—that is to say, not merely influence, but life, consciousness, and love." Réville lectured Arnold that "man no longer worships powers of which he has discovered the nature to be impersonal" (CPW 7:160). A writer in the *Edinburgh Review* reminded Arnold that all existing entities must be either persons or things. We know that persons are superior to things. Would Arnold have us worship a thing? (CPW 7:160). Arnold's reply is straightforward: "We assure M. Réville that *we do not profess to have discovered the nature of God to be impersonal, nor do we deny to God conscious intelligence*. We assure the Edinburgh Reviewer that *we do not assert God to be a thing*. All we say is that men do not know enough about the Eternal not ourselves that makes for righteousness to warrant their pronouncing this either a person or a thing (CPW 7:160; italics added).

Arnold's reluctance was well-founded, for, as Max Müller was then exhaustively demonstrating, men easily and naturally attribute operations that engage their notice to authors who live and think like themselves.[22] Adopting Max Müller's nature myth theory, Arnold points out that "we make persons out of sun, wind, love, envy, war, fortune. . . . But this, we know, is figure and personification. Being ourselves alive and thinking, and having sex, we naturally invest things with these our attributes, and imagine all action and operation to proceed as our own proceeds" (CPW 7:162). Arnold acknowledges, however, that "this is a tendency which in common speech and in poetry, where we do not profess to speak exactly, we cannot help following." Furthermore, he adds, it is a tendency "which we follow *lawfully*. In the language of common speech and of poetry, we speak of the Eternal not ourselves that makes for righteousness as if he were a person who thinks and loves. *Naturally we speak of him so, and there is not objection at all in our doing so*" (CPW 7:162; italics added).

In the terms of contemporary linguistic analysis, Arnold is saying that it is a mistake to use "person" univocally, or scientifically when referring to God, for one cannot, as Paul Van Buren reminds us, "go looking for 'God' or for his evidences, just as it would be wrong . . . to look for a mind with a powerful microscope or X-ray machine." In each instance, "the evidence that counts lies in the circumstances in which the word is used."[23] Anthropomorphic God-talk used in the language of common speech and of poetry will not demand the same logical standards of coherence employed in literal, scientific speech.

The evidence is abundantly clear that Arnold did not conceive of God as *a* person, nor did he think of God as less than personal—"nor do we," he assured M. Réville, "deny to God conscious intelligence." God is not a *thing*, Arnold assured the Edinburgh Reviewer. Arnold's position here is perhaps best represented by the terms used by Paul Tillich, who speaks of God as "the ground of everything personal." Tillich points out that "since personality (*persona, prosopon*) includes individuality, the question arises in what sense God can be called an individual." Tillich's solution to this difficulty is to insist that the phrase "personal God" does not mean that God is *a* person. It means, rather, "that God is the ground of everything personal and that he carries within himself the ontological power [Arnold's "stream of tendency"] of personality. He is not a person, but he is not less than personal."[24]

It is clear that Arnold considered it natural and appropriate to speak of God *religiously* in the language of personal relations. However, he wisely resists any tendency toward a univocal use of personal language about God. Here he was willing to err in the direction of agnosticism. "He who pronounces that God must be a person or a thing, and that God must be a person because persons are superior to things," simply doesn't realize how anthropomorphic he is! Such a person "talks as idly as one who should insist upon it that the law of gravitation must be either a person or a thing." But, again, Arnold's wit breaks through his annoyance and he asks: "Because it is a law, is it to be pronounced a thing and not a person and therefore inferior to persons? and are we quite sure that a bad critic, suppose, is superior to the law of gravitation?" (CPW 7:195). To insist on using words in too literal and univocal a sense is to attempt to know and to do what we lack the means of knowing and doing. Personality, first of all, entails the idea of individuality—to be individuated as a particular member of a species, a subdivision of a genus. But, as all philosophical theologians insist, God being incorporeal is not a member of a genus or species.

Neither were the dangers of anthropomorphism lost on the Jewish nation, as its prohibition against graven images testifies. Furthermore, the term "person" (*persona*) was used of God in the Christian church for the first time during the Trinitarian controversies and then only in reference to the Trinity of persons in the one Divine Nature. Classical, orthodox Christianity did not speak of God as *a* person, as C. C. J. Webb has shown:

> It is so often taken for granted nowadays that the Personality of God is a principal tenet of Christianity that it is not without surprise that we find the expression not only entirely absent from the historical creeds and confessions of the Christian Church, but even, until quite modern times, in the estimation of all but the minority of Christians who reject the doctrine of the Trinity, regarded as unorthodox. Nevertheless, it is beyond question that historically it was in connexion with the doctrine of the Trinity that the words "person" and "personality" came to be used of the Divine Being; and that God was first described as "a person" by certain [Socinian] theologians of the sixteenth century.[25]

Arnold was on solid ground in resisting the demands of the Bishop of Gloucester that he insist upon "the blessed truth that the God of the universe is a person." But he was less wise in failing to recognize the significance of and to bring out more fully the crucial fact that Christians could rightfully ascribe to God attributes which it only made sense to speak of as belonging to personal agents. Arnold's fear of anthropomorphism, which he shared with a generation of sensitive late Victorian agnostics, is responsible for this theological blind side. Nevertheless, while he wished to protect the otherness and transcendence of God, it is also evident that he insisted on the providential immanence of God in human history. Arnold's belief in divine providence entailed belief in a transcendent purpose and will, i.e., personal agency.

Gordon Kaufman has shown how both theistic concerns can be protected only by the employment of models drawn from interpersonal experience.

> The personalistic image . . . interprets man's relationship to that which ultimately limits him as being like his relationship to the finite selves with which he interacts. Such selves always transcend in their subjectivity and freedom what is directly accessible to one in his experience. . . . This is the most powerful experience we have of *transcendence of the given* on the

finite level, the awareness of genuine activity and reality *beyond* and *behind* what is directly open to our view. . . . Likewise, on this model God cannot be identified with what is accessible within our experience. . . . Indeed, only when it is grasped and interpreted in concrete personalistic terms does the Limit become understood as the expression of a being transcending our world, that is, an active God. Thus, the constitutive *experience* underlying the word "God" is that of limitation; the constitutive *image* which gives the term its peculiar transcendent reference is personalistic. These fused into one concretely religious apprehension of our finitude provide us with the root referent for the word.[26]

Arnold did not possess either the interest or the conceptual bent to explore the question of divine transcendence and immanence in this manner, but his position is not substantially different from Kaufman's. In any event, Arnold believed in both God's transcendence and God's personal agency.

"THE METHOD AND SECRET OF JESUS": METANOIA AND NECROSIS

Toward the end of his life, Arnold discovered a spiritual kinship with Leo Tolstoi. The attraction was mutual, for Tolstoi was greatly pleased with *Literature and Dogma*. The kinship had to do in part with their views on art and on metaphysics but, more especially, with their common devotion to the method and secret of Jesus. In his essay on Tolstoi, Arnold remarks that for both men the true life is found in "union with God to which we aspire" and that "we reach it through union with Jesus and by adopting his life" (CPW 11:297). Arnold's theology was distinctly Christian in that for him knowledge of and union with God was uniquely mediated through Jesus—his person, teaching, and work. Arnold agreed with Tolstoi that "questions over which the churches spend so much labour and time—questions about the Trinity, about the godhead of Christ, about the procession of the Holy Ghost, are not vital; what is vital is the doctrine of access to the spirit through Jesus" (CPW 11:297).

Arnold recoiled, however, from Tolstoi's effort to extract from the Sermon on the Mount a stringent rule of life based on what he called the Five Commandments of Jesus. For Arnold this smacked too much of the letter of the law, something exterior and not of the spirit, not something inward and feeling. "Christianity," he insisted, "cannot be packed into any set of commandments." Christianity is a *source*, and "no one supply of water and refreshment that comes from it can be called the sum of Christianity." The reason, Arnold had found, lies in the character of Jesus and the nature of his teaching, for "not less important than the teachings given by Jesus is the temper of their giver"—the temper of *epieikeia* (CPW 11:302).

It was Jesus whom Arnold sees as restoring the great intuition of Israel that there is an Eternal not ourselves that makes for righteousness and that to righteousness belongs happiness. But Jesus did so by means of his wonderful temper, urging greater inwardness and spontaneity of feeling, "a life-giving change in the inner man" in place of legalism. To Arnold, Christ's temper is best conveyed by the Greek word *epieikeia*, which the Bible translates as "gentleness" and which Arnold calls "sweet reasonableness." It means at once that which is convincing and prepossessing, "that which has an air of consummate truth and likelihood, and which, by virtue of having this air, is prepossessing" (CPW 8:28). Christ "put things in such a way that his hearer was led to take each rule or fact of conduct by its inward side, its effect on the heart and character. . . . The meaning of what had been mere matter of blind rule flashed upon him" (CPW 6:219).

Arnold believed that the word *epieikeia* best characterizes Christianity as a religion as well, for "true Christianity wins, . . . not by going through a long debate with a person, . . . and making him confess that, whether he feels disposed to yield or no . . . he ought to yield. No, but it puts something which tends to transform him and his practice, it puts this particular thing in such a way before a man that he feels disposed and eager to lay hold of it" (CPW 8:28).

Arnold hit upon that attraction and power in Jesus' person which indeed gave to his words "an air of consummate truth," what we today would call *charisma*. But Arnold's skill in inventing striking phrases failed him miserably in this instance, for "sweet reasonableness" does not begin to convey that air of truth and that energizing power which he perceived in Christ's *epieikeia*. Critics have winced at his talk of Jesus' sweet reasonableness and understandably have reacted with irritated derision. What Arnold attempted to convey about Jesus' unique attraction by this misbegotten phrase was, nevertheless, important and insightful.

According to Arnold, Jesus restored the great biblical intuition about God and man by transforming the idea of righteousness through the conjunction of what he called Jesus' *method* of inwardness and his *secret* of self-renunciation. It was, in fact, the method and secret which "produced the total impression of Christ's *epieikeia*" and which the disciples tried to describe in such words as "full of grace and truth." Between Israel and Christ there was no question as to what to aim at; for both it was the commandments of God. But Jesus introduced a method "by which to determine on what the keeping of the real commandments of God depended." That method was *inwardness*, the searching of conscience, to which belongs its corollary, the Greek word *metanoia*, change of heart—"the setting up an immense *new inward movement* for obtaining one's rule of life: *A change of the inner man*" (CPW 6:288-89). For the disciples, as for those who followed them, such an inner searching and change of heart were revolutionary.

Jesus' method of inwardness necessarily called for a rule of action, and this is what Arnold called Jesus' *secret*. It is what St. Paul discovered in Christ and what became the foundation of his teaching. He called it the word of the cross, or *necrosis*, "dying." The rule of action which Paul gave was: "Always bearing about in the body the *dying* of Jesus, that the life also of Jesus may be made manifest in our body" (II Corinthians 4:10; CPW 6:201). Paul's words, of course, refer to those paradoxical and exacting words of Jesus: "He that will save his life shall lose it; he that will lose his life will save it," and, "Whosoever will come after me, let him renounce himself, and take up his cross daily, and follow me" (Luke 9:24, 23).

To Arnold, the value of Jesus' secret is that it is surprisingly true. Men and women have found it to be true in their experience. In renouncement *is* life. And we have the testimony not only of our own experience but of the sages from Plato to Goethe as well. "Die and come to life!" says Goethe; "for so long as this is not accomplished thou art but a troubled guest upon an earth of gloom" (CPW 6:295). Goethe, of course, borrowed this from Jesus, and it was Jesus who, above all others, discovered that in dying lies life, peace, joy:

> Never certainly was the joy, which in self-renouncement underlies the pain so brought out as when Jesus boldly called the suppression of our first impulses and current thoughts: *life, real life, eternal life*. So that Jesus not only *saw* this great necessary truth . . . he saw it so *thoroughly*, that he saw through the suffering at its surface to the joy at its centre, filled it with promise and hope, and made it infinitely attractive (CPW 6:296).

While others have seen that self-renouncement was necessary, "Jesus, above everyone, saw that it was *peace, joy, life*" (CPW 6:296). The truth of *necrosis* as a rule of life will, Jesus taught, "be found to commend itself by *happiness*, to prove itself by happiness" (CPW 6:298).

Arnold concludes his reflections on Jesus' intuition with these words: "This total stamp of 'grace and truth,' this exquisite conjunction and balance, in an element of mildness, of a method of inwardness perfectly handled and a self-renunciation perfectly kept, *was found in Jesus alone*" (CPW 6:300; italics added). It is evident that Arnold perceives Jesus as in some sense unique, as "above everyone," as archetypal, the inimitable revelation or mediation of the Eternal not ourselves that makes for righteousness.

If Arnold so perceives Jesus, the question remains: How, then, does he see Jesus' relation to God? Does he understand it in the terms of the definition of the Council of Chalcedon (A.D. 451)—i.e., in terms of the two distinct natures, divine and human, united in one person? Does he conceive of the relationship in the traditional terms of the doctrine of the incarnation? The answer is that he does not. Arnold rejected what he called the miracle of the incarnation. However, at the same time he consistently maintained that Jesus was sent from God and uniquely revealed the will and way of God for man. Arnold's understanding of the person of Christ tends to be, to use the technical term, adoptionist, and in this he has much in common with numerous Modernist theologians who, while rejecting metaphysical and supernatural or substantive conceptions of the incarnation, are nevertheless insistent on retaining belief in Jesus' unique revelatory vocation and even on using the incarnational imagery, since it may actually help to express and to protect this truth.

The *Guardian* had reminded Arnold that the miracle of the incarnation is "*the* fundamental truth" for Christians. On the contrary, Arnold responded, "In insisting on 'the miracle of the Incarnation,' the *Guardian* insists on just that side of Christianity which is perishing" (CPW 6:146). Again, in Arnold's estimation, the reason it is perishing is that doctrines such as the two natures in Christ or Christ as the divine Logos, the second person of the Trinity, are creedal formulations, abstract concepts, which more and more lack experiential reality and truth. The formularies strive for scientific exactitude, but "the very terms of which these propositions are composed, are such as science is unable to handle. But that the Jesus of the Bible follows the universal moral order and the will of God, without being let and hindered as we are by the motions of private passion and by self-will, this is evident to whoever can read the Bible with open eyes" (CPW 6:42).*

Arnold consistently held that the Jesus depicted in the New Testament is, "in the jargon of modern philosophy, an *absolute*," by which he meant that Jesus transcends mankind: "We cannot explain him, cannot get behind him and above him, cannot command him" (CPW 6:145). Yet Jesus' uniqueness is not to be understood in terms of a substantive or metaphysical divine nature—"Veiled in flesh the Godhead see," as Wesley's hymn speaks of the incarnation. No, Christ's personal uniqueness is seen not in terms of a static nature but through his life and work; dynamically and relationally in the vocation that he carries through even unto death on the cross. Arnold understands Christ's divinity as he believes did St. Paul—i.e., in Christ's *obedience*, in his perfect sinlessness. "For us, who approach Christianity through a scholastic theology, it is Christ's divinity which establishes his being without sin. For Paul, who approached Christianity through his personal experience, it was Jesus Christ's being without sin which established his divinity. . . . He [Jesus] was led by the spirit of God; he was dead to sin, he lived to God; and in this life to God he persevered even to the cruel bodily death of the cross" (CPW 6:40).

Arnold's position is best understood in the nineteenth-century tradition of liberal Protestant christology, as exemplified in Schleiermacher and Ritschl. For both theologians, to know Christ's person is to know his personal vocation, his work, or, as Luther said, to know his benefits. Ritschl taught that the attribute of divinity in Christ "is to be found in the service He renders, the benefit He bestows, the saving work He accomplishes."[27] Schleiermacher similarly held that Christ is known only in his effect upon us, by the impress of his unique God-consciousness, which was perfectly realized in that it gained faultless control over his entire person. In this sense we can properly speak of Jesus' perfection and sinlessness. Schleiermacher envisioned Jesus Christ as the full historical realization of archetypal humanity; Christ embodies concretely the new race of men and thus becomes for mankind the exemplar of God's will, the medium for the communication of God's redemptive power. For Schleiermacher, Jesus is exemplar (*Vorbildlichkeit*) in that he stands in a continuum with the rest of

---

* Arnold, like most theologians of his time (and indeed since), takes an uncritical view of what historical research can do to establish or justify the New Testament picture of Jesus' moral perfection or uniqueness. Notions of sinlessness, uniqueness, etc., are obviously theological judgments drawn from necessarily limited historical data enshrined in traditions whose authors had other than historical purposes in mind. For a trenchant discussion of these matters, see Dennis Nineham, *The Use and Abuse of the Bible* (London, 1976).

the human race, and yet Jesus is not simply a moral example to be followed. He is the *unique medium*; what Arnold and Schleiermacher (*Urbild-lichkeit*) both call the ideal image or ideality of Jesus Christ. Implied in this *Urbild* is the fact that man does not posit his own exemplar. What is at work here is divine prevenience. Therefore, it is proper to speak of Christ not only as exemplar but also as redeemer in that he gives a new impetus and power to man "in the flesh."[28] Arnold's depiction of Christ as the unique, divinely prevenient ideal image and exemplar of God's redemptive power is strikingly similar to Schleiermacher's doctrine, and it is highly likely that here Arnold is, in part at least, dependent on Schleiermacher, whose work he knew.*

Jesus' words as reported in the Johannine Gospel, "He who has seen me has seen the Father" (John 14:9), are for Arnold true words, since in Jesus, as in no one else, we see the eternal word of righteousness spoken and enacted. In the New Testament, it must be remembered, Jesus never claims to *be* God—rather, to reveal "him who sent me." Jesus thus reveals God by being transparent to the divine word and will.

Arnold believed that the favorite way of speaking of Jesus' uniqueness in the New Testament is through the expressions "sent from God"; "the Father hath sent me"; "God hath sent me." This "identified Jesus and his salvation with the Messiah," and "for his disciples therefore and for Christendom after them, Jesus was and is the Messiah or Christ." Arnold had no "difficulty in supposing [Jesus] to have applied to himself each and all of the terms which the Jews . . . used to describe the Messiah,—*Messiah* or *Christ*, God's *Chosen* or *Beloved* or *Consecrated* or *Glorified One*, the *Son of God*, the *Son of Man*; because his concern . . . was with his countrymen's idea of salvation, not with their terms for designating the bringer of it" (CPW 6:308).

The christological terms and titles used in the New Testament and by Jesus himself are many and varied, serving different purposes in varying contexts. However, Arnold concludes that in using such titles as Son of God, Jesus "did not at all mean that the Messiah was a son of God *merely in the sense in which any great man might be so called*, but he meant that these questions of theosophy were useless for his hearers. . . . All that they were concerned with was that *he* was the Messiah they expected sent to them with salvation from God" (CPW 6:309; italics added).

---

* Thomas Arnold and the Noetics were deeply influenced by Schleiermacher and passed this on to Matthew. See CPW 6:268, 456 and 7:293, 480.

The terms used to describe Jesus as the Messiah—i.e., as sent from God—were, moreover, active, dynamic, relational terms which heightened and reshaped people's awareness of God's demand, his power, and his saving promise. "How far," Arnold asks, has "the pseudo-scientific language of our creeds, about *persons*, and *substance*, and *godhead*, and *co-equal*, and *co-eternal*, and *created*, and *begotten* and *proceeding* . . . at all to do with what Jesus said or meant?" (CPW 6:311). What Jesus uniquely revealed as the one sent from God was the very word of the Eternal not ourselves that makes for righteousness, namely, that "he that will save his life shall lose it" and that in renouncement, in self-giving, is life, joy, peace. Arnold felt that language and concepts used in the ancient creedal formularies failed to convey this fundamental truth of Christianity. Furthermore, these concepts attempt to speak in scientific terms about the intrinsic nature of God and his relation to Jesus, terms which in modern times increasingly appear inauthentic, increasingly lack credibility.

Maurice Wiles, Regius Professor of Divinity in Oxford and a noted patristics scholar, suggests, in words reminiscent of Arnold, that we have reached a point in our knowledge of the sources at which "we may need to be more ready to rest content with talk about that which we receive through Jesus Christ and to be more reticent in our speech about his own inherent nature."[29] What the believer receives through Jesus Christ, Wiles points out, includes belief in the reality of God, that God has a purpose for the world, and that he elicits a response in faith and love:

> The central figure within history who focuses for us the recognition and the realization of these things is Jesus Christ. In Christian history all this has undoubtedly been held together and vividly expressed by the doctrine of the unique incarnation of God in Jesus Christ. I have been arguing that that particular doctrine is not required for the whole pattern of belief to be true, or indeed for our having good grounds for believing it to be true.[30]

This is to say, Arnold's rejection of the *terms* in which the doctrine of the incarnation has been traditionally expressed does not entail rejection of what is uniquely revealed of God through Christ. For as Wiles concludes, "there will be continuity of religious reality in the conviction that it is supremely through Jesus that the character of these purposes of God and the possibility of this experience of grace have been grasped and made effective in the world."[31] This, expressed in similar terms, is exactly Arnold's conviction.

Any consideration of Arnold's view of Jesus Christ touches not only on the question of Christ's person but also on his work. For Christianity is committed to the belief that Jesus is essentially and uniquely involved in what is called God's work of atonement, redemption, or reconciliation. This doctrine is inseparably connected with other beliefs about man's estrangement and sin and God's prevenient action or grace. Arnold's views of human sin, grace, and Christ's work are often dismissed as the typical palliatives of a nineteenth-century religious humanist who has experienced neither the horror of sin not the glory of grace, and who holds up the moral example of Jesus as a thoroughly realizable human possibility. T. S. Eliot, for example, tells us that "the vision of the horror and the glory was denied to Arnold,"[32] and Robert Shafer reminds us that, contrary to Arnold, "Christians, of course, have always . . . asserted that no efforts of our own can be sufficient to overcome our lower selves, inherently sinful as we are."[33] What does Arnold believe about sin and grace? Is his understanding of the work of Christ a thoroughly subjective theory of moral influence? This facet of Arnold's religious doctrine also requires a more careful scrutiny than it has yet received.

On 3 March 1865 Arnold wrote to his mother, "No one has a stronger and more abiding sense than I have of the 'daemonic' element—as Goethe called it—which underlies and encompasses our life" (L 1:249). Like Mozart's music, Arnold's poetry and essays reveal a steady awareness of the empty, mean, and tragic side of existence poised on the edge of all the affirmations. Beneath the debonair and often flippant exterior was a man who saw the hard and horrific side of English life. If Arnold encountered less sensational forms of malevolence than did Eliot's generation, he knew well the banal but no less haunting forms of evil. "It is," Trilling says, "truly life that Arnold sees—a life in which Wragg, poor thing, had her existence in a ditch, a life which included the horrors of St. Helens and Spitalfields, the hideous schools, the hymns of the chapel and the lucubrations of the episcopal study, the lowness and meanness of the forms the human spirit can take."[34]

Arnold knew the reality of human moral infirmity, even viciousness. He was convinced, however, that the Genesis story of the origin of sin and the fall of Adam and the New Testament and patristic accounts of Christ's cosmic conflict with the devil and the powers of sin and death were myths no longer serviceable. They are now, he felt, an embarrassment, and we must do without them. Here Arnold's critical tact fails him. His imagination could not, apparently, see the same rich meanings conveyed in these myths that he was able to perceive, for example, in the birth stories and the eschatological prophecies. Like Schleiermacher, Arnold looks not to Adam but to Christ, the Second Adam, as the archetype of humanity who convicts men of their sin or disordered wills—fearful, perhaps, that notions of Adamic original sin preclude genuine moral freedom and responsibility. In any case, moral sin is real for Arnold.

In *Culture and Anarchy* Arnold points out that the "wonderful spirit" of Israel and of Hebraism is its sense of sin, its preoccupation "with an awful sense of the impossibility of being at ease in Zion." "It is all very well," he reminds sanguine optimists, "to talk of getting rid of one's ignorance, of seeing things in their reality . . . but how is this to be done when there is something which thwarts and spoils all our efforts? This something is *sin*; and the space which sin fills in Hebraism . . . is indeed prodigious" (CPW 5:168).

Arnold compares the Hellenic conception of human nature—thinking clearly, seeing things in their essence—with Hebraism, which "speaks of becoming conscious of sin, awakening to a sense of sin," and he concludes that "it was the Hellenic conception of human nature which was unsound" (CPW 5:168-69). It is clear from the context that Arnold regards the Hellenic view as false in its exaggeration of human perfection, just as in Puritanism the Hebraic awakening to sin becomes a "sterile fact, a fact on which it is possible to dwell too long." He insists, however, that it is too often the case that we do not have a strong enough sense of sin's reality. He cites with entire approval St. Paul's great insights in this regard:

> The motions of what Paul calls "the law in our members" are indeed a hydra-brood; when we are working against one fault, a dozen others crop up without our expecting it; and this it is which drives the man who deals seriously with himself to difficulty, nay to despair. . . . Paul knew, too, that nothing outward, no satisfaction of all the requirements men may make of us, no privileges of any sort, can give peace of conscience. . . . He knew, also, that the law of the moral order stretches beyond us and our private conscience. . . . Therefore though I may know nothing against myself, yet this is not enough, I may still not be just (CPW 6:36).

Evidence such as this supports the conclusion that Arnold recognized the reality of sin, it pervasiveness and its intractability. The doubt remains, however, because one also encounters passages which appear thoroughly Pelagian, which imply that by one's own efforts, and apart from grace, one can take the necessary steps to overcome "the law in our members."

Arnold remarks, for instance, that "to a world stricken with moral ener-vation, Christianity offered its spectacle of an inspired self-sacrifice . . . conformity to the image of a self-sacrificing example" (CPW 5:169). In passages such as this, Arnold can be read as simply proposing Jesus as a moral example; divine grace does not appear to be required or presup-posed. These instances perhaps explain why a sympathetic critic of Ar-nold's religious thought can interpret his view of sin and grace as a purely human, psychological process. "To Arnold the state of grace is rather that regenerate moral insight and the practice (conduct) which bring man into harmony with the eternal moral law. Faith is simply a psychological pro-cess (most particularly the love men feel for Jesus, the great exemplar of moral goodness) which invests the otherwise rather barren stoicism of renunciation with an emotion of joy."[35]

Such an interpretation does not sufficiently take into account the scores of passages in *Literature and Dogma* where Arnold speaks of the prevenient action of God. It is implied, of course, in all that he says about the Eternal not ourselves. He speaks of the Hebrew intuition of God as the power by which we have been "upholden ever since we were born" and whose "mercy is over all his works." "He is the power that 'saves both man and beast, gives them drink of his pleasures as out of the river,' and 'with whom is the well of life.'" It is this same prevenience of divine action or grace that Arnold sees as playing a central role in the thought of St. Paul. It is, the "element in which we live and move and have our being, which stretches around and beyond the strictly moral element in us." It is, "by this element we are receptive and influenced, not originative and influencing. . . . So we get the thought of an impulsion outside ourselves which is at once awful and beneficent" (CPW 6:37). "We have seen," Arnold concludes, "how strong was Paul's consciousness of that power, *not ourselves*. . . . The sense of life, peace, and joy which comes through identification with Christ, brings with it a deep and grateful consciousness that this sense is none of our own getting and making. *No, it is grace, it is the free gift of God*" (CPW 6:58-59; italics added).

Arnold assents to St. Pauls's teaching that as moral agents, "for whom exist . . . effort and failure, vice and virtue, we are impotent and lost and that we are saved through that in us which is passive and involuntary; . . . it is by an *influence*, and the emotion from it, that we are saved" (CPW 6:59). This influence Arnold speaks of earlier as "the elemental powers of sympathy and emotion in us, a power which extends beyond the limits of our own will and conscious activity" (CPW 6:47). This is the prevenient power of grace that in us is morally originative and influencing.

Arnold's understanding of the work of Christ is not at all singular; it stands in a long tradition that runs from Abelard and Thomas à Kempis through Schleiermacher and the Anglican Modernist Hastings Rashdall. What these teachers have in common is the perception of the profound moral truth that love begets love; that in yielding to the attraction of the gift of grace, as it is given and revealed in its supreme manifestation in Christ's *necrosis*, men respond to this gift in lives of self-sacrifice and service. Abelard expressed it thus: "His Son took our nature, and in it took upon Himself to instruct us alike by word and example even unto death and so bound us to Himself by law; so that kindled by so great a benefit of divine grace, charity should not be afraid to endure anything for his sake."[36] Arnold uses the Abelardian analogy of love in speaking of the prevenient action of grace:

> Every one knows how being in love changes for the time a man's spiritual atmosphere, and makes animation and buoyancy where before there was flatness and dullness. . . . And not only does it change the atmosphere of our spirits . . . but it also sensibly and powerfully increases our faculties of action. . . . This, I say, we learn from the analogy of the most everyday experience;—that a powerful attachment will give a man spirits and confidence which he could by no means call up or command of himself (CPW 6:38-39).

For Arnold the crucial text is I John 4:19, "We love, because he first loved us." On this passage he comments: "As we did not make the law of righteousness, so we did not, the writer means, make 'the fulfilling of the law,' which is love. It arises in us from the way the 'not ourselves' affects us" (CPW 6:336). Arnold unquestionably believed in and saw the need of the prevenient action and grace of God, as he often repeated: "We may most truly say, with the author of the *Imitation*: 'Left to ourselves, we sink and perish; visited, we lift up our heads and live'" (CPW 6:181).

There are, to be sure, conceptions of Christ's work in the Aberlardian tradition that historians of dogma call subjective, by which they mean that the love and grace of God is merely exhibited in Christ, to be morally appropriated; the focus of attention is shifted to the human response. This is not Arnold's view. Arnold believes that Christ's sacrifice, as St. Paul represents it, involves the fact

> that by it Jesus died to the law of selfish impulse, parted with what to men in general is most precious and near. Paul's second notion is, that whereas Jesus suffered in doing this, his

suffering was not *his* need, but ours; not for *his* good, but for ours. In the first aspect, Jesus is the martyrion—the testimony in his life and in his death, to righteousness, to the power and goodness of God. In the second aspect he is the *antilytron* or ransom. But, in either aspect, Jesus Christ's solemn and dolorous condemnation of sin does actually loosen sin's hold and attraction upon us who regard him—makes it easier for us to understand and love goodness, to rise above self, to appropriate Christ, to die to sin (CPW 6:67).

Arnold emphasizes the fact that Christ's expiation and condemnation of sin is *prevenient.* It is, he says, "made irrespectively of our power or inclination to sympathize with it and appreciate it." Its effect, however, is that "presently there comes a change. Grace . . . , that awful and beneficent impulsion of things within us and without us, which we can concur with, indeed, but cannot create, leads us to repentance towards God, a change in the inner man." It is only then that we "put on Christ " and "follow the eternal law of the moral order which by ourselves we could not follow" (CPW 6:67-68).

In *Literature and Dogma* Arnold gives this affecting summary of his understanding of Christ's work:

> And no grand performance or discovery of a man's own to bring him thus to joy and peace, but an attachment! the influence, of One full of grace and truth! An influence which we feel we know not how, and which subdues us we know not when; which, like the wind, breathes where it lists, passes here, and does not pass there! Once more, then, we come to that root and ground of religion, that element of awe and gratitude which fills religion with emotion, and makes it other and greater than morality—the not ourselves. . . . *No man can come to me,* as Jesus said, *except the Father which sent me draw him* (CPW 6:310-11).

Arnold's soteriology has a kinship with that of Abelard and Thomas à Kempis in their common emphasis on God's revelation in Christ as always directed to the enkindling of a moral response in the soul which transforms life. To so accentuate the demonstration of and response to divine grace in Christ is neither to deny nor to underestimate the antecedent and objective side of the divine action. It is implied and presupposed. Neither Abelard nor Schleiermacher nor Arnold is guilty of placing exclusive stress on the exemplary dimension of Christ's work. Speaking in defense of an essentially Abelardian understanding of the work of Christ, Maurice Wiles make this observation: "In the world of historical experience, the passion has done much and continues to do much; nor are there grounds for limiting its potential effectiveness in the future. . . . May it not be that what we need is precisely a combination of these two things: a demonstration of that which is eternally true about God and effectiveness as an historical phenomenon in producing an appropriate response to that truth about God?"[37] This, in short, is what Arnold is proposing in *Literature and Dogma.*

"IN HIS WILL IS OUR PEACE"

Arnold concluded his lay sermon on 29 November 1884, honoring Canon Barnett of St. Jude's, Whitechapel, by reminding his audience that they should always lay to heart the great truth of the Hebrew prophets and of Jesus, that the Prince of this world is judged. "More and more," he assured them, "it has become manifest that the Prince of this world is really judged—that the Prince of this world, which is the perpetual idol of selfishly possessing and enjoying, and the worlds fashioned under the inspiration of this idol, are judged. One world and another have gone to pieces because they are fashioned under the inspiration of this idol, and that is a consoling and edifying thought" (CPW 10:253).

This Liberal Anglican view of history was bred in Arnold's bones from childhood through youth. It became the mainspring of his moral vision. It is a common theme in his correspondence—for example, when he writes to his mother that the fall of France "is mainly due to that want of a serious conception of righteousness . . . the consequences of which so often show themselves in the world's history. . . . The fall of Greece, the fall of Rome, the fall of the brilliant Italy of the fifteenth century . . . are all examples." Nothing, he concludes, "gives more freshness and depth to one's reading of the Bible than the sense that this is so" (L 2:48).

Arnold felt that "the master-impulse" of Israel was "the great natural truth that righteousness tendeth to life." This truth is what separates man from nature ('Man must begin, know this, where Nature ends' [P, 44]). Arnold writes that "other creatures submissively follow the law of their nature; man alone has an impulse leading him to set up some other law to control the bent of his nature" (CPW 3:236).

Twenty years later he jotted in his notebook the words of Samuel Johnson: "To man is permitted the contemplation of the skies, but the practice of virtue is commanded" (NB 399). Arnold perceived "the law of righteousness" as "the very law and ground of human nature" (CPW 6:30). And he looked to the role of conscience, no less than did Newman, as the locus of the *imago Dei* and as the only reliable and persuasive way to knowledge of God. Jesus it was who plumbed the truth of conscience, the law of righteousness, through his method and his secret. Yet all too often men hear the words of the prophet, "O that thou had'st hearkened to my commandments! Then had thy peace been as a river," and think, Arnold writes to his sister Jane late in 1881, "that the 'peace as a river' is to be had without having 'hearkened to the commandment'" (L 2:195). But that is to forget Jesus' secret, to evade the word of the cross.

Stirb und werde—Die and become—from Goethe's poem "Selige Sehnsucht," was one of Arnold's treasured quotations. He cited it often in his books and recorded it several times in his notebooks. Like similar quotations from Thomas à Kempis and Bishop Wilson, it was a favorite because he associated it with *necrosis*. Arnold came early to the conviction—a conviction that was at once exacting and consoling—that man has no natural claim on life, on its rights or happiness. Christianity, he came to know through his own experience, has "nothing to do with the gospel of the rights of man, of the natural claim of every man to a certain share of enjoyment. Nothing but an infinite dying, and in that dying is life (CPW 7:145).

As Arnold studied the writings of St. Paul in the late 1860s, he found in the letters the consummate expression of the spiritual meaning of Jesus' word of the cross. That theme he came to see as "the *clef-de-voute*" of Paul's theology, and thereafter it was to dominate not only *St. Paul and Protestantism* but also Arnold's conception of the essence of Christianity. St. Paul's understanding of the appropriation of Christ's secret became Arnold's own:

> If any man be in Christ, said Paul—that is, if any man identifies himself with Christ by attachment so that he appropriates him, enters into his feelings and lives with his life,—he is a new creature; he can do and does what Christ did. First, he suffers with him. Christ throughout his life and in his death presented his body a living sacrifice to God; every self-willed impulse blindly trying to assert itself without respect of the universal order, he died to. You, says Paul, are to do the same. . . .
> If you are one with him by faith and sympathy, you can die to them also. Then, secondly, if you thus die with him, you become transformed by the renewing of your mind, and rise

> with him. The law of the spirit of life which is in Christ be-
> comes the law of your life also, and frees you of the law of sin
> and death. You rise with him to that harmonious conformity
> with the real and eternal order . . . which is life and peace and
> which grows more and more till it becomes glory. If you suffer
> with him, therefore, you shall also be glorified with him (CPW
> 6:47-48).

Arnold believed that a man must die to live and that in renouncing, in self-sacrifice, are resurrection, life, peace. He did not, of course, believe in what he called the "materialized" resurrection of Christ, in the literal empty tomb and bodily assumption, but he believed in the resurrection of Jesus as his indisputable victory and the vindication of his message and work: "He *has* risen, his cause has conquered; the course of events contin-ually attests his resurrection and victory. . . . *The prince of this world is judged*; the victory of Jesus is won and sure. Conscience and self-renouncement, the method and secret of Jesus, are set up as a leaven in the world, never-more to cease working until the world is leavened" (CPW 7:371). The crucifixion and resurrection of Christ were no pious fictions for Arnold, nor did he consider it mere sentiment to speak of dying and rising with Christ. He believed they possessed all the truth and grandeur of a natural law.

While self-denial and renouncement are spiritually essential, Arnold believed they are nevertheless only penultimate. For renouncement gives birth to resurrection, life, joy. The great natural truth of the Bible is, after all, that "righteousness tendeth to life," by which Arnold means, "to right-eousness belongs happiness." He believed that true healing and joy in-deed come to those who, freed from obsession with their ordinary or lower self, find fixity and joy in the way of the best or higher self. And the exemplar of this higher self is Jesus Christ, his method and his se-cret—conformity to which brings with it satisfaction, happiness, a sense of hitting the mark: "The breaking the sway of what is commonly called *one's self*, ceasing our concern with it and leaving it to perish is not, Jesus said, being thwarted or crossed, but *living*. And the proof of this is that it has the characters of life in the highest degree,—the sense of going right, hitting the mark, succeeding. That is, it has the characters of *happiness*" (CPW 6:293).

Here Arnold follows Aristotle in the conviction that the exercise of one's true end or being is accompanied by happiness or joy, which is the proof of its rightness. "Jesus not only saw this great necessary truth of there being, as Aristotle says, in human nature a part to rule and a part to be ruled; he saw it so *thoroughly*, that he saw through the suffering at its surface to the joy at its centre" (CPW 6:296).

This speaks to F. H. Bradley's criticism of Arnold. Bradley was greatly offended by Arnold's conviction that to righteousness belongs happiness. He reminded Arnold that "what is ordinarily called happiness does not follow virtue" and "in every-day experience that its opposite is so."[38] Arnold, of course, did not mean by happiness what is ordinarily called happiness. He meant that affection which the great religious traditions have called blessedness and which involves a sense of well-being, a new attunement of the soul, an overcoming of the world.

R. R. Niebuhr describes the religious experience of blessedness in his phenomenological analysis of the religious affections. He features those unique qualities of spiritual rejoicing which Arnold, too, refers to repeatedly. Religious joy suggests "motion, energy, power, together with directionality of this energy"; it discloses "the sense and conviction of being part of something larger . . . of sharing in the life and strength of others. It is a promise . . . of the power and freedom to be a contributor to the whole, to be a doer of deeds, an agent." Niebuhr even uses Arnoldian imagery, speaking of joy as the feeling of being a part of the river of life, "of liberation into the stream of life," "a feeling of the union of one's own power with power and energy itself" that issues in a profound sense of effectiveness and accomplishment. Niebuhr concludes that the most conspicuous feature of spiritual joy is "an inner sense of motion. Here joy directly opposes dreading with the latter's attendent sense of stagnation. Spinoza defined the affection as 'the transition of man from a lesser to a higher state of perfection.'"[39] It is this unique affection of joy which Arnold found in St. Paul and Augustine and Isaac Barrow. "This truth," writes Arnold, "cannot be gainsaid; and to reject the truth itself, because of frequent perversions of it, is a fatal error" (CPW 7:234).

Students of the phenomenology of religion point out that the form or structure common to religious anthropology is the contrast between the ordinary, empirical self or ego and the true or real spiritual self. The great religions have as their aim the sacrificing of the private self or ego to that which is absolute and enduring. The structure and pattern is found not only in preliterate religion but in classical Hinduism, Buddhism, and Confucianism, as well as in the biblical religions. Arnold recognized it as *the* sign of man's spiritual awareness, for it has to do with the awakening of conscience:

> It will generally be admitted that all experience as to con-
> duct brings us at last to the fact of the two selves . . . contend-
> ing for the mastery of man: one . . . a movement of man's
> ordinary or passing self, of sense, appetite, desire; the other, a
> movement of reflection . . . leading us to submit inclination to
> some rule, and called generally a movement of man's higher
> or enduring self. . . . The thing is described in different words
> by different nations and men relating their experience of it,
> but as to the thing itself they all agree (CPW 8:154).

The images of the buried life and the true self, central to Arnold's
poetic imagination, shift to the ordinary self and the best self in the later
elegies and in the prose writings. In Culler's analysis, Arnold associates
the ordinary self with life on the "burning plain," where the true or best
self is suppressed by egoistic craving and Romantic self-obsession. By the
1860s the best self Arnold associates with the overtly religious image of
the City of God, which, is for him the will or reign of Christ.[40] The poem
"East London" brings this out most directly where the best self sets up "a
mark of everlasting light" as its pole star; not the self that lies deep within
the ego, but a knowledge and an imitation of another, greater self (P 525).
In 1866 Arnold inscribed in his notebook Coleridge's words: "An approving conscience is the sense of harmony of the personal will of man with
that impersonal light which is in him, representative of the will of God"
(NB 40). The impersonal light became for Arnold "being conformed to
the image of Christ," to that higher or real self agreeing with the will of
God (CPW 6:331).

> "How is man advantaged," Jesus asked, if he gain the whole
> world and forfeit *himself*. . . . And by recommending, and still
> more by himself exemplifying in his own practice, by showing
> active in himself . . . the two qualities by which our ordinary
> self is indeed most essentially counteracted, *self-renouncement
> and mildness*, he made his followers feel that in these qualities
> lay the secret of their best self; that to attain them was in the
> highest degree requisite and natural, and that a man's whole
> happiness depended upon it (CPW 6:220).

To learn through experience the secret of the best self was for Arnold
to discover the natural truth of Christianity and the way to human happiness. Men persistently have deceived themselves in believing that happiness is to be found in enhancing and safeguarding the interests of the
self. But "it turns out that the only real happiness is a kind of impersonal

higher life, where the happiness of others counts with a man as essential to his own. He that loves his life does really turn out to lose it" (CPW 8:157). In the secret of the best self, Arnold envisioned the whole eschatological drama of Christianity spiritualized, its true existential meaning and import disclosed:

> Eternal life? Yes, the life in the higher and undying self of man. Judgment? Yes, the trying, in conscience, of the claims and instigations of the two lives, and the decision between them. Resurrection? Yes, the rising from bondage and transience with the lower life to victory and permanence with the higher. The kingdom of God? Yes, the reign amongst mankind of the higher life. The Christ the son of God? Yes, the bringer-in and founder of this reign of the higher life, this true kingdom of God (CPW 8:156).

At no point does Arnold more clearly reveal his kinship with nineteenth-century liberal Protestant theology than in the regulative role which he assigns to the figure of the kingdom of God as the reign of the higher life. He called it "the fundamental matter of the primitive gospel" of Christ himself, and he saw it as symbolizing the great communal hope for the renovation of our corporate life. "It is," he wrote,

> a contracted and insufficient conception of the gospel which takes into view only the establishment of *righteousness*, and does not also take into view the establishment of *the kingdom*. And the establishment of the kingdom does imply an immense renovation and transformation of our actual state of things. . . . This, then, which is the ideal of the popular classes, of the multitude everywhere, is a legitimate ideal. And a Church of England, devoted to the service and ideals of any limited class—however distinguished, wealthy, or powerful,—which is perfectly satisfied with things as they are, is not only out of sympathy with the ideal of the popular classes; it is also out of sympathy with the gospel (CPW 8:77-78).

If historians of religion are indeed correct that the world's great faiths share the common insight that human suffering and evil have fundamentally to do with illusions concerning the self or a misordering of the self's will, then Arnold touched on and addressed the heart of the human problem. Today we are living still in that aspect of Romanticism which Arnold came increasingly to oppose; namely, Romantic obsession with the self. The ego remains at the center of our attention, and yet we continue uncertain and confused about who we are. It is ironic that an age so obsessed with the self has no adequate image of an ego-ideal or larger social or "higher self."

Arnold was taught by his father, but he also learned in his own experience, that human well-being and happiness are found not in self-absorption but in those disciplines, renunciations, and duties of life that require sublimation, self-loss, and commitment to a higher corporate vision. To look within to find freedom and authenticity without any cost is not only illusory, it is a sign of "cheap grace." As Lionel Trilling has vividly expressed it, with an elegance and rightness reminiscent of Arnold, it is as if each one of us wished to be a Christ "but with none of the inconveniences of undertaking to intercede, of being a sacrifice, of reasoning with rabbis, of making sermons, of having disciples, of going to weddings and to funerals, of beginning something and at a certain point remarking that it is finished."[41]

Like the great Christian humanists of the Renaissance, Arnold shaped a self by disciplined effort, not by instinct or freedom of impulse; by what Pater called "imitative energy," the knowledge and imitation of another, greater self. He was helped in this by habitually meditating on those directing and energizing aphorisms and moral teachings from the religious classics which were a part of his daily reading. This effort and discipline resulted in a sense of well-being that is reflected in Arnold's quiet confidence, his "humor of perspective in which the eternities laugh at time," his unflinching, no-nonsense courage, tempered by tenderness.

NOTES

1. Janet Courteney, *Freethinkers of the Nineteenth Century* (1920) 89.
2. See, e.g., the remarks of Krook, *Three Traditions of Moral Thought* and Cockshut, *The Unbelievers*.
3. John Henry Newman, *Apologia* 30.
4. Stephen, *Studies of a Biographer* 104-5.
5 Russell, *Matthew Arnold* 262.
6. Gordon Kaufman, *God the Problem* (Cambridge, MA, 1972) 78.
7. Kaufman 77.
8. Ludwig Feuerbach, *The Essence of Christianity*, trans. George Eliot (New York, 1959) xxxviii.
9. Robbins, *The Ethical Idealism of Matthew Arnold* 98-99.
10. Albrecht Ritschl, *The Christian Doctrine of Justification and Reconciliation*, trans. H. R. Macintosh and A. B. Macaulay (Edinburgh, 1900) 3:212; italics added.
11. Édouard LeRoy, *Dogme et Critique* (Paris, 1907) 19, 25.
12. David Edwards, *Leaders of the Church of England, 1828-1944* (London, 1971) 42.

13. Trilling, *Matthew Arnold* 357.

14. Robbins, 109-10.

15. John Henry Newman, *Parochial Sermons* (London, 1839) 1:233.

16. Scott, "Arnold's Vision of Transcendence" 274.

17. James Martineau, *Essays, Reviews, and Addresses*, (London, 1891) 4:289.

18. R. H. Hutton, *Criticism on Contemporary Thought and Thinkers* (London, 1900) 1:220.

19. J. Llewelyn Davies, "Mr. Arnold's New Religion," *Contemporary Review* 21 (1873):857-58.

20. Robbins, chap. 5.

21. Henry Dunn, *Facts, Not Fairy-Tales: Brief Notes on Mr. Matthew Arnold's "Literature and Dogma"* (London, 1873) 31.

22. Friedrich Max Müller, *Lectures on the Science of Language*, 2nd series (London, 1864).

23. Van Buren, *The Edges of Language* 133.

24. Paul Tillich, *Systematic Theology* (Chicago, 1953) 1:244-45.

25. C. C. J. Webb, *God and Personality* (London, 1918) 61.

26. Kaufman 63-64, 68.

27. Ritschl 396-97.

28. Friedrich Schleiermacher, *The Christian Faith*, 2nd rev. ed., ed. and trans. H. R. Mackintosh and J. S. Stewart (Edinburgy, 1948) 377ff.

29. Maurice Wiles, *The Remaking of Christian Doctrine* (London, 1974) 50.

30. Wiles 118.

31. Wiles 122.

32. Eliot, *The Use of Poetry and the Use of Criticism* 106.

33. Robert Shafer, *Christianity and Naturalism* (New Haven, 1926) 195.

34. Trilling 9-10.

35. Robbins 82.

36. J. G. Sikes, *Peter Abelard* (Cambridge, 1932) 208.

37. Wiles 80.

38. F. H. Bradley, *Ethical Studies* (London, 1876) 283.

39. Richard R. Niebuhr, *Experiential Religion* (New York, 1972) 99, 103.

40. Culler, *Imaginative Reason* 268-70.

41. Lionel Trilling, *Sincerity and Authenticity* (London, 1972) 172.

6 "A Modernist Before the Time": Arnold's Place in Modern Religious Thought

> I more and more learn the extreme slowness of things, and that though we are all disposed to think that everything will change in our lifetime, it will not. Perhaps we shall end our days in the tail of a current of popular religion, both ritual and dogmatic. Still, the change, for being slower than we expected, is not the less sure.
>
> Arnold to M. E. Grant-Duff
> 22 August 1879

> I persist in thinking that the prevailing form for the Christianity of the future will be the form of Catholicism; but a Catholicism purged. . . . Its forms will be retained, as symbolizing with the force and charm of poetry a few cardinal facts and ideas, simple indeed, but indispensable and inexhaustible.
>
> *Irish Catholicism and British Liberalism*

Lionel Trilling judged that "Arnold's religious writings do still speak to men" who, rejecting dogmatic orthodoxy, are yet impelled to connect their religious vision "with something beyond the merely temporal and the wholly conditioned."[1] Arnold's religious writings did speak to numbers of the educated class, including many eminent theologians and ecclesiastics, in Britain and America, for two generations after 1870. References to his religious essays and discussion of his striking ideas are scattered throughout the best religious literature of this period—with a mixture of censure and praise. However, between 1930 and the present the situation is quite otherwise. One searches in vain for mention of Arnold in the important religious literature of the past half-century.

How, then, can we best understand Arnold in relation to the movements of religious thought of the past century and a half? Are we now able to locate him in a definite religious tradition or school of thought, or is he original, an eclectic maverick who defies classification? The answer is, paradoxically, both simple and complex. Arnold stands unmistakably in the tradition of modern Protestant liberalism with its roots both in Kant's metaphysical skepticism and his effort to establish religious belief on moral experience, as well as in Schleiermacher's experiential grounding of theology in religious feeling and the affections. The keys to this liberal tradition are *the experiential and the moral foundations of religious belief.*

178

In his, at the time, influential *The Rise of Modern Religious Ideas* (1915), Arthur C. McGiffert summarized the modern Protestant liberal position simply yet authoritatively, placing Arnold centrally within it. The position is one, he wrote,

> which interprets the larger whole in terms of moral purpose and makes religion consist in the the recognition of this divine purpose and virtue life in sympathy with and devotion to it. Matthew Arnold's description of God as "the power not ourselves that makes for righteousness" illustrates this position and in the teaching of the German theologian Ritschl, it finds its completest and most consistent theological formulation. We are religious when we rise above our separate or single selves into the consciousness of a divine purpose, and, when we devote ourselves to its accomplishment we put religion into practice and are righteous in the highest sense. The influence of this conception upon the religious thought and life of the present day it would be hard to exaggerate.[2]

What is critical to this theological position is the perception of God as the ground of moral values, envisioned essentially in terms of moral influence rather than in abstract, susbtantive, or metaphysical terms. God is known neither by scientific demonstration nor by mystical vision but rather by the exercise of conscience and moral will. It was this approach to theology that informed the writings of John Baillie, who, with William Temple, is regarded as foremost among British theologians of the first half of the twentieth century. Baillie commended Arnold for his insistence on founding religion in moral experience and for his refusal to consider any antithesis between the two. Referring specifically to Arnold's work, Baillie suggests that "this tendency to look upon religion as being essentially and in the first place a practical thing is the most characteristic contribution which the last two or three generations have made to religious thought."[3]

The dominant movement of liberal Protestant thought between 1870 and World War I was the Ritschlian school. Albrecht Ritschl (1822-89) was the foremost Protestant theologian between Schleiermacher and Karl Barth. His writings had a leading influence for a half century, and while theologians and clergy attracted to his work did not conform to a strict party line, they did reflect common tendencies traceable either to Ritschl himself or to the neo-Kantian currents of thought dominant at the time. We know that Arnold was not familiar with Ritschl's work; he does, however, reflect the philosophical soundings of his day which have much in common with the Ritschlian program. The parallels are striking. For example, Arnold shares with the Ritschlians an abhorrence of metaphysics and speculative theology; the rejection of ecclesiastical dogma as normative for faith; a practical, moral conception of religion and thus a sharp contrast between religious and scientific knowledge; the restriction of theological knowledge to the contents or effects of God's action on the moral consciousness and affections; the perception of Jesus' life and message as the normative revelation of the Christian "idea" or gospel; and the use of the kingdom of God as the regulative principle of the Christian community and its moral activity. In all of these ways Arnold's religious thought is representative of classic nineteenth-century Protestant liberalism.

Arnold was not, however, simply a liberal Protestant. He was an Anglican deeply attracted to aspects of Catholic spirituality and tradition, religious tendencies that Protestant liberalism neither found congenial nor could nurture. Arnold's religious position is, therefore, more complex. It has a kinship as well with the Anglican and Catholic Modernism that briefly flourished between 1890 and 1910 and with certain aspects of Anglican Empirical Catholicism of the 1920s and 30s. A. O. J. Cockshut has commented that "we shall never understand Arnold if we liken him to the Protestant modernists—let us say to Dean Inge. Inge was for clearing away accretions of custom and habit. . . . [Arnold] loved the liturgical traditions, the accumulated moral wisdom of Christendom, which seemed to the Protestant modernists childish and out of date. Arnold was nearer to the spirit of the Catholic modernists."[4]

Cockshut is correct if he means by Protestant Modernists not those Englishmen who were following the lead of Ritschl but those who represented a more extreme form of liberal rationalism. Arnold had, as early as 1863, denounced this latter type of theological liberalism:

> [Christianity] will even survive the handling of the "liberals of every shade of opinion." But it will not do this by losing its essence, by becoming such a Christianity as those liberals imagine, the "Christianity not Mysterious" of Toland; a Christianity consisting of half-a-dozen intellectual propositions, and half-a-dozen moral rules deduced from them. It will do it by retaining the religious life in all its depth and fulness in connexion with new intellectual ideas (CPW 3:78).

What Arnold shares in common with turn-of-the-century Catholic and Anglican Modernism is an antipathy to metaphysics and scholastic theology; the belief that religion has essentially to do with living experience and that doctrines containing spiritual truth derived from such vital experience can never be wrong—no matter what science of history may say about the nature and claims of the original sources of revelation; the recognition that religious language is essentially symbolic, analogous, and not scientific; the rejection of any sharp antithesis between natural and revealed religion; the recognition of the critical need to adapt Christianity to the intellectual needs of the time and the radical implications of this fact for the development of doctrine; and, most significantly, the importance of the corporate life and worship of the church, what George Tyrrell called "the collective subconscious of the 'Populus Dei.'"

Mrs. Humphry Ward, Arnold's niece and author of the popular novel *Robert Elsmere* (1888), was correct in saying that her uncle "was a Modernist long before the time."[5] Moreover, much in Arnold's work attracted the later Catholic and Anglican Modernists—although it is also true that they rejected aspects of his reconstruction as shallow, too Protestant, and thus lacking the very Catholic wholeness that Arnold himself praised and defended so often. Nonetheless, such a theologian as George Tyrrell, the most brilliant of the English Modernists, was influenced by Arnold's writings at a critical period in his own movement from orthodoxy, a fact that is reflected in his published work. Writing to his friend, the Abbé Henri Bremond, Tyrrell declared: "We all know that Matthew Arnold is a Doctor of the Church."[6] Bremond later surmised that a third of Tyrrell's work was to be found in Arnold.[7] Bremond's suggestion has been widely quoted, and, though open to misunderstanding, it points to an important truth. The truth is that Tyrrell discovered in Arnold a valuable spiritual confrère. In Arnold, Tyrrell found encouragement and support for his own ideas and also some striking ideas and phrases which he was able to adapt to his own religious apologetic. The two men shared a religious temper of mind, the difficult balance of Catholic spirit and modern, critical intelligence.

Nicholas Sagovsky has studied the relationship between Arnold and Tyrrell in detail and sees a crucial kinship.

> Was there a third of Tyrrell in Arnold? If one remembers the convergence of interest on the points that Arnold hammered home in *Literature and Dogma*, especially the key distinction between scientific and religious language, the wider attunement to doubt and faith in the contemporary world, the common concern with the "organic" society and implicit self-

appointment to the "clerisy," the common concern for the "Catholicism of the future," rid, at last, of "spiritual materialism," the knowledge that they stood "between two worlds," then the answer must be "yes." . . . The area that Tyrrell *recognized* in Arnold, must, if one is to speak in such Arnoldian terms, cover quite a third of all that Tyrrell has to say.[8]

The point that is significant here is that a thoroughly *Catholic* Modernist, such as George Tyrrell, saw in Arnold a spiritual colleague, the balance of criticism and Catholic ideals. It is worth further noting that the Anglican Modernists who were drawn, not to the German Ritschlians such as Adolf von Harnack, but to the Catholic Modernists, also saw a kinship with Arnold. One was Percy Gardner, Professor of Classical Archaeology in Oxford and President of the Modernist Churchman's Union (later the Modern Churchman's Union) between 1915 and 1922. Arnold's influence is detected in Gardner's several Modernist books. What he especially owed to Arnold was his convictoin about religious criticism, joined with a Catholic devotion. In Gardner's opinion, Arnold was "the greatest critic of our age."[9]

A sense of inclusiveness, a balance of the rational, the moral, and the aesthetic, of thought and devotion, of tradition and the modern, was what both Arnold and the Catholic Modernists found lacking in Protestantism. Arnold wrote to the French Protestant pastor Ernest Fontanès that his ideal for Catholic countries would be "the development of something like old Catholicism, retaining as much as possible of old religious services and usages, but becoming more and more liberal in spirit" (L 2:114). It was also Arnold's hope for the future of the Church of England.

Arnold found the religious life of Catholics and Protestants to be much alike in essentials. In the accessories, the outward form and setting, there is, however, a very great difference, and to these externals Arnold attached immense significance:

> Catholicism has these so different from Protestantism! and in Catholisicm these accessories have, it cannot be denied, a nobleness and amplitude which in Protestantism is often wanting to them. In Catholicism they have, from the antiquity of this form of religion, from its pretensions to universality, from its really widespread prevalence, from its sensuousness, something European, august and imaginative; in Protestantism they often have from its inferiority in all these respects, something provincial, mean, and prosaic. . . . The signal want of grace

and charm in English Protestantism's setting of its religious life is not an indifferent matter; it is a real weakness (CPW 3:97-98).

Arnold's strong attraction to worship with its "consecration of common consent, antiquity, public establishment, [and] long-used rites" (CPW 5:197) sets him apart from Protestantism. He felt deeply that "unity and continuity in public worship are a need for the human race, an eternal aspiration of Christendom" (CPW 8:110) which could not be nurtured by "the Protestantism of the Protestant religion." Arnold predicted that Catholic worship would prevail long after the intellectual liabilities of Catholic dogma "tired out men's patience." The old forms "thrown out at a dimly-grasped truth, approximative and provisional representations . . . which are now surrounded with such an atmosphere of tender and profound sentiment, will not disappear" (CPW 8:162).

Arnold especially valued the public and corporate aspect of Catholic worship. "Instead of battling for his own private forms for expressing the inexpressible and defining the undefinable, a man takes those which have commended themselves most to the religious life of his nation" (CPW 5:239). Catholic worship is not left to the will and pleasure of chance individuals. It is, rather, expressly designed to rise above that level, to be a schooling in a religious devotion that reflects the experience of the ages. While Catholicism and Protestantism both possess the kernel of the Christian substance, Catholicism alone adorns it by "the gradual work of time and nature." "In the beauty and poetry of its clothing of the germ [Catholicism] has an immeasurable superiority" (CPW 8:341). And this is because "the need for beauty is a real and now rapidly growing need in man; Puritanism cannot satisfy it, Catholicism and the English Church can" (CPW 8:343).

Arnold perceived in Catholicism a power which he associated with the unity and "beauty of its age-long growth, a growth . . . unconscious, popular, profoundly rooted, all-enveloping" (CPW 8:333). He wrote to his sister Fan that the need to maintain a "connexion with the past in one's religion is one of the strongest instincts in human nature," and that Protestantism had severed that vital connexion (L 2:131). The sense of a profoundly rooted, and yet popular, all-enveloping and universal spiritual reality is what, he acknowledged, gives Catholicism its grandeur and power.

Arnold expressed his attraction for this side of Catholicism in a masterful passage. If one goes to the reading room of the British Museum and to that sacred quarter housing its theological books, one finds "an immense Catholic work, the collection of the Abbé Migne, lording it over that whole region, reducing to insignificance the feeble Protestant forces which hang upon its skirts." The Protestant representatives all appear so divided against one another, and how they are "dwarfed by the Catholic Leviathan, their neighbor!" Migne's "work embraces the whole range of human interests; like one of the great Middle Age Cathedrals, it is in itself a study for a life." It is this fact which draws the man of imagination and why he "will always have a weakness for the Catholic Church." On the other hand, the Protestants "at once call up in our mind the thought of men of a definite type as their adherents," but "Catholicism suggests no such special following." On the contrary, "Catholicism suggests,—what shall I say?—all the pellmell of the men and women of Shakespeare's plays" (CPW 3:213-14).

Arnold was convinced that Catholicism was the form of Christianity most capable of reaching the people. This, of course, was also the source of its popular superstition. But Arnold was not as troubled by this as by the faults he perceived in Protestantism and the English Church. "The bulk of its superstitions come from its having really plunged so far down into the multitude, and spead so wide among them. If this is a cause of error, it is also a cause of attachment. Who has seen the poor in other churches as they are seen in Catholic Churches?" (CPW 8:331). The Church of England, Arnold feared, lacked this universal, democratic, all-embracing appeal. In 1871 he wrote to Cardinal Newman: "Do not you think that what is Tory and anti-democratic in the Church of England is one of her great dangers at the present time; and a danger from which the Catholic Church . . . is much more exempt? I mean, though the R. Catholic Church may in fact have been anti-democratic in modern times on the Continent, there seems nothing in her nature to make her so; but in the nature of the English Church there does" (UL 57-58).

What antiquity, public establishment, and commonality conveyed to Arnold was above all the excellence of unity. "If there is such a thing specially alien to religion, it is divisions; if there is a thing specially native to religion, it is peace and union. Hence the original attraction towards unity in Rome, and hence the great charm and power for men's minds of that unity once attained" (CPW 8:331-32).

Arnold was drawn to those qualities in Catholic spirituality and tradition which he saw as essential to the nurturing of the religious life, but he never personally wrestled with the question of whether or not to go over to Rome. There was much in the Roman Church that repelled him—its Ultramontanism and sacerdotalism, and its superstition and dogmatic pretension. Yet Arnold believed and prophesied that these excesses of Catholicism were not permanent and would in the future be an embarrassment to Rome.

> Its dogma and its confident assertion of its dogma are no more a real source of strength and permanence to the Catholic Church than its Ultramontanism. Its real superiority is in its charm for the imagination,—its poetry. I persist in thinking that Catholicism has, from it superiority, a great future before it; that it will endure while all the Protestant sects (in which I do not include the Church of England) dissolve and perish. I persist in thinking that the prevailing form for the Christianity of the future will be the form of Catholicism; but a Catholicism purged, opening itself to the light and air. . . . Its forms will be retained, as symbolizing with the force and charm of poetry a few cardinal facts and ideas, simple indeed, but indispensable and inexhaustible (CPW 8:334).

Augustin Renaudet has remarked of the religious *modernisme* of Erasmus that it was neither wholly Protestant nor wholly Catholic.[10] What Erasmus wanted was a *troisième église*, a third church that would be spiritual Catholicism profoundly reformed by the Protestant principle of critical light and prophetic protest against absolutist claims. This, too, was Arnold's vision and hope. "Protestantism," he wrote, "had hold of Jesus Christ's 'method' of inwardness and sincerity, Catholicism had hold of his 'secret' of self-renouncement. The chief word with Protestantism is the word of the method: *repentance, conversion*; the chief word with Catholicism is the word of the secret: *peace, joy*" (CPW 6:352). Like Erasmus, Arnold saw that the need was for a third way which would join the two in an unerring balance; a Catholicism transformed by uniting the spirituality of Catholicism with the moral conscience and light of Protestantism at its best.

A too exclusive focus on the moral and critical side of Arnold's religious reconstruction will fail to plumb the true depths of his spiritual life and ideal. Arnold was a religious liberal, but a liberal with a difference. He could direct his sharpest and even bitterest sallies against those "shallow Liberals" who failed to grasp the ancient, traditional, abiding truths of Christianity and its genuine redemptive power. We must remember that compared to W. K. Clifford, Moody and Sankey were for Arnold "masters of the philosophy of history" (CPW 7:381). The liberal rationalist will pounce on Christianity's "mishandling and disfigurements"; he will see it as "an obsolete nuisance to be discouraged and helped to die out" but Arnold knew that a profound sentiment in the people has rebelled, and rightly will continue to rebel, against the rationalists "because the people are conscious not of their vain disfigurements of the Christian religion, but of its genuine curativeness" (CPW 8:331).

Arnold united in his own person the effort to balance what he saw as the unique contribution, the "light," of liberal Protestantism with the spiritual profundity of a Catholicism transformed. In the last year of his life he wrote to Lionel Tollemache: "I consider myself, to adopt your very good expression, a Liberal Anglican; and I think the times are in favour of our being allowed so to call ourselves."[11] We know from his letters and diaries and the comments of his friends that, at least from the time of his marriage, Arnold's daily and weekly routine was punctuated by religious devotions: morning prayers, the reading of the Bible and the spiritual classics, regular attendance at Sunday services, preferably the early Communion service, and the reading of sermons to his family on Sunday evenings. While much of this no doubt represented for Arnold a type of secret discipline that for him was singular in its meaning, these habitual practices of the religious life were not perfunctory, nor were they undertaken to keep up appearances or to pacify his family. He often expressed the pleasure and the spiritual refreshment that these occasions afforded. During the year in which he was deep in preparation of *St. Paul and Protestantism*, he confessed to his friend Frederick Temple, then Bishop of Exeter, that were he still a young man he would take religious orders.[12]

Despite the very different contexts there is a kinship between Dietrich Bonhoeffer's experience of the tension between a profound interior spiritual life, a *disciplina arcana*, and what he observed of the world's coming of age and Arnold's sense of the travail of living between two worlds. The secret discipline of the interior life, Arnold discovered, was the means of knowing religious truth. It was a spiritual path that simply yet severely— in the words of the Prayer Book—required that one truly and earnestly repent of his sins, be in love and charity with his neighbor, and intend to live a new life. At the time of his death many close acquaintances remarked on the odd contrast between Arnold's public image, "decked and adorned as if for a triumph," and the spiritual *necrosis* so characteristic of the private man. Arnold's dual persona, H. F. Lowry has remarked, was like that of the young bride of Giocopone di Todi, compared, in Arnold's "The Austerity of Poetry," to the Muse:

Such, poets, is your bride, the Muse! young, gay,

> Radiant, adorn'd outside; a hidden ground
> Of thought and of austerity within.   (CL 27; P 532)

What friends and relatives especially remembered about Arnold were his untold acts of self-renouncement and kindness. His niece, Mrs. Humphry Ward, recalled the time which the young Arnold gave, day after day, to his invalid sister when he "might so easily have made one or other of the trifling or selfish excuses we are all so ready to make." This, she observed, "was only a prophecy of those many 'nameless unremembered acts' of simple kindness, which filled the background of Matthew Arnold's middle and later life, and were not revealed, many of them, even to his own people, till after his death—kindness to a pupil teacher, an unsuccessful writer, a hard-worked schoolmaster or schoolmistress, a budding poet, a schoolboy."[13]

John Morley recollected how Arnold "was incapable of sacrificing the smallest interest of anybody else to his own," how "he stood well aloof from all the hustlings and jostlings by which selfish men push on." Arnold "cast no burden upon others, and never shrank from bearing his own share of the daily load to the last ounce of it."[14]

Since the beginning of the early modern era Christian humanism has persistently affirmed that the first step to being a Christian is not in knowing the doctrine, but rather in *metanoia*, in what Arnold called "the immense inward movement for obtaining one's rule of life," which rule is Jesus' secret of *necrosis*, dying. Arnold is perhaps best understood as standing in this modern tradition of Christian humanism in which Christianity is first and foremost "a temper, a behavior," and for whom the words of St. John's Gospel—"If any man wills to do his will, he shall know the doctrine"—is the sine qua non.

The characteristics often associated with Christian humanism and with Arnold, but which often have displeased the critics of both, are well described by a modern cultural historian:

> We *are* troubled . . . by the frivolous lightness of his humanistic style when he writes about things sacred. . . . It is hard for us to accept piety with such a strong aesthetic tinge as serious. [His] religious sentiments, it seems to us, more often moved in a muddling sphere of poetic learning than cried toward heaven out of the deep. . . . His theology seems too vacillating and too vague. . . . He placed little value on definitions. As a consequence he had no desire to advance toward a profound and clearly defined philosophical foundation of his beliefs,

and the direct, mystical basis of his theological thinking was
also weak. He was just as little a rationalist. His beliefs were
rooted in deep ethical needs. . . . Sacred truth cannot bear subtle
definitions. It was but little service to piety for one to attempt
to penetrate further than was seemly, into the cave of the un-
fathomable mystery.[15]

The person Johan Huizinga is here describing is not Arnold but the
Christian humanist, Desiderius Erasmus. One could expatiate on the extraordinary relationship between the humanistic and spiritual principles
and ideals of the two men. A brief enumeration of some of these will
suggest the extent of their religious kinship. Both men viewed Christianity in essentially moral terms and were suspicious of both rationalism
and mysticism; they disliked scholastic metaphysics and "theologism"; both
recognized the profound spiritual importance of tradition, comprehen-
siveness, and Christian unity; they both were engaged and yet detached
observers of their age; they shared a passion for the disinterested truth of
scholarship and knowledge and yet found themselves deeply involved in
a mission to edify and to put something in the place of reductive criticism;
in this mission they used humor, scorn, and irony, but they also shared a
faith in the morally directing and energizing power of key precepts or
maxims which they collected and used; as humanists they were alike in
their devotion to the classics and were drawn especially to the spiritual
resources of the Stoic philosophers, but it was a Stoicism touched and
transformed by Christian sentiment; they shared a love of simplicity and
a dislike of a materialistic and commercial spirit, of narrowness and "the
one thing needful"; both men were noted for their defense of religious
toleration. Arnold was one with Erasmus in affirming "the old and true
Socratic thesis of the interdependence of virtue and knowledge" (CPW
8:162) and the harmonious expansion of all human powers. Both men
worked to achieve this balance and the breadth that culture alone could
give to religion, but they also sought to reconcile autonomous classical
culture with the moral and spiritual temper of Christianity. Arnold's treatment of this in "Pagan and Mediaeval Religious Sentiment" and in "Hebraism and Hellenism" would have delighted Erasmus. In 1859, as part
of his educational tour of Holland for the Newcastle Commission, Arnold
had been attracted to the way in which Dutch youth were schooled in
Christelijke en maatschappelijke, or Christian and social values.[16] The word
Christelijke conveyed a decidedly Erasmian sense of Christian humanism.

Aby Warburg suggests that the central intellectual problem of the Renaissance was to find a compromise formula, "an *Ausgleichsformel,* that would enable men to live comfortably with classical forms and Christian convictions, trust in man and trust in God, vigorous secular energies and a tenacious ascetic ideal."[17] Erasmus epitomized the quest for such a formula, but this was also a burning problem in the High Victorian age, perhaps best seen in the dialectical tension of Arnold's essays on religion and culture and in his own life. It is this quest for the interdependence and balance of these competing values and forces which accounts for the fact that students of both Erasmus and Arnold have so often observed and commented on the unique juxtaposition of strong traditional and yet intensely reformist predispositions in the life and work of both men. It is a telling mark of the Christian humanist.

H. F. Lowry has written about this aspect of Arnold which is so distinctive of the Christian humanist—and which truly bespeaks Arnold's legacy to the religious need of our own day.

> Out of his own integrity, [Arnold] heightens reason until it becomes itself transformed and includes some deeper quality of the soul. Upon the shelves of his study is Voltaire in seventy volumes, and near to him Saint Francis of Assisi. One month he studies Locke and, another, the Benedictine Rule. In his pocket diaries he puts one day a cynical *mot* of La Bruyère or La Rochefoucauld, and next day he enters, "Blessed are the pure in heart, for they shall see God." . . . It is because he owns, in the far range of his life and work, this rare balance of opposing qualities that we can give him first our confidence; and, by this same balance, he gives light and leading to a time that needs it more perhaps than did his own (CL 51-52).

Arnold's life and his work as a religious critic do have a claim upon us. Historically, his essays in religious criticism were in several imporant respects pioneer works in the English-speaking world, the breaking of new trails which later critics and scholars could explore in depth and with the specialist's finer equipment. Arnold helped free Christian belief from a crude literalism and a moribund theologism. He saw how things were moving and perceived important religious exegencies in the period prior to the turn of the century. But more importantly, Arnold's insights on religious language, his perception of the need of an experiential beginning to any theological construction, his sagacious and subtle understanding of the interdependence of religion and culture, and his soundness in recognizing the moral dimension of the hermeneutical task as central and indispensable—all these remain as enduring contributions to religion and to the work of Christian criticism in the present time and in the future.

NOTES

1. Trilling, *Matthew Arnold* 432.

2. Arthur C. McGiffert, *The Rise of Modern Religious Ideas* (New York, 1915) 74-75.

3. John Baillie, *The Roots of Religion in the Human Soul* (London, 1926) 51.

4. Cockshut, *The Unbelievers* 72.

5. Ward, *A Writer's Recollections* 235.

6. Letter to Bremond, 28 Dec. 1905; cited Nicholas Sagovsky, *Between Two Worlds: George Tyrrell's Relationship to the Thought of Matthew Arnold* (Cambridge, 1983) 31.

7. Letter to Alfred Loisy, June 1913; cited Sagovsky, *Between Two Worlds* 15.

8. Sagovsky, *Between Two Worlds* 148. The religious connections between Arnold and Tyrrell are also discussed in David Schultenover, *George Tyrrell: In Search of Catholicism* (Shepardstown, W. Va. 1981).

9. Percy Gardner, *Exploratio Evangelica* (London, 1907) vii.
The most authoritative account of the history of English Modernism in the early decades of this century summarizes the principal Modernist tenets. They could be taken as Matthew Arnold's credo: "The English Modernist believed in a God who was in everything and that everything was in God, but a God who worked only through the evolutionary process. . . . He had no doubt about the existence of Jesus Christ, though he was prepared to admit that if it were proved that Jesus had never existed, that would not mean the end of his religious faith. His Christology was a degree Christology and adoptionist. His Jesus was not an eschatological figure but rather 'The Lord of Thought' who proclaimed the Fatherhood of God and the Brotherhood of Man. His doctrine of the atonement was Abelardian or exemplarist. He had no hesitation in accepting all that biblical criticism had to say. He maintained that he believed in the supernatural, but not in the miraculous. His Jesus, therefore, did not perform miracles. He was not born of a Virgin and his resurrection was a spiritual one. The tomb was not empty. He had a strong belief in the life after death and was a universalist. He was not so naive as to think one could exist without dogma, but he wished dogmatic definition to be kept to a minimum. He thought there was such a thing as essential Christianity. For the English Modernist ethics were more important than doctrine. Life was more important then belief. He did not relish ecclesiasticism or see a great divide between the secular and the sacred." (Alan M. G. Stephenson, *The Rise and Decline of English Modernism* [London, 1984] 7-8.) Depending on how it was interpreted, the only tenet about which Arnold might express a reservation would be a strong belief in life after death. On the subject of Arnold and the afterlife, see John Speller, "Arnold and Immortality," *The Arnoldian* 10 (1983):21-25.

10. See Renaudet's *Etudes erasmiènes* (1939) and *Erasme et l'Italie* (1954).

11. Russell, *Matthew Arnold* 263.

12. E. G. Sanford, ed., *Memoirs of Archbishop Temple* (London, 1906) 1:278.

13. Ward 46.

14. John Morley, "Matthew Arnold," *The Nineteenth Century* 38 (1895):1053.

15. Johan Huizinga, *Men and Ideas* (London, 1960) 314.

16. Honan, *Matthew Arnold* 303.

17. Cited Peter Gay, *The Enlightenment: An Interpretation* (New York, 1967) 270.

Index